NATURE AND GRACE

NATURE AND GRACE

BY MATTHIAS JOSEPH SCHEEBEN

TRANSLATED BY CYRIL VOLLERT, S.J., S.T.D.

Professor of Theology
St. Mary's College, St. Marys, Kansas

B. HERDER BOOK CO.

15 & 17 SOUTH BROADWAY, ST. LOUIS 2, MO.
   and
33 QUEEN SQUARE, LONDON, W. C.

Library of Congress Catalog Card Number: 54-7471

234.1
SCn

COPYRIGHT 1954 BY B. HERDER BOOK CO.

Printed in the United States of America
by Vail-Ballou Press, Inc., Binghamton, New York

FOREWORD

BY THE TRANSLATOR

Time has evaluated the theological achievement of Matthias Joseph Scheeben, and has recognized in it an importance that is attributed to no other theological works written in the German language.

Throughout Europe, especially in Germany, Catholic theology had reached its nadir at the end of the eighteenth century. Under Kant, the philosopher of Protestantism, the despair of human nature that was Luther's legacy turned into a despair of human reason. Kant had hoped to save religion by freeing it from the clutches of science and philosophy; he succeeded only in laying a foundation for hostility to all dogma. Despair of nature was matched by the despair of supernature that is the canker of rationalism.

The intellectual leadership of Germany had passed to the Protestant North. Catholicism did not escape its influence. Rationalism, idealism, sentimental moralism, and Protestant theology were corrupting Catholic thought.

Catholic theologians were poorly equipped to meet the grim onslaughts of the Enlightenment. Scholastic philosophy, formerly so effective an instrument of theological speculation, lacked the lusty vigor it had possessed during the Middle Ages. It neglected the new physical sciences that were being cultivated. It had grown perilously ill by trying to assimilate indigestible chunks of the philosophies of Descartes, Leibnitz, and Wolff. It failed to draw sufficiently on the patristic wealth that was being made increasingly available. Worst of all, the gloomy conviction prevailed that scholastic methods were outworn and powerless to check the infiltration of rationalism and secularism.

Those who still cherished scholastic theology had slight interest in the scholarly pursuits that attracted the men of their day. They were indifferent or bewildered when challenged by the new sciences. They refused to give up their fondness for the interplay of ideas that had scarcely any contact with life and reality. Eventually the break with medieval theology was almost complete. The great books of the Golden Age were no longer read. Few men appreciated the true nature of Scholasticism. The distinction between what was permanently valuable in Scholasticism and the trivialities or aberrations of eighteenth-century Scholastics was overcast.

Deprived of the vitality animating Scholasticism, theology tended to become a purely positive science, content to expose the scriptural and patristic bases of dogma. Yet some thinkers of metaphysical temperament refused to renounce all speculative cultivation of theology. Since the bridges leading back to Scholasticism were down, Catholic theologians, sincere in their yearning for a Catholic restoration, sifted German philosophy for elements that might prove usable for a new elaboration and synthesis of Catholic teaching. Many discerned in the system of Schelling an approach to the Catholic view of the world. Others hoped that they could manipulate the sentimental philosophy of Jacobi and the dialectic of Hegel, so as to do what Albert the Great and Thomas Aquinas had done with Aristotle. After abortive attempts that reached

deep into the nineteenth century, they were forced with
bitter disappointment to the realization that the philosophies of the Enlightenment were unable to promote an
understanding of the supernatural, and hence possessed no
value for dogmatic theology.

Faced with such disasters, theologians at length perceived that they would have to abandon all plans to exploit the new German philosophies. Their misgivings were
confirmed by repeated ecclesiastical pronouncements that
called for a study of the past. They decided to turn back
to medieval Scholasticism, to the ages in which faith and
theology had flourished so gloriously. The rediscovery of
the twelfth and thirteenth centuries was inaugurated. Under Adam Möhler, Joseph Kuhn, and Heinrich Klee, the
great men of the Tübingen school, theology was liberated
from Schelling's oppressive influence, and foundations
were laid for a reconstructed theology. After painful grop-
ings, heartbreaking failures, and partial triumphs, Neo-
Scholasticism was firmly established in Germany by Joseph
Kleutgen who, in his *Theologie der Vorzeit*, restored the
idea of the supernatural and convinced his country's theologians of its supreme importance.

While in Germany the power of reason in the supernatural domain was exaggerated, efforts undertaken in
France and Italy to revive the theological sciences veered
toward the opposite extreme of traditionalism and ontolo-
gism. These tendencies, however, were soon stifled by the
resurgent Scholasticism, which insisted on reasoned motives and foundations of faith, and vigorously rejected attempts to confound the logical and ontological orders. In
Spain, continuity with the Middle Ages had never been
wholly severed. In Italy, particularly in Rome, the Dominicans had remained loyal to the great Thomistic traditions

of their Order. In the Eternal City, too, scholastic thought
was strongly fostered by the re-established Society of
Jesus, especially by Liberatore and Taparelli.

Up and down Europe, Catholic scholars were reaching
back to the philosophical and theological resources of
Scholasticism. Encouraged by papal exhortations and by
ecclesiastical condemnations of the errors of the times, Neo-
Scholasticism labored with mounting success to rescue
Catholic theology.

At the time theologians were still cautiously feeling their
way and occasionally stumbling along strange paths in
search of their ancient heritage, Matthias Joseph Scheeben,
who would hurl the last seedy dregs of rationalism out of
theology, was residing at the German College in Rome
and pursuing his studies at the Gregorian University.

Sheeben was born March 1, 1835, in Meckenheim near
Bonn. He made his elementary studies in Münstereifel and
his secondary studies in Cologne. On the basis of his excellent scholastic record he was sent to Rome in 1852, at
the age of seventeen, and for the next seven years attended
lectures at the Gregorian University as a student of philosophy and theology.

In Rome at that time a great intellectual renascence was
developing. Taparelli and Liberatore, then teaching at the
Gregorian, were champions of Italian Neo-Scholasticism.
Other very influential professors were Secchi, Tongiorgi,
Perrone, and Ballerini. The great Kleutgen was then living
in the Eternal City; the first two volumes of his *Theologie
der Vorzeit* accompanied young Scheeben at his initiation
into the sacred sciences.

Passaglia and Schrader were Scheeben's regular professors during the first two years of his theological course;
the rest of his studies were mainly under the direction of

Cerciá and Franzelin. The latter had a special influence on Scheeben; he was the prefect of studies at the German College and presided at the weekly disputations conducted there. With his wealth of patristic erudition, he had a large share in cultivating Scheeben's love for the Fathers of the Church.

The scientific bent of the German College was in the direction of tradition. The library possessed good editions of the Fathers and all the great authors of medieval Scholasticism. The works of later Scholastics were also on the shelves. During his term as librarian, Scheeben had excellent opportunities to become acquainted with the new books issued by the prominent theologians of the Catholic restoration in Germany. With his native openness of mind, he early learned to combine reverence for the past with keen awareness of the contributions of contemporary scholars.

The young theologian was singularly fortunate in his teachers, who were among the militant pioneers of the Neo-Scholastic movement. From his professors he received a sound introduction to the true genius of Christianity. To the incentives received in class, he added his own taste for independent speculation and did much private reading and research. He felt that if the past was to be revived, it should be not only the past of the twelfth and thirteenth centuries, but the past of the third, fourth, and fifth centuries; the past not only of the West, but of the great Fathers of the East, the past of those early ages when Christian life and thought had not yet been confined to neat, man-made channels of abstract formulas, but flowed in their original freshness. He summoned forth the noble spirits of the ancients to associate with them on terms of intimacy and to make their knowledge his own.

Under the stimulation of such minds, the living and the dead, the leading idea of his life, the idea of the supernatural order, began to dominate the young student and his ambition crystallized: to make the drab naturalistic world glow again in the light and beauty of grace, to bring back to the consciousness of men the glorious destiny of their conformation to God.

Scheeben was ordained in Rome on December 18, 1858. The following summer he returned to Germany, armed with doctorates in philosophy and theology. For a year he acted as rector of the conventual church of the Salvatorian Sisters in Münstereifel and taught religion in the school the nuns conducted for young women. In 1860 he was appointed professor of theology at the archiepiscopal seminary of Cologne, and shortly thereafter began his amazing career of theological scholarship.

A few minor theological writings were followed by the publication of *Nature and Grace*, the first of his major books. In it he describes the supernatural as a sharing in God's nature: the supernatural implies a state of being, life, and knowledge resembling that of God. This volume, which is highly original in conception and method, at once ranked Scheeben among the leaders of speculative theology.

To supply a patristic foundation for *Nature and Grace*, Scheeben published a new edition of *Quid est homo*, by Antonius Casinius, S.J., adding an introduction and notes. In his desire to spread a knowledge of the supernatural, he wrote *Die Herrlichkeiten der göttlichen Gnade;* the work is popular in scope and became enormously successful. An English translation, *The Glories of Divine Grace*, appeared during Scheeben's lifetime and has gone through several reprintings.

A series of articles that had been running in the periodical, *Der Katholik*, during 1861 and 1862, served as the skeleton of what was to become Scheeben's most famous book, *The Mysteries of Christianity*. This volume, a monument to Scheeben's theological intuition and incredible industry, presents a conception of Christian truth as a whole that alone would admit the author to the company of the world's foremost theologians. In a measure of success unsurpassed by any theological work, it penetrates into the interrelations, the laws, the organism, and the consequences of the great mysteries of Christianity. With consummate skill, Scheeben displays in a masterly synthesis the richness and variety of the Christian revelations as a unified system of truths flowing from the mystery of the Trinity. The book is a striking proof that a high degree of initiative and of speculative power can be developed on the basis of tradition and within the framework of ecclesiastical teaching. There is no other work quite like it in the vast history of Christian literature.

In addition to his theological treatises, Scheeben took delight in tracing out the operations of grace in the lives of the saints. A series of short ascetical and hagiographical studies appeared in 1867, and several articles in *Der Katholik* are the product of his pious meditations amid the grind of his scholarly researches. He was also active in an editorial capacity. At the beginning of his sojourn in Cologne, he was appointed director of the *Katholischer Volksfreund*, a magazine devoted to the edification of the faithful. In his zeal to promote the sanctification of his fellow-priests, he founded the periodical, *Kölner Pastoralblatt*, and edited it up to his death.

During the controversies incited by the decrees of the Vatican Council, he defended the teaching of the Church in a large number of articles and brochures. At this time he accepted the editorship of yet another periodical, *Das ökumenische Konzil von 1869*, of which two volumes of some 600 pages were issued annually. Scheeben himself wrote practically all of the first four volumes.

In the midst of this feverish activity Scheeben was contemplating a further project which was to take form in the greatest of his works. For many years there had been ripening in his mind the plan of gathering together the results of his theological investigations and reflections in a vast synthesis. The incentive for actually beginning the work was supplied when Benjamin Herder, an intimate friend of Scheeben's, urged him to write the volumes on dogmatic theology for the Herder "Theologische Bibliothek." The first tome of Scheeben's *Handbuch der katholischen Dogmatik*, the most profound and valuable treatise on dogmatic theology in the German language, was published in 1873. The second followed in 1878, and the third, issued in two parts, in 1882 and 1887. The three volumes, embracing over 3000 pages of small type, take in the whole theological tradition of Christianity.

Concurrently with this, the great work of his life, Scheeben continued to write for periodicals and encyclopedias. He published over twenty articles in *Der literarische Handweiser* and contributed regularly to *Der Katholik*. He wrote several pieces for the *Staatslexikon der Görresgesellschaft*, and had some thirty articles in the second editon of the Wetzer and Welte *Kirchenlexikon*.

The supernatural is the main theme of Scheeben's works from first to last. He judged the correct description of the revealed mysteries so necessary that he consecrated all his theological writings to the purpose of showing their force and importance for the sacred sciences, and of emphasiz-

ing their meaning for the daily life of man. His most notable contribution to Neo-Scholasticism is his service in
bringing the supernatural, in its full purity and beauty,
back to the center of theological thought. By his doctrine
as well as by his method he sought to destroy the lingering
influence that rationalism and the Enlightenment had exerted on Catholic theology. He was neither philosopher
nor apologist but a theologian; theology made no sense to
him apart from the revelation of Jesus Christ. He tried to
attract men to the faith, not by proofs built on historical
or apologetic foundations, but by opening and displaying
its inner treasures. The considerable success he had in this
venture is owing to his penetrating insight and vivid description of the supernatural; and that is why his theology
appeals so powerfully to modern man, sick to death with
naturalism.

The supernatural, of course, is so essential to Catholic
life that it could never be wholly overlooked. Yet we can
correctly speak of a resurgence of the supernatural in the
last century. During preceding ages attention had been
largely restricted to controversies with Protestantism and
Jansenism. It was only after the conquest of these errors
and their culmination in the sterility of rationalism that
theologians could again devote their energies to a fuller
study of the supernatural.

A revival of theology as the science of the supernatural
could not be achieved by demonstrating the fact of the
supernatural order, but had to bring out its value, beauty,
and vitality. It had to span the gap between theory and
action, between the apprehension of supernatural truth
and its realization in supernatural living.

Against the prevailing neglect of the supernatural,
Scheeben endeavored to show that the mysteries of Chris-

tianity abound in light. He insisted that these mysteries constitute the richest treasure of our spiritual life; that dogma is not alien to life, but is the source and inspiration of the fullest life attainable by man—supernatural life with Christ and in Christ.

He brought back to the consciousness of his contemporaries the undistorted ideals proposed by Christianity. He taught Catholics to appreciate their heritage. He again unveiled the image of the true man, who is the deified man, a child of the heavenly Father and a member of the Incarnate Son. He never wearied of pointing out that Christian life is a participation in the divine life. This is his most important message to the modern world. In the name of life, attacks have been launched against religion for decades. Christianity has been pilloried as a storehouse of dead concepts, as a system of life-killing logic. Scheeben's works demonstrate the appalling stupidity of such a caricature. The life of the Catholic is life in God. The faith is not a concatenation of ideas hostile to life or a collection of repressive moral prescriptions. All the laborious speculations of the great theologians are only attempts to bring the living reality of the faith home to our consciousness; all the precepts of the moral code are but aids to the preservation, enhancement, and perfecting of supernatural life.

Scheeben's theological synthesis is best proposed in *The Mysteries of Christianity*, his most original work, but was clearly formulated from the outset of his career and was sketched in his first book, *Nature and Grace*. There he shows that theology is in quest of knowledge of the divine nature and its supernatural communication. This communication proceeds in three stages. The first is the total and substantial communication of the divine nature in the Blessed Trinity, from the Father to the Son, and from the Father and the Son to the Holy Spirit. The divine Trinity is the origin, the center, and the term of the supernatural economy of salvation, which is based on a merciful communication of the divine nature to men. The second stage of the communication, the hypostatic union, is realized in the Incarnation, the union of a human nature with the divine nature in the unity of one Person, the Word. The Incarnation, in turn, is the source and model of the third communication. This third communication consists in the participation of men in the life of God by their mystical union with the Incarnate Word. It is the union of men with the God-man in the mystical body of Christ, a union that is to culminate in supernatural beatitude, which consists, not in the progressive flowering of human nature, but in the glorification of human nature by the divine nature in the beatific vision.

The powerful synthesis that is the supreme achievement of Scheeben's genius is the reason for the recognition accorded to him as the chief theologian of the supernatural order. In addition, he had the merit of restoring sanctifying grace, the study of which had been obscured by preoccupation with actual grace, to its rightful place in the sacred sciences. He also succeeded in drawing the attention of theologians to uncreated Grace and to the teaching of the Greek Fathers on the deification of man. These are the main contributions that account for his unique position in the development of theology.

Scheeben died July 21, 1888, at the age of fifty-three, in Cologne. His name is rightly associated with St. Albert the Great, St. Thomas Aquinas, and John Duns Scotus, who in the Middle Ages had shed such splendor over that ancient city.

CYRIL VOLLERT, S.J.

St. Mary's College
St. Marys, Kansas

AUTHOR'S PREFACE

THE scope and plan of this work are apparent from the Table of Contents and the Introduction. In the brevity required of a preface I can hardly hope to arouse the reader's interest in the subject. The title indicates simply that a systematic, scientific treatment of nature and grace is envisaged. The exposition will be as profound and comprehensive as I can make it; nature and grace must furnish the basis for a reasonable chart of life and growth. My cherished aim is to bring out the supernatural character of the Christian economy of salvation in its full sublimity, beauty, and riches. The main task of our time, it seems to me, consists in propounding and emphasizing the supernatural quality of Christianity, for the benefit of both science and life. Theoretical as well as practical naturalism and rationalism, which seek to throttle and destroy all that is specifically Christian, must be resolutely and energetically repudiated.

The concept of man's nature influences the whole area of philosophy. Similarly the concept of man's place in Christianity is supremely important for its entire system of mysteries. If these mysteries lie beyond the reach of nature and reason, man can gain no part in them through the sole resources of his nature. He must receive a sort of new nature and must be raised by it to a higher sphere; when that is done he can take on new, mysterious relations with supernatural things and enter into a new, higher life.

Grace imparts to man this higher state and this higher life. It invests nature with a kind of second, nobler nature which we may fittingly call supernature, and so lays the foundation of an essentially superior order of things for man that differs from the natural order in every respect.

We have undertaken in this work the task of bringing out the difference, opposition, and union of these two orders of things that mean so much to man. One of them has nature, the other has grace or supernature as its basis and center. The application of this doctrine to the clarification and mutual interconnection of all the mysteries of faith and Christian life can be only suggested here; a fuller treatment must await the future.[1] But even the points that are developed in this book will be enough to show the incalculable value these mysteries have for our practical as well as our speculative life.

In consulting source materials I have made ample use of the teaching on grace so dear to the Greek Fathers. Usually, in the question occupying us, the doctrine developed by the Latin Fathers against the Pelagians is almost the only one employed. St. Augustine tends to be regarded exclusively as the Doctor of Grace. He richly deserves the title; yet we must not forget that the standpoint he took was dictated by circumstances. In his controversies with the Pelagians he did not and could not envisage grace as distinct from pure nature; he had to set grace against that Pelagian distortion of nature, that idol of the absolutely independent free will, which was haughtily indifferent to good. The Greek Fathers, on the contrary, considered grace in its supernatural and divine excellence, as a perfection that surpassed even what was true in the

---

[1] This promise has been fulfilled in Scheeben's masterpiece, *The Mysteries of Christianity* (St. Louis: B. Herder Book Co., 1951).—Tr.

created world of nature. They saw grace in its relations
with the mysteries of the Trinity, the Incarnation, and the
Eucharist. Against rationalistic Nestorianism they pointed
out that grace, like the Incarnation, has a supernatural,
mysterious connection with the Godhead; against the
Manichaeans, Gnostics, and Eutychians they brought to
light the difference and opposition between nature and
grace. They insisted that grace does not merge with nature
and that it even possesses a certain autonomy. With
remarkable penetration and incisiveness these Fathers,
notably Cyril of Alexandria, triumphantly combated the
naturalist and rationalist tendency that marked Nestorius
and that had earlier appeared among the Arians. They
remain the best allies in our conflict with modern rationalism. Yet they have been studied least of all.

Among outstanding theologians who have treated the
subject, St. Thomas merits chief mention; indeed, he drew
up the plan and established the principles we follow. After
him come the classic work of Dominic Soto, *De natura et
gratia,* composed at the time of the Council of Trent; the
monumental work of Francis Suarez, *De gratia,* in twelve
books; and Isaac Habert, *Theologia Graecorum Patrum de
gratia.* The Jesuit, John Martinez de Ripalda, has dealt
expressly and copiously with our subject in his great work,
De ente supernaturali.

The present treatise takes a form that is speculative in
development; I hoped that this procedure would be the
easiest way toward the acquisition of clear concepts. But
the whole edifice rests squarely on theological foundations:
the Scriptures, the Fathers, and the teaching of the Church;
nothing has been fabricated out of thin air. The certitude
of the assertions depends solely on the arguments adduced
in their favor; of set purpose, no attempt has been made

to fix the theological qualifications of the opinions, although in itself this is an important item. The author did not trust himself to propose such censures, as he is too keenly aware of the incompetence of his judgment; he hopes rather that his views, proposed in the form of a simple investigation, may for that reason be more fairly examined and criticized. Some of the ideas will strike many readers as being novel and unknown. But they are not innovations; they are the teachings which make up the oldest and most venerable fund of doctrine about the mysteries of Christianity to be found among the holy Fathers. The true mind of these ancient Fathers and of the great Scholastics has eluded the new spirit of our century. In any case, the author has the intention of teaching, not what he has learned by his own efforts, but what he has received from illustrious men in the Church.

He perceives only too clearly how unequal his poor powers are to the task of satisfactorily carrying out the enterprise he set himself. Nevertheless he has dared to undertake it, with the purpose of focusing the attention of scholars on these points, that others who are abler with the pen may write about them more worthily. He may often have strayed from this difficult path; if so, it is incumbent on experts to pass pertinent judgment, on the author to acknowledge his mistake, and on you, dear reader, to condone the error. And if you are willing to add to your forgiveness the friendly service of pointing out such errors, you will find him more anxious to learn than eager to speak.

Here I should like to bring these preliminary remarks to a close. However there is one item about which I believe I ought to come to an agreement with my readers from the outset. Throughout this work I have ventured to use the word "supernature" to stand for grace in the proper sense, the grace of divine sonship by which we share in the divine nature. I employ the word to stress the distinction between grace and nature. The sequel will make its meaning clear and will justify it. I beg the gracious reader to bear with me patiently when I come to explain the term; for in a certain respect, especially in the application I make of it, it may appear to be novel and for that reason may alienate some minds.

As has been indicated above, grace is here considered as the foundation of a truly higher, supernatural order of life in contrast to the natural order. If the exposition is to be successful, we must be able to designate this property of grace clearly and distinctly with a technical term that is short and precise. The word "grace" can be drawn down to the level of nature and natural things, and in point of fact is frequently misunderstood. It covers God's unmerited love of us, all the effects of that love including the natural ones, and any state in man that is pleasing to God, even on the plane of simple morality. It can also refer to anything that is supernatural, such as God's supernatural love of us and all its consequences. We could, of course, be content with expressions canonized by Sacred Scripture and ecclesiastical usage, like "sanctifying grace," "grace of divine sonship," and "participation in the divine nature." These expressions are free enough from ambiguity; but they are not sufficiently sharp and concise to serve as technical terms for our purpose. A good term must bring out what the Apostle designated by "new creature," and the Fathers by "new nature," "divine race," and the like. In a number of modern languages we are fortunate enough to have not only the adjective "supernatural" as opposed to "natural," but also the substantive "supernature" as opposed to "nature," although this term has gained currency only in recent times. It has all the advantages we could wish. The course of our exposition must show whether the extensive employment of the word is really as useful or even necessary as it seemed to be to the author.

At first sight the term "supernature" may appear hard to understand and even to open the door to gross misunderstandings. Our conviction is that it is hard to understand only for those who have no clear idea of a supernatural order of life among men, and that it will subsequently be clarified and vindicated by its evident utility and basic intelligibility. As for the other objection, there is no word that is not open to misunderstanding. Indeed, the relative vagueness of the other expressions that are usually employed in this connection subjects them to outrageous misinterpretation. Supernature can refer to the higher nature of another being that stands above a lower nature, and can therefore designate the highest nature of all, the divine nature. For that very reason supernature, when found within the domain of nature, is the lower human nature's participation in the perfection proper to the supreme divine nature.

This work is commended to the fair judgment of the reader and to the blessing of God, to whose greater glory in the mysteries of His grace it is dedicated. A friendly reception will hearten the author to undertake further investigations, starting from the points that have been established, to shed clear light on the meaning and interconnection of the other mysteries of Christianity, and thus to contribute his mite toward the promotion of genuine Christian learning and Christian life.

CONTENTS

CONTENTS

PART FOUR

UNION OF NATURE AND GRACE

INTRODUCTION

THE vast, seething commotion among religious questions of the present age, which is still vacillating between two extremes, is but the continuation of a conflict that has grievously occupied and shaken the Church during these latter centuries. This is a situation that unfortunately has received too little attention. The battle that has been fought on the ethical field for several centuries has in recent times spilled over into the intellectual sphere.

On the ethical terrain two hostile views were locked in struggle, with the Catholic teaching holding the center. One view was that man's nature carried within itself at least the seed of all good which it could ever reach, including the Christian good; no more than some favorable influence from outside was needed to develop that seed to full maturity. This was the Pelagian (and later the Socinian) view; but its characteristic features took final shape in Semipelagianism, in which, tragically, many theologians of the modern era have seen their own minds reflected. Opposed to this view was another which maintained that man's nature, as disfigured by original sin, is utterly incapable of any true good or noble morality; it does not even contain a good seed, which would at least enable it to begin to produce, if not completely to develop, good fruit. This was the Lutheran and Jansenist view.

The Church had waged war against the first view a thousand years earlier, in the person of one of its greatest champions, St. Augustine. A brilliant victory had been won and within the space of a few years the haughty error was suppressed. Yet the heresy had sprung up again and found room enough to run through all the phases of uninterrupted growth from rank profusion to specialized culture. Stage by stage, with greater care and foresight, the Church had to renew the battle against it. The true malignancy of the canker was perceived more and more clearly. At length the error was plucked out by the roots; the teaching of Augustine as set forth in his last books prevailed and was raised to the level of dogma. According to this teaching, by original sin man lost all capacity and power for the good to which he had been destined by his Creator and for which he had originally been equipped. He did not even retain the seed which, under the action of outside influences, could develop and thus realize its inherent potentialities.

But this very teaching of the Church and its whole substructure as supplied by St. Augustine were exploited to the advantage of the other error. The Church had established the doctrine that the true life of the soul had not only been obstructed by original sin but had been completely eradicated, down to the last root, and that consequently the soul had lost all its power and tendency to reach its original destiny. The heretics drew the false conclusion that the soul had forfeited all higher life, all power for all true morality and religion, as well as the capacity for any good; it had become evil and corrupt either in its substance (Luther), or in its faculties (Baius), or in its inclinations (Jansenius). As this error gradually evolved and drew out its subtle inferences, it was painstakingly and decisively combated by the Church. From its high vantage point, ecclesiastical scholarship won the dogmatic battle even before it concluded its campaign against the first error. The victory was clinched by the thoroughgoing and detailed condemnation of the teaching of Baius. This proclamation clarified the entire issue with so clear and searching a light that it forestalled the refined subtleties which spun a web of captious sophisms around the condemned propositions, as they were fabricated not only by the heretical Jansenists but also, sad to record, by certain theologians in the Church. It further furnished a norm for judging all other theories spawned by the same basic error. This was made possible by the explanation that God could have created man with no other gifts than those he now receives at his birth; that even now man is a good work produced by God and enters the world with a capacity for good, having within himself the power to labor for its development; that he is still endowed with an inborn ability to perform morally good acts, and even possesses the faculty of eliciting the highest of all acts in the sphere of ethics, love of God as the author of nature.

Where is the signpost pointing out the road which the Church has trod between two such apparently contradictory teachings, one of which must seemingly be accepted as true if the other is rejected as false? Where is the lofty vantage ground which the Church has occupied to engage them both in simultaneous battle? It was radically the same in both conflicts, that against the Pelagians and that against the Baianists and Jansenists; but against the former the position was inadequately (and materially) conceived, whereas against the latter it was adequately (and formally) conceived. It was the viewpoint of the original supernatural destiny for which man was to labor and according to which the goodness of his actions had to be judged. From this standpoint the Church taught, especially through St. Augustine's writings against the Pelagians, that fallen nature had completely lost the ability, supernaturally communicated to it in the beginning, to reach that destiny which the first man could have attained with the aid of the endowment originally given to him by God, and which has again been opened to fallen man by grace; left to itself, however, the soul was dead to that destiny. At this stage man's supernatural destiny was still regarded materially rather than formally; that is, it was thought of as a destiny which is supernatural, but the full extent to which it is supernatural was not always realized. The point at issue was not to show what nature can do, but only to prove that the perfection which the Pelagians ascribed to nature, ability to work for such a destiny, is beyond the competency of nature. But this very fact, that our supernatural destiny was not considered in its formal aspect, lent to the opposite error a spurious importance when the Church later came to grips with the problem. Thereupon the Church took pains to bring out the true supernatural character of our destiny. It explained that man, in consequence of original sin, lost only his ability to work for his supernatural destiny; but another sphere of activity was still possible, the natural sphere; ability and power to act in this domain, though somewhat curtailed, still remained in the seed of nature.

This distinction between a natural and a supernatural sphere of activity, between a natural and a supernatural ethical order, as also between a twofold capacity and equipment in man, a distinction that appears most striking in the state of elevated man in Paradise and of fallen man, is the two-edged sword the Church took up when it sallied forth to join battle with both errors; it not only cut them down but thoroughly hacked them out by their roots. Although the Church was not forced to an explicit formulation of this distinction until the second error confronted it, we must acknowledge that the first error could have been eradicated more easily and decisively if the distinction had received prominence at that time. For, to some extent at least, one of the main difficulties facing the Semipelagians, in the supposition of fallen man's absolute inability to work for his real end, was the fear of falling into Manichaeism (the Lutheranism of ancient times). This fear could not be completely eliminated unless the assurance was forthcoming that man was able to work in another field of activity that still remained open to him. As in the case of many other dogmas, the distinction between the two ethical orders incontestably owes its sharper conception and formulation to a polemic against opposing heresies.

The doctrine of two different orders of spiritual man's destiny and activity was the secure, but also the necessary standpoint from which the Church and its teachers launched their attack against Luther, Baius, and Jansenius. But the enemies, especially the Jansenists, had perceived the importance of this position, just as the Church itself had, and therefore turned all their artillery and picked columns against it. And we must admit that they conducted the campaign with fanatic energy and marvelous ingenuity; they fought it out on poorly mapped terrain that had not been thoroughly explored by the Latin Fathers, and knew how to find and utilize its difficulties to their own advantage. In spite of their assaults, Catholic theology held its ground; it was aware of the ascendancy of its position and strained every nerve to beat back the charges of the enemy as well as to protect and fortify its lines against future attacks. The enemy disguised himself and changed uniforms a thousand times in an effort to gain the upper hand by deception and treachery. And all the while certain theologians who had been led astray by the morbid

spirit of the age or refused to attune their minds to ecclesiastical teaching, sought to introduce a subtle and specious
form of the error into the Church. But the right cause
triumphed, and at length received renewed confirmation
from the bull, *Auctorem fidei,* of Pius VI.[1]

Theology had won this position as the climax of a griev-
ous struggle that had lasted for three hundred years, and
with it as a base solved the great ethical questions which
agitated minds in those days. Why should we not make it
our own, to solve the vexing intellectual and ontological
problems of the present century? From the time when
these problems first began to interest me and I as yet had
no confidence that I could see more deeply into them, the
realization was forced on me that in spite of the generous
efforts which had been expended on our stormy German
soil by men of true talent and serious purpose, that hard-
won achievement of past centuries had attracted scarcely
any notice and had influenced thinking even less. Even if
the solution did not have all the importance that, as I hope
to show in this work, really belongs to it, at least it merited
earnest consideration. Everything else, whatever its source
or nature may be, is hailed as an experiment leading toward
progress, and scholars use it and believe they must draw it
into their own orbit. This is the reason why questions bearing on religious knowledge, on faith and understanding, on
reason and revelation, and hence on the mysteries themselves, particularly the chief mysteries such as the divine
Trinity, the nature and effects of original sin, the necessity
of the Incarnation, and the meaning of the sacraments,
have in many cases not met with the satisfactory solution
and clarification that had been expected. Investigators did
not go back to the basic truth of two different spheres and

1 Denz., 1516.

orders of knowledge and being. They neglected to build on the glorious foundations laid by our forefathers or to stand on their shoulders. Many disdained to carry farther a project inaugurated by others (although that attitude has been given up by now) and wished to strike out on a new line of their own. And in more recent times, unfortunately, in spite of the most sincere intentions, unremitting labor, and praiseworthy acumen, many did not feel confident that they could rediscover the solid terrain from which the tempests of the century had dislodged them. The inevitable result of all this was that down to our own time an enervating indecision ruled in this domain, and thinkers could not find the safe middle ground between two extremes that were no less antagonistic than Jansenism and Pelagianism were in the field of ethics.

On the one side the fact is indisputable that nature lost not only a part but all of its power to reach the truth in which it originally lived and ought ever after to have lived. To regain possession of this truth it unconditionally needed a foundation that could not be laid again except by Christ, and could not be made over to us except by external and internal revelation. On the other side the Church has repeatedly rejected the teaching that robs fallen nature of all capacity for knowledge and blinds it to all noble and religious truth, as though outside and alongside the truth offered to us by Christ it did not have its own proper sphere of knowledge about divine and spiritual things. Here again the Church proposes two doctrines that seem to contradict each other; yet both have been simultaneously upheld by the Church. Even if we had no definitive evidence about the mind of the Church, this fact alone would impose the conclusion that the Church recognizes, in the intellectual as well as the moral domain, two radically different and opposite orders of spiritual activity that have nothing in common. For the higher order can be completely abolished without the lower order being affected except by the loss of the advantage coming to it from its connection with the higher order.[2]

As long as we do not accept the doctrine of two provinces and orders of knowledge, or regard the higher merely as a more perfect evolution of the lower without a new foundation of its own, or look on the foundation of the order that is left as a simple expedient for promoting the naturally restricted development of that order; in general, as long as we recognize only one basic order of knowledge and yet desire to remain faithful to the positive teachings of the Church, we shall not be able to reconcile those teachings but must fall into one or the other of the extreme errors condemned by ecclesiastical authority, depending on which one we retain.

One alternative is to hold that nature still possesses an active power of knowledge extending to its own sphere, and that grace and revelation are no more than aids favorable to the development of natural powers within their own domain. All known truths will be drawn into the realm of nature, which can employ its own resources to grasp them and can find within its own circle concepts or ideas corresponding to them. Revelation can be necessary only to develop reason more surely, easily, and quickly, and can at most furnish a few positive data about some of God's special designs for the human race. But its object cannot belong to a higher sphere, and its object is not enveloped in any obscurity other than that which in general shrouds

---

[2] We shall see later how these two orders of truth are to be understood, how they agree or disagree, and how they are mutually dependent or independent.

the deeper essence of familiar things from our minds. The upshot of all this is our modern rationalizing tendency in theology, which seeks to draw all revealed truths down to the level of reason, to demonstrate them with rational principles, and to squeeze them into the mold of pre-existing concepts. This tendency is, in the intellectual domain, more or less what Pelagianism is in the field of ethics. The Church has repeatedly spoken out its mind against it in a way to leave no room for doubt.

But if, in the same hypothesis of a single order of truth and knowledge, we turn to the other fundamental position maintained by the Church, that nature lacks the inherent power of rising to the exalted region of those truths which invest the Christian religion with its characteristic features, we inevitably come to the diametrically opposed view, that nature, unsupported by divine helps from within and without, is incapable of knowing the slightest religious truth, and that reason, in Luther's phrase, is "nothing but futile darkness." We favor that position which believes that it opposes rationalism as its contradiction, though not as its contrary, and claims to hold the only key for entirely escaping that error. This attitude was unable to win much headway among German philosophers, but met with a friendly reception in neighboring countries that were more exposed to Jansenist influences.[3] This last extreme could indeed be called in as an ally for undermining rationalism; but even more easily could rationalism unhinge traditionalism and other systems that disparage natural reason, whatever their names may be. Pitch nature out, but it will always

---

[3] In saying this, I have no intention of casting reproach on a number of advocates of "Traditionalism" whose minds were otherwise attuned to the Church. But the interior, and to some extent the historical, connection of their teaching with Jansenist views about the corruptness of our nature is unmistakable.

come back. We cannot gainsay nature. The will can, within limits, take evil to itself as a second nature; but reason cannot. That is why the thinking mind repels traditionalism, whereas it may yield to the seductions of rationalism. However, as long as the two above-mentioned teachings of the Church stand together, neither of the two errors can dislodge the other, since both come to a halt at the same spot. The seeming opposition between the two teachings of the Church remains until we discern that third point of view which enables us to bring them both into harmony and so to topple over the foundation of the two corresponding errors. We have to show that there is one order of truths whose light has set for us, and another whose light still shines for us.

Thus it becomes clear why I said in the beginning that to settle our intellectual crisis we must go back to the achievement of past centuries, and in the spirit of the Church distinguish between two orders of knowledge and truth, as well as between two kinds of ethically good actions in man. But for an adequate understanding of the two orders in the ethical and intellectual spheres we must penetrate to a deeper level in which both are united in a common basis. From that point we shall be able to survey the entire field of the forces locked in struggle, and at the same time acquire a new, more profound insight into the object and sources of our religious knowledge and love, particularly of that knowledge and love which I have designated as the higher, and which have the so-called mysteries of faith for their object and principle.

The powers of knowledge and love are rooted together in the substance and nature of the soul; for nature is the common source of all the powers in a being. The more perfect the nature, the more perfect its powers. Therefore the perfection and extent of knowledge and love are proportionate to the degree of perfection in the soul and its powers of comprehension, through which it can enter into a more or less intimate union with outside beings, to receive them into itself by knowledge and to embrace them with love.

Accordingly the perfection and extent of our knowledge and love of God depend on the relation of our nature with Him. And if we wish to rise to a particularly perfect knowledge and love of God that is specifically distinct from that which we possess through our essential relation to Him as creatures to Creator, we must receive a certain kind of second nature from God. I repeat, we must receive a sort of new nature, not by the addition of a new substance or by the implanting of radically new faculties in the soul, but by a transfiguration and elevation of our whole nature with all its faculties to a higher sphere. We must be spiritually born of God and clothed with the garments of His children. Then we shall no longer stand afar off like servants, but will be welcomed like children to His fatherly presence, and will be admitted to those secrets of His majesty and love which, while we were still remote from Him, were closed and foreign to us.

In other words, to gain a thorough, solid grasp of the distinction between the two orders of knowledge and morality, we must trace them back to their common foundation, a double ontological order. This is the source and norm of our knowledge and love in their subjective and objective, their formal and material aspects. Subjectively and formally, knowledge and love proceed from the power a being possesses conformably with the excellence and fullness of his nature; objectively and materially, the realm of things and relations which constitute the object of intellectual and ethical activity accords with the perfection and nature of the acting subject, since his activity does not extend beyond limits with which he has some contact in his concrete existence.

Since we are now speaking of religious knowledge and love, and therefore mainly of knowledge and love of God and of all other things so far as they are referred to Him, the twofold order must be based on a double ontological order of man with regard to God. This means that man enters into a twofold relationship with God through a twofold nature he receives from Him. In the first place, man receives human nature from God, along with his existence, and thereby enters into relationship with Him as the Creator of this nature. But human nature, as spiritual, necessarily includes a definite power and tendency toward knowledge and love and is their source. The measure of this knowledge and love is nature itself, for nature itself is their proximate object, and beyond that God is their object, so far as He stands in relationship with nature.

However, as we shall see, man receives from God not only a nature proportionate to his proper mode of being, but a higher nature (which is accidental, not substantial) whereby he is refashioned on the model of the higher, divine nature. This sort of second nature which is superior to his own proper nature (we shall later call it supernature) first causes in man the dawning of a new light that makes him capable of a higher knowledge and love. It further places him in a new, special relationship with God, who now draws near to man in His own essence, and not only as Creator of a nature foreign to Him. Thereupon, conformably with his higher power of knowledge and love, man is admitted into a higher world of objects in which he can move about. Thus the question, why and how there are two orders of knowledge and love with reference to God, is clearly settled by answering that two different orders of being are established in the relationship of the rational creature with God.

Christianity claims this higher order of being, knowledge, and love, or, in other words, this superior ontological, logical, and ethical order, exclusively as its own. Consequently the exposition of the distinction between the two orders, natural and supernatural, gets its greatest and deepest meaning from the conception of Christianity itself. Christianity cannot be comprehended in its due nobility and its true, inner quality unless its real, specific difference from all that is merely natural and rational, that is, from all that lies in the realm of nature and reason, is clearly perceived. Christianity presents itself in its perfection as something that is absolutely supernatural and mysterious; and it is supernatural as an institution because it has as its end something that is absolutely supernatural and mysterious. This supernatural character and mysterious depth of Christian finality, and hence the necessity of its supernatural constitution, particularly its function as intermediary with regard to God, revelation, and grace, rightly form the object of the chief and vital question dividing the Church from rationalists and indifferentists. This question has deservedly occupied our theologians and apologists, especially in our day. But the crisis has not yet been completely settled, and it will not be settled until the supernatural order is frankly, adequately, and radically distinguished from the natural order. The standpoint that has been given must serve as the basis for a definition of the supernatural and the mysterious in general and in particu-

lar; and the definition must be such that its very simplicity
and aptness commend it, even if there were no urgent need
of it.

As regards Christian ontology, the previously mentioned
elevation of human nature (*exaltatio humanae naturae in
consortium divinae naturae*), that is, the higher mode of existence which is not essentially required by human nature,
is supernatural. Further, the resulting activities and relations, especially those referring to God, are supernatural.
From our own point of view, we can say that God's existence is supernatural when it enters into a relationship not
merely with our inborn nature, but with our elevated nature. We can also designate as supernatural those works
and institutions of God which contribute directly to the
establishment of man's supernatural union with God.

With regard to Christian epistemology, the same order
is mysterious, that is, it is hidden from natural reason which,
by itself and its natural resources, cannot know such an
order. It lies above the reach of reason, for it surpasses
reason as much as it surpasses nature. Reason is not only
unable to comprehend the supernatural perfectly, but can
at best find among its concepts very deficient analogues for
the realities of the supernatural order.

Finally, Christian ethics owes its special, superhuman
holiness to the fact that it measures up to the supernatural
and mysterious relationships which rest on the elevation
of human nature brought about by its participation in the
divine nature, and therefore can be known only by faith,
not by reason, the instrument of nature. Since all that is
specifically Christian is identical with what is supernatural,
mysterious, and holy in Christianity, we can use this general norm to discern which truths are genuinely characteristic of Christianity. Such are all truths that refer to man's

supernatural union with God, or that come to light in this union.

This procedure will bring out the full, characteristic excellence of Christianity. I shall venture even farther and say: this is the only way we can grasp the inherent value, meaning, and interconnection of the truths of Christianity, and consequently organize a truly Christian body of knowledge. Whenever these truths are not assigned their own exclusive sphere and are intermingled with truths of the natural order, they are necessarily confused with the latter, and therefore not only lose their organic union with truths of their own kind but suffer a dimming of their own light. And in fact we know by experience that those theologians who do not base their theology on these definitions of the supernatural either fail to put together a sound, orderly system of Christian truths or, if they make the attempt, inevitably disfigure the dogmas themselves.

The foundation of the natural order of things is nature, and the domain of natural knowledge, including that of natural ethics, is fixed by nature. In a similar way the foundation of the supernatural order of things and hence of the supernatural sphere of knowledge and ethics is the elevation of human nature to a participation in the divine nature.

My intention is to bring out the supernatural character of Christianity in its true genius and in its influence on the whole range of its doctrines as well as on the Christian life that stems from them. I shall begin by discussing as thoroughly and adequately as I can the two orders of life corresponding to the states of pure nature and of elevated nature in man. I shall particularly endeavor to exhibit and emphasize the true grounds on which each of the two orders is constructed and the center around which each revolves, that is, the ontological or metaphysical element of which I spoke above. In the natural order this element is plain enough; no one has ever philosophized about the natural order of life in man without starting from, or at least reverting to, the nature of man on which it rests and to which it conforms. But in the supernatural order this point is often neglected; no foundation analogous to nature is looked for, and that is the reason why a clear, sound idea of the supernatural order is so rarely achieved.

PART ONE
PRELIMINARY NOTIONS

Chapter I

NATURE AND THE SUPERNATURAL

NOTHING is more necessary and important at the beginning of our investigation than clear definitions of the meanings of words to be employed and a firm resolution to shut out the fundamental ideas of any elements that can beget confusion. The terms we have to define are mainly "natural" and "supernatural," "nature" and "supernature." The first three turn up often in life and science, and are therefore used and applied in a bewildering variety of senses. The last, in the form given, is not indeed new, but is seldom found; yet its content has long been familiar to theological science. Even the form of the word is deeply rooted in the teaching of Holy Scripture and tradition. By using this word, I hope to throw light on the entire doctrine and, by firmly settling its meaning, to fix more easily the sense of the other terms.[1]

"NATURE"

The word "nature" has, as everyone knows, many meanings. It comes from the Latin *natura*,[2] which is the same as

[1] Joseph Kleutgen has carefully worked out these definitions. But his procedure was more polemic and did not envisage the end I have in mind. See his *Theologie der Vorzeit* (Münster: 1854), II, pp. 6–9.—Cf. also Scheeben, *Handbuch der katholischen Dogmatik*, Drittes Buch, nos. 593–609.

[2] The various stages through which the meaning of the word *natura* runs are summarized by St. Thomas in several passages, for example,

19

the Greek *physis*; the two even share their etymological history. As *natura* comes from *nasci* [to be born], *physis* comes from *phyein, phyesthai*. Both words properly denote origin by begetting and birth. They further denote the begotten being and, correlatively, the begetting principle; more exactly, they signify what the begetter communicates to the begotten by generation, what the begetter gives and the begotten receives. Since an offspring quite similar to the parent is produced by generation (like begets like), something that is specifically or numerically the same is found in the principle of generation and in the begotten being.

Therefore *physis* denotes the essential, vital form that is capable of being communicated; and, since each species generates only within its own limits, designates the essential, vital principle that determines the species itself, that is, the form, and hence the specific essence of a thing. However, since generation occurs only among living beings, and since life is communicated by generation, the word "nature," even when it designates the essence and substance of a thing, has a special connotation; it signifies the essence and substance, not simply as such, but with reference to life and activity, as the principle of motion, as the

---

in his *Quaestio disputata de unione Verbi incarnati*, art. 1: "The solution of this question requires, first, a consideration of the meaning of *natura*. . . . We should note that the word 'nature' is derived from *nascendo* [being born]; hence the nativity of living beings, that is, animals and plants, was first called *natura*, as though the word were *nascitura*. Then the term 'nature' was extended to the principle of this nativity. And because the principle of such nativity is internal, the name 'nature' was further employed to designate the interior principle of movement. . . . And because natural motion, especially in generation, has as its term the essence of a species, the essence of a species, signified by its definition, is called nature."—See also *Summa theol.*, IIIa, q. 2, a. 1.

root and basis of the entire life. Hence it indicates a certain state of the substance arising out of its essence rather than the essence itself. This is to be borne in mind, as it will solve some weighty difficulties. Moreover, since generation does not occur among all beings, nor even among all living beings, and is not found at all in spiritual beings, seeing that life cannot be communicated in this way from creature to creature unless matter is present to receive life, *natura* or *physis* properly signifies the essence and species of things that are composed of animated matter and an animating, moving principle; only such beings, the living members of the material world, are capable of generation. As is evident, the word primarily and mainly signifies the form, the determining and moving principle in composite beings (the *forma substantialis,* that is, the *forma determinans principaliter essentiam substantiae compositae*).

By a certain analogy, this meaning of the word is extended to purely material things, which contain matter that is capable of being determined in many ways. This matter is modified, shaped, and molded from without by an act analogous to generation, in such a way that not only its external form is altered, but primary forces spring up and fade out in it somewhat as in the communication of life among living beings.

Therefore "nature," as a concrete and collective noun, signifies in the first place the collectivity of all beings living in matter. It signifies, further, the orderly aggregate of all material things in general, with their forces and relations, their motion and life, embracing the world of material things that are subject to the contrast between generating and being generated, as well as to the distinction between animated or simply determined matter and animating or

determining form. None of this is found in the purely spiritual world in which, because of its simplicity, matter and
the tensions arising from matter have no place.

But if we understand "nature" in a somewhat wider sense,
to express in a general way the essence of a thing and the
principle of life of any kind whatever, the word may be
applied to spirits; and not only to created spirits, but to the
uncreated, creating Spirit. Thus it acquires a transcendental
universality. In this extension, however, it is no longer used
as a concrete and collective noun, but becomes abstract
(and a universal that is realized in many inferiors). In this
sense it is employed in direct opposition to the concrete
existent, that is, the *suppositum,* subject, or individual
thing; it signifies the specific character which individual
things share in common, and through which they occupy
a definite rung in the scale of being, possessing their definite rank, influences, and relations in their association with
other beings.

Here we may recall how St. Augustine, in his controver-
sial works, used the word "nature" according to its transcendental universality in several different meanings. This
variety was imposed on him by the diversity of the controversies in which he engaged; and he never made it his
particular business to seek a conciliation among the different senses by undertaking an analysis of the term. In all
his writings against the Manichaeans, nature meant for
him the essence and substance of created things, especially
of spiritual beings, with their essential powers; it meant
the true product of creation in the narrower sense. Accordingly he maintained that nature itself could not be disfigured or destroyed by evil. But when the Pelagians came
on the stage, the scene shifted at once, and nature appears
suddenly as that which God established, as the condition

of life which the created being originally received from the Creator's bounty, the vital principle and the tendency to good originally conferred on the creature by the Creator, prescinding from the question whether these two endowments belonged to the essence and substance of the creature or were something supernatural. Understood in this sense, nature can be destroyed and annihilated by a sin of nature; the higher, supernatural freedom bestowed on nature can perish, and its life can be uprooted. If the point of view adopted against the Manichaeans had been preserved, none of these considerations could be urged against the Pelagians. We shall later have occasion to resume this problem.

"NATURAL"

If the meaning of the word "nature" veers off in so many directions, the same must be true of the term "natural."

We generally say that that is natural which pertains to nature, arises from nature, or is conformable to nature. We apply the term "natural" to the beings that belong to the totality of material nature, or we extend it to include all created beings that belong to the network of the so-called *natura naturata,* that is, created nature. We can call an effect natural, either because it arises spontaneously from any nature whatever, or because it takes place in a way we describe as a natural mode of acting (particularly in sensible nature), to distinguish it from the voluntary mode of acting proper to spiritual beings, or because the effect is brought about by the powers of some lower nature or combination of natures without the special influence of a higher nature (in opposition to the miraculous).

We can also call qualities and faculties natural, either because they emanate from nature considered as the essence of a thing (or at least are not beyond its capacities); or because they are not foreign to the thing's essence but are compatible with it and are therefore conformable with nature; or because they are joined to a thing by its nature regarded as the generation and origin of the thing.

Furthermore, a good can be called natural, either because it is destined for a thing from the beginning; or because a thing can and ought to attain the good by its own natural powers; or because a thing is susceptible of the good, especially when it finds in such a good the highest perfection it is capable of, even though the attainment of that perfection surpasses its own unaided efforts.

Lastly, the orientation of a being to its end and to the totality of everything pertaining to the end is termed natural. This ordination to an end is natural, either because the being is capable of the end and strives for its possession by its own efforts, or can be made capable of it by the action of a higher cause. For, as we shall see, the created spirit has a twofold end, just as God is its ideal in a twofold way. The created spirit can imitate its model in a manner that is commensurate either with the power of its own nature or with the power of the divine nature. But in the narrower and usual sense we apply the term "natural" to an ordination toward an end which matches the nature and essence of the created being, that is, which can be acquired and reached by a being's own powers and activity. This natural orientation comprises something that is natural in the sense that it belongs to nature as a component element, namely, its principles and powers; something that is natural because it proceeds from nature as an effect, that is, its activity; and something that is natural as corresponding to nature, as the proportionate object of its powers and activity. In the natural orientation of a being to its end, therefore, the various shades of meaning implied in the etymology of the word are to a large extent associated and recapitulated.

"SUPERNATURAL"

Contradictorily opposed to the natural is not, strictly speaking, the supernatural, but the non-natural, that is, that which does not pertain to nature, or does not proceed from nature or correspond to it. This fact is to be kept in mind when we understand nature in its general comprehension as the essence of things with reference to their activity. In that case we regard nature in the abstract, as the essence itself, which as such does not include everything that determines and modifies nature as it is actually found in existing beings, namely, their individuality. Whatever thus determines nature in individual things does not belong to nature so far as it coincides with the essence, and to that extent is not natural. Yet it is natural in the sense that it is closely connected with nature and does not lie above nature.

Only that can be called supernatural which is above nature, extends beyond nature, and is higher than nature. Thus, if we regard nature as the material world order, we can designate as supernatural a being that is elevated above this nature in dignity, power, and activity. Such are spirits, especially those spirits which are not confined within the boundaries of matter, as our souls are, and are therefore not restricted in their activity, and which, moreover, are not visible, as natural things are.

The term "supernatural" can also be applied to a cause that does not belong to the kingdom of material nature and consequently is not tied down to the laws of matter. Such are in general the higher spirits, and especially that cause which is so high above the whole world of nature that the foundation and development of nature, as well as the laws of its activity, are given, sustained, and completely governed by it. This cause is God, the Creator and Lord of nature.

An effect may be called supernatural when it exceeds the powers of nature and cannot be achieved by these powers. An example of such an effect is the production of being by creation, which is a prerequisite of all activity exercised by created nature; also certain special phenomena, like the resurrection of a dead person, which nature cannot cause. Furthermore, an effect may be called supernatural if it could have been produced by natural powers, although as a matter of fact it was brought about not by them, but by a supernatural cause. This is what is known as *supernaturale per accidens.*

These assertions about causes and effects that surpass nature may be applied to nature regarded, not only as the totality of the material world, including man, but also as the sum total of all created beings, whose existence is not nature itself but is something received from God. Consequently we may say that an effect is not simply and absolutely supernatural unless it necessarily or at least actually proceeds immediately from that cause which stands above all other causes. Likewise, a cause is not simply supernatural if there is another cause higher than it to which it is subordinated.

If we take a further step and understand "nature" in its most general, transcendental extension, and at the same time in its most proper connotation, as the principle of motion in a thing, as a thing's aptitude and tendency for activity that are rooted in its essence, or as its life and movement toward its end, then whatever is in nature while nevertheless surpassing nature is its supernatural endowment. Such is every quality, every capacity, every aptitude and inclination, every activity and life, every relation and title, in a word, everything that does not belong to the essence of the thing or is not founded on the essence. On the contrary, all those things are natural which a being has or can and ought to have; everything it possesses in reality or in hope, everything it is fitted by its nature to be or to have in virtue of its nature, that is, its natural origin, owing to the essence communicated to it.

Everything that constitutes a thing's essence as a component part is natural in this sense. All the faculties emanating in greater or lesser degree from such a part are natural. The proportionate development and activities of these faculties are natural, even though outside influences may be needed. The relations which the thing has to all other things by reason of its essence are natural. And the destiny which the thing must reach, to avoid injecting a false note into the harmony of the universe, is likewise natural.

On the other hand, those qualities and adornments that do not constitute the essence of a thing, but are so exalted that they greatly surpass what the thing is equipped by its origin to have, are supernatural. Those powers which in no way emanate from a thing's essence and substance but transcend its level are supernatural. That activity which in value and dignity far excels any action lying within the capacity of the natural powers in supernatural. Those relations to other beings and to God which raise a being far above the sphere and order it would have if left to itself, conduct it to a higher domain, and open to it associations of which previously it had no inkling, are supernatural. Finally, the last end (and in the case of rational creatures, full consummation in beatitude) which a being is meant to attain is supernatural, if the destiny is such that the being can neither make itself capable and worthy of it by its own dignity or its preparatory activity, nor reach it by its own powers.

These things, which are essentially supernatural in themselves by reason of their elevation above nature, must also be at least relatively supernatural when they are regarded as effects, for they cannot be produced by the nature in which they occur, but only by a higher nature. In part, too, they are supernatural as causes, since the supernatural powers placed in nature bring about effects that surpass the powers of nature itself.

This is the supernatural with which we have properly to do. It consists in that dignity, those qualities, powers, activities, and relations which are found in nature but are so superior to anything within the province of nature, that is, anything grounded on and flowing from the essence and substance of a thing, that they pertain to a higher order of their own.

Yet all this gives us no more than a negative idea. Unfortunately, not a few theologians who otherwise grasp the truth aright and perceive it clearly, stop at this point and make no endeavor, by going into the matter more thoroughly, to rise to a positive concept. But only by doing so will their conception be based on a firm, solid foundation.

What is above one nature and is therefore supernatural for it, may not be supernatural for another, more perfect nature. The reason is, that a more perfect being naturally has a higher endowment, superior powers, and a more eminent circle of relationships. Hence what is supernatural for one being may be natural for another. Thus immortality is supernatural for men, because one component part of his essence, the material body, is continually on the march toward dissolution. But immortality is natural for an angel, a pure spirit, whose entire essence is on a higher plane, because no opposition between matter and the principle of life has place in him. Again, the face-to-face vision of God as He is in His essence, without medium or mirror of any kind, is supernatural for every created spirit, because finite nature, by its natural capacity, can receive only feeble, broken rays of the infinite Sun. But this vision of the divine essence is natural to God, who is completely present to Himself. Hence it is clear that a good or perfection which is supernatural for a lower nature is natural for a higher nature. Accordingly the concept of a supernatural good consists positively in the fact that it is a good which in itself is due exclusively to a higher nature, and is shared with a lower nature only because the latter is raised, in a sense, above its own dignity and power to the level of a nature that is superior to it.

"SUPERNATURE"

We have now arrived at the point where we can explain the last of the terms mentioned above and thus clarify the last of the preliminary notions required for our exposition. An elevation and union of a lower nature with a higher nature could perhaps be restricted to particular aspects. For example, God could have endowed man with the immortality of the angels, without at the same time giving him freedom from unbridled concupiscence of the senses, or vice versa. In that case the elevation of the lower nature would be partial; the supernatural good would be a sort of external adornment of the lower nature, and would not invest it with a wholly new dignity and nobility in consequence of which this adornment would be its own and would, so to speak, initiate it into the rank of the higher nature to which that perfection rightly belongs. God could also, at least in abstract conception, bestow supernatural faith on the created spirit, and thus grant it some share in the inherently infallible knowledge that is proper to Himself alone and unlocks the deepest secrets of the divinity, without raising the entire soul to Himself in such a way as to communicate to it all the riches of His divine life. The soul would then receive a gift that is proper to the divine nature; but it would not be elevated to a godlike eminence and would not, on account of its exalted rank and position, receive along with this one gift all the other communicable gifts that pertain to divinity. It would not share in the divine nature to such an extent that in every respect, in its existence, powers, activity, destiny, and relations it would enter into a higher sphere. None of these relations would be essentially due to the created spirit, none would be inherent in it or natural to it; they would continue to be divine properties that in themselves belong exclusively to the divine nature and are accordingly natural to God.

But if the lower nature is raised in all these respects to the level of a higher nature, and especially if this elevation modifies the lower nature so deeply and affects its inmost being and essence so powerfully that the limits of possibility are reached; if God, purest light and mightiest fire wishes thoroughly to permeate His creature with His energy, to flood it with brightness and warmth, to transform it into His own splendor, to make the creature like to the Father of spirits and impart to it the fullness of His own divine life; if, I say, the entire being of the soul is altered in its deepest recesses and in all its ramifications to the very last, not by annihilation but by exaltation and transfiguration, then we can affirm that a sort of new, higher nature has come to the lower nature, because it has been granted a participation in the essence of Him to whom the higher nature properly belongs.

This, then, is what I call supernature. It is that quality and transfiguration accruing to the nature of a lower being which permeate the being throughout its breadth and depth and raises it (so far as that is possible) to the plane of a higher nature. We should carefully note that the nature of the higher being that is superior to the lower nature can also be called supernature. But here we are regarding supernature and nature as two opposites found in one and the same being that in a certain sense has two natures. The first is the basic life, along with everything involved in it, that belongs to a being by reason of its essence; the second is the basic life, with its accompanying perfections, that transcends the being's native endowment. The latter is not rooted in the essence of the being's own nature but is communicated by the nature of a higher being, in such a way that the lower nature is raised above its condition and is enabled to participate in the higher nature.

To explain why I do not confine myself to the term "the supernatural," I wish to point out that the word "nature," as employed in a metaphysical sense, can have two meanings. Even the word "essence" has two meanings, one of which has long been designated as the genuinely metaphysical, the other as the physical sense. According to the former, essence is the root idea underlying all that belongs to a being, that from which everything else proceeds as from its source; according to the latter, essence is the aggregate of all that really pertains to the inner structure of a thing. In like manner the word "nature" can mean either the totality of all that bears on the development of life and the motion of a being—hence the several powers, the activity, the tendency toward a proportionate end, and so on; or it can signify that which forms the substructure of all this, the basic force and fundamental orientation toward an end, from which all the individual faculties in their proper sphere, all tendencies, all activities, all relations to the end, and all the objects coming into contact with these activities issue as from their principle.

We must understand the word in this narrower yet correct sense if we accept the position that there is found in the lower nature, not merely a simple collection of supernatural qualities and activities, but a coherent, harmonious life underlying these supernatural phenomena. As rationality (*intellectualitas*) is the foundation and center of the whole natural life of the spirit, on which all the vital faculties and activities depend, so in the supernatural order we discern something that we can call supernature in the more restricted sense, in terms of which the various supernatural powers, their activities, and their end are defined.[3]

[3] However, as we shall see later, the end in the supernatural order is not, as in the natural order, defined in terms of nature or quasi-nature. Nature finds within its original endowment all it needs to reach its necessary end, but must be further equipped with grace by supernature in order to attain the supernatural end.

CHAPTER II

COMPARISON AND ANALYSIS

THE foregoing discussion of supernature enables us to furnish a much better definition and to provide a sounder substructure for the other three concepts pertinent to our subject matter, especially that of the supernatural. We are in a position to define and delimit the supernatural [1] by supernature, just as we define and delimit the natural by nature. The natural is that which belongs to nature, proceeds from nature, or corresponds to nature. Similarly the supernatural is that which belongs to supernature, proceeds from it, and corresponds to it. We shall appreciate in due time the importance of this definition for gaining clear, fundamental ideas of the supernatural order of grace. At present I shall merely remark that this is the only way the word "supernatural" can be assigned a precise, definite meaning that is not open to ambiguity; practically all the other definitions that are not directly connected with this one fail to circumscribe and fix its meaning satisfactorily. Yet a good definition is extremely necessary, especially in our day, when all notions on this subject are so confused.

Let us endeavor to shed further light on the two terms "supernature" and "supernatural," especially in their opposition to nature and the natural.

[1] We are here speaking of the supernatural in the stricter sense, particularly as it refers to man's supernatural life.

The word "supernature" is not as strange as it may have seemed at first sight. We often say that such and such a habit has become second nature for a man who has developed so deep-rooted and positive an inclination or skill in a certain line that it resembles aptitudes which ordinarily come from nature alone, although in this case it does not really stem from nature. This example serves very well as a clarification and justification of the expression, but at the same time it can lead to a misunderstanding. It serves as a clarification, because the most notable feature of the elevation of nature I call supernature is that it imparts to nature new capacities and powers, and hence opens up a new and permanent field of activity in a higher sphere. It also serves as a justification; for we learn from it that supernature is not, as I foresee that someone will object against me, a new substance in the natural order; and it is certainly not the divine substance uniting itself substantially with nature. The example itself excludes all that. Nature does not formally signify a thing's substance as such, as I pointed out above, and strictly understood does not even signify the essence as such. Rather, nature properly signifies essence so far as an essence, by reason of its characteristic structure, is a definite foundation or principle of life and of movement toward its end and within its sphere. Nature is a vital power and disposition for activity and movement, arising out of an essence. Thus we say that something is second nature to a person when he inclines toward it with his whole being and all his powers, or when it becomes as habitual with him as his own natural activity. In this way supernature is the vital power and inclination toward a definite end that are imparted by a higher Being. They surpass the vital power and aspiration of nature; but because they confer no new essence and no substance, they must be attached to the natural vital power and aspiration and have them as substructure. And because the new vital power is not added in such a way that it exists alongside the natural one but is adapted to and received by the latter, which it merely raises to a higher sphere of activity, another objection vanishes: namely, that the essence is substantially changed by the accession of the new power.

In itself, and also partly because of the point that has just been made, our example can easily lead to a misunderstanding. Since a person can acquire a strong inclination through habit, and since no basic powers are newly deposited in the soul by supernature, the idea may occur that supernature is a new nature only in the sense that it lends to existing vital energies a positive orientation toward something higher; or that it merely enhances such powers within their own sphere and brings them into association with the nature of the higher Being, that of God, with the result that the lower nature would then imitate the higher nature and become similar to it. For instance, if a man knows and loves God with his natural powers and seeks in his way to become holy and perfect as God is holy and perfect; if he follows the law and rules of his reason which is a mirror of the eternal law-giving reason, so that he conscientiously imitates God and eventually, by the progressive development of his natural powers of knowing and loving God, becomes like to Him, he may suppose that he has done full justice to the idea of supernature. In reality, however, the exalted notion of supernature, as made known to us by revelation and also as recognized by sound philosophy, would not thus be clarified, but on the contrary would be watered down and explained away.[2]

[2] An interesting instance of such a conception is found in Staudenmaier, *Christliche Dogmatik* (Freiburg: 1848), III, 482 ff., at the end of his teach-

Even if a situation such as that just described could be called supernatural, it cannot be called a result of supernature. It may be termed supernatural in many respects, most of which, however, are foreign to the mind of the Church and stem from heretical principles, or at least from principles that are incompatible with ecclesiastical teaching. A life led by a man who turns to God with his higher faculties can be called supernatural by one who keeps company with the rationalists, meaning that such a life does not spring from nature regarded as the world of matter and sense and is not tied down to this world but rises above it. Furthermore, it is brought into being by the absolutely supernatural cause (that is, the cause that transcends all other causes) by the creation of nature, and its original seed grows and is sustained by the continuous influence of this cause. Again, this life is directed to a supernatural end (that is, to the nature which is superior to all other natures), and man in some measure becomes like this supreme nature by knowing and loving it. The Jansenist, too, can call this state of affairs supernatural, because it exceeds the capacity and merit, not of pure, innocent nature as it came forth from God's hand, but of nature as perverted and deranged by man's sin. The implication is that in this perverted nature the development of all the natural powers in the direction of good is completely arrested and can again proceed freely only with God's extraordinary assist-

---

ing about creation, where he discusses, according to the doctrine of Sacred Scripture and the Fathers, how man's perfection is a divinization. This means for him the full development of the natural powers of knowledge and love by which man becomes like to God and hence divinized. He had the good intention of clearing this doctrine of the taint of pantheism, and in this respect his explanation has much to recommend it. But by refusing to admit any middle ground between pantheistic commingling and a mere moral union with God by the development of the natural faculties, he imparts a rationalist coloring to his teaching.

ance that overcomes the power of fallen nature. A few Catholic theologians contend, quite incomprehensibly, that supernatural sanctity is actually supernatural rather than natural because it is not given along with nature, but requires the free decision of the will for its realization.

But all this is not supernatural in the sense demanded by the present subject matter and firmly maintained by the Church. As we are now using the term, "supernatural" refers to a good that is indeed found in the lower nature, but is not conferred by the creating nature along with and through the lower nature, and therefore does not unite the lower nature with the higher nature and make the former like the latter merely according to the inherent capacity of the lower nature. That good is supernatural which is communicated by the higher nature to the lower nature apart from and independently of creation; the good by which the lower nature is made like to the higher nature, not *secundum modum suum* but *secundum modum eius*, that is, not according to the measure of the lower nature's power, but according to the measure of power which the higher nature wills and is able to produce, in order to give to the lower nature what the latter does not possess and cannot attain by itself.

We can draw no more from the example mentioned above than this: a new direction, as positive as though it were a new nature, can be imparted to the natural faculties without destroying them. The example is very defective,[3]

[3] More to the purpose is the example which the holy Fathers, with reference to the reception of a new nature, transfer from other material natures to human and spiritual nature. Thus Irenaeus uses the illustration of a tree on to which a sprig of a better variety or even of another species is grafted, so that the tree grows and produces blossoms and fruit not of its own kind but conformably with the nature of the tree from which the sprig was cut. Other Fathers suggest the example of metal which, when immersed in fire, does not lose its own essence but takes on the glow

and the application is made *a minori ad maius,* not *a pari.* If we can say that a man takes on a second nature when he merely gives to his existing powers a special direction that resembles the constant inclination and aspiration of nature, with greater right and in a richer sense we can use the term when not only a direction is given to existing powers but new, higher powers are infused which raise the entire organism of nature to a higher plane and make it capable of a wholly new kind of activity. On the other hand, to do full justice to the meaning of the word, which suggests that nature is raised to a higher level and enters into possession of a sort of second, higher nature, we must say: The existing powers, besides receiving a definite development and formation orientating their activity toward the higher level, have been given a new sphere for their activity, because they have been filled with a new, higher power that comes to them from outside and above. The lower nature is made like the higher nature, but not merely in the sense that it can imitate the higher nature according to the measure of its own inherent power; through the power that is inherent in the higher nature and is communicated as an accidental perfection to the lower nature, the latter is raised so high that it is, so to speak, on a par with the higher nature. Formerly it was capable of a bare outline and shadow of resemblance with the higher nature; now it can receive a completely rounded out and living image of that nature.

Here we touch on a point that is supremely important. Around it are concentrated the greatest difficulties respect-

---

and the qualities of fire, so that it gives forth light and heat as though it were fire. In this way the soul, under the action of the divine nature, receives a quality by which it flowers into a life that is more god-like than human or creaturely, absorbs divine light and heat, and thus takes on a sort of second nature that resembles God's nature.

ing the conception of this doctrine and also its demonstration in Scripture and tradition.

Nature, no less than supernature, as we have asserted, can persevere in union with the higher and be like it, by means of the supernature which makes such union and resemblance possible. And I add that nature, to be capable of supernatural union and resemblance with the higher nature, must be like the latter even naturally, by its very essence. For supernature is not a substitution or change of essences; the essence of nature remains, it is only elevated and transformed. Therefore it must have a capacity for such elevation and transformation; and, as was said above, fundamental powers must already be present in it to form the substructure of the new powers. Thus a stone or even an animal cannot be raised to a supernatural knowledge, because such beings are not capable of any intellectual knowledge, even on the natural level. To receive supernatural knowledge, a being must have a capacity for knowledge, and hence must possess a faculty of intellectual cognition emanating from its essence; this is the faculty that is elevated by the higher light illuminating it and is thereby introduced into a new sphere.

Therefore the nature that is to be elevated must have some innate kinship and similarity with the nature to which it is to be raised, if it is to be capable of that higher kinship which relates it to the higher nature on a footing of equality, so far as that is possible, and causes it to resemble the higher nature more perfectly. Accordingly the two orders of nature and supernature are related and similar.

This is the reason why supernature is not contrary to nature (and hence unnatural) but is quite in harmony with nature, and can even be called natural, in the sense that it is conformable with nature and is not unnatural. It can also be called natural in the sense that it perfects nature and leads nature to its highest consummation, not within the sphere proper to nature, but by exalting nature above its station and so bringing it to a perfection of which nature is susceptible, though lacking in itself the power and capacity to attain it. In a word, the supernatural may be called natural to the extent that it is not unnatural. And it is not unnatural, first, because nature, while not aspiring to the supernatural by its own forces, is capable of reaching the supernatural through the influence and operation of another, higher nature. This is obediential potency, which is actuated under the guidance of a higher being to which unreserved obedience is given.[4] A second reason why it is not unnatural is that it is not bad but is something good for nature; a good which nature may not demand as belonging to it by right, but lovingly, gladly, and thankfully receives as a welcome gift that has been offered. Therefore, although the two orders are not so connected that the lower encloses the higher, they are united in such a way that the higher encompasses the lower and presupposes it as its substructure and prerequisite condition.

That relationship and similarity and connection of nature and supernature involve the consequence that an eye which is less practiced or fails to view the matter in the right light and from the correct angle, cannot, for all its keenness and penetration, keep them quite separate, especially if the observer becomes immersed in details. The difficulty of marking such differences in detail is the cause that so long arrested the full development and formulation

---

[4] St. Thomas discusses obediential potency in the *Summa theol.*, Ia, q.115, a.2 ad 4; IIa IIae, q.2, a.3; IIIa, q.1, a.3 ad 3; q.11, a.1; *De veritate*, q.29, a.3 ad3; *Compendium of Theology*, chap. 104.

of this doctrine, and gave to its adversaries, particularly the Jansenists, so much room to move about in. As long as generalities are in question, a logic that is somewhat skilled finds it easy to come to grips with all the objections arising from the confusion and interchange of fundamental concepts, especially by sharply analyzing the many-sided meanings of words like natural and supernatural. By this procedure a general solution can rather easily be given to the difficulty which conceives supernature as a heightening of the natural powers because it modifies them, or as a habit or state by which natural energy is merely developed and supported in its own field of activity, as in the case of the so-called acquired virtues (the name the older theologians gave to the natural, moral virtues acquired by the efforts of the natural powers).

We remarked above that such a conception is inadmissible. The reason is that a simple heightening of a faculty leaves it in the sphere which it occupies, and elevates it only by aiding it more readily to overcome all the obstacles in the way of its activity, so that it can rule its own domain with greater ease, security, and firmness. This is the case with the moral virtues, with regard to which our inherent power is so tempered by repeated trials that it performs its proportionate acts with greater facility and sureness. But such an enhancement does not enable the faculty to perform acts of a higher kind than it could perform previously. However, not only a simple strengthening of a power, but an elevation of it to a higher sphere, can be called a heightening of it. Hence the expression is equivocal, and is perhaps the term most likely to introduce confusion into a subject that is already delicate enough without such ambiguity.

A like equivocation is found in the words "capability,"

"capacity," and generally in terms that express potentiality. For potentiality is twofold: *ad fieri* and *ad facere, quae fit* and *qua fit, quae agitur* and *quae agit,* or, as Aristotle puts it, the power to produce all things and the power to become all things. In modern languages we can say that there is a twofold power or capacity, to receive or to give existence, to become or to cause to become. And thus we have in us a capability or capacity for the supernatural, but not in the same way as for the natural. We have in our nature an active ability and capacity to produce natural effects by our own forces; but we have no such ability to produce the supernatural. We have only the ability and capacity to receive supernatural powers (and without any claim for their realization), and only the ability to perform supernatural activity through powers received from above.

With respect to the rule for determining what belongs to nature or to supernature, the general norm is to observe which powers nature has and must have in virtue of its essence, how far these powers extend, and what end must be appointed for them if nature is to reach its suitable development and achieve rest and perfection. For only that is due to a thing which it can attain by its own resources, not what is in any way possible for it. All that must be assigned to nature as incentive, material, and object of the exercise of its powers falls within its province, and nature can lay greater or lesser claims to such things according to the degree of their necessity. Also the similarity, relationship, and union which it has with a higher nature by its essence, powers, and activity, are natural.

Whatever is outside this list—hence the powers that do not emanate from the essence, and in general all that is unattainable by the unelevated powers emanating from the essence—is supernatural, and, if it pertains to a symmetrically organized life, counts as supernature. Consequently the union, similarity, and connection with a higher nature, which are commensurate, not with the lower but with the higher nature, are supernatural, so far, I repeat, as the higher nature grants to the lower nature a share in perfections that are proper to it to the exclusion of other natures.

This general rule is easily established, but is not so easy to apply in detail. However, we can say this much: There is a natural and a supernatural knowledge of God, a natural and a supernatural justice and love of God, a natural and a supernatural blessedness. It is certain and beyond all doubt that this is so, and that the blessedness we are meant to attain and the knowledge, love, and justice by which we are to attain it, are not natural but supernatural. But why one blessedness, knowledge, and love should be natural, and the other blessedness, knowledge, and love should be supernatural, and how they differ in detail, to such an extent that the natural perfections are attainable by natural powers whereas the supernatural perfections are not, is not so easy to show and constitutes an extremely difficult problem. Earnest effort is required to penetrate into the depths of the soul's superior life; at the same time, the excessively sharp scalpel must be shunned. That is why the author who has studied this subject most minutely and with greatest acumen said at the close of his investigation: "I do not wish to press any farther, as otherwise I shall draw blood." [5]

[5] This is John Martinez de Ripalda, in his work, *De ente supernaturali* (republished in 6 vols., Paris: L. Vivès, 1871-72), which was formerly so renowned but is now practically unknown. The treatise is remarkable for its immense erudition, clarity, coherence, logic, and wealth of contents. These high qualities are deserving of praise even in points where the doctrine is not developed with the depth and simplicity of style characteristic of Suarez, especially in the second, sixth, and seventh books of his great work, *De gratia* (vols. VII to X of the *Opera omnia,* Paris: L. Vivès, 1866).

The ordinary explanation, somewhat superficially proposed in theological manuals against the Jansenists, represents as supernatural the act that is elicited with the aid of supernatural grace and is meritorious for supernatural, eternal life. This is quite true, but does not completely satisfy the scientific intellect. Therefore I shall endeavor to avoid the logic-chopping by which the otherwise flourishing Spanish Scholasticism of recent centuries (which has devoted special attention to this field) has sometimes obscured rather than clarified the question, and shall give my support to the system, so plain and simple, yet drawn with such genius from the deepest sources of Christianity, which some of the leaders of that school have constructed on the model supplied by St. Thomas. The Angelic Doctor was almost the first who began to develop this whole doctrine in its proper traits, and was also the one who penetrated into it most searchingly with the profound insight of his genius and fashioned it into a system, which his followers have only to expand.

To proceed step by step from what is better known to what is less known, and at the same time to set off the two orders against each other adequately, I shall first present the order of nature in its full dimensions. I shall begin by showing what it is, what it embraces, and what it can embrace. Then I shall show what it does not embrace and what its boundaries are; in this way we can better perceive where the supernatural order starts. Lastly, we shall consider nature according to the substructure of its substantial essence, its powers, its end, and its activity.

We are mainly concerned, as is evident, with human nature, which is not only under the divine nature but is also under the angelic nature, and which consequently can become supernaturally similar to the latter, especially by the suppression of the defects that naturally grow out of our bodily composition. However, since such elevation is not effected by a power proceeding from the angels themselves but is brought about by a power conferred by God, and since, moreover, this power in the present order of things is a result of the transformation and elevation common to the human soul and to angels, that is, the same participation in the supreme, divine nature, we need not examine our relationship with angelic nature more closely, and have only to regard elevated nature in its relation to God as the absolutely highest nature. Accordingly the main question concerns the elevation of the soul to the divine nature. The raising of our corporal nature to a higher grade will occasionally come into the discussion as a subordinate consideration.

PART TWO
NATURE AND NATURAL LIFE

CHAPTER III

GENERAL PRINCIPLES

NATURE, as we have said, is a substantial state springing from and determined by the essence of a thing, along with its aptitude for life, activity, and movement toward an end commensurate with the essence. It is that which confers on a thing its definite place in the scale of being and its relation with other beings over it, alongside it, and under it. It is therefore the substructure and foundation of all capacities, powers, and tendencies inherent in an essence.[1]

Many heretics wrongly believe that they exalt grace by contending that it displaces and destroys nature. That amounts to praising God as Giver of grace while insulting and disparaging Him as Creator. Praise of God's grace does not require any depreciation of nature. Grace itself is inevitably debased and robbed of its true heavenly, divine splendor by the attempt to make it nothing but a means to prop up a wretched, corrupt, or feeble nature and restore it to health and vigor. How can grace be noble, high, divine, and heavenly if it produces nothing but what is natural, even though we may be in desperate need of a supplement to nature? Need invests a thing with a relative, external value, but does not confer an absolute, inner worth.

---

[1] On the entire matter discussed in Part Two, see the detailed and valuable analysis of the subject as presented in the classic works of Dominic Soto, *De natura et gratia*, lib. I, and Suarez, *De gratia*, lib. I.

Grace is too sublime to be used merely for a natural purpose. Grace produces effects and goods that are of far higher excellence: not human or earthly goods, but divine and heavenly goods. It transforms children of men and servants of God into children of God, and gives them, in place of the natural, menial love of God they can have by themselves, the holy, free, and filial love that marks the children of God.

Our intention is not to extol grace at the expense of nature. Rather, we shall do justice to nature and give it its due; thereby we shall also do justice to grace and more easily and surely vindicate for it its rightful position of pre-eminence. Both endeavors require of us a clear, definite, and sharply delineated philosophical notion of nature. Such a concept will immediately place at our disposal two clear, simple principles which, if we maintain them resolutely and logically, not allowing them to be obfuscated by various prejudices and specious difficulties, and if we take them as firm, incontestable starting points, will lead us surely and happily to our desired goal.

Nature is the principle of activity necessarily proceeding from the substance and essence of a being; it has a definite power and tendency by which it strives for a definite end and a definite development and perfection. Two principles are involved in this conception. Each being has received from the Creator, in and with its essence, a good nature equipped with power; this nature is as indestructible as the being itself. This principle safeguards the rights of nature against its enemies. Furthermore, each nature has assigned to it a development and perfection proportionate and corresponding to its powers. This principle also vindicates nature's rights, but in such a way that it keeps nature in its proper place with respect to grace. For it indicates that not any and every development and perfection pertain by right to nature, but only such as are definitely fixed and circumscribed, beyond which the supernatural domain of grace begins.

Let us examine these two principles somewhat more closely; we shall then pass on to a more detailed discussion of man's nature.

To begin with the first principle, we remarked above that they who regard nature as powerless or hold that it is in itself capable of nothing but evil, disparage and affront the Creator's work. For in the beginning God made all things good, and everything that He makes later is also good, so far as it comes from the Creator's hand. Therefore I do not have to delay over the blasphemous contention of those heretics who decry the substance of man himself as wholly or partly evil, whether they consider it evil as existing without God, or as coming from the hand of God, or as made evil in consequence of personal or hereditary sin. The last is not entirely foreign to the otherwise subtle Jansenist view, which can without injustice be called the new Manichaeism.[2]

Accordingly the substance and essence of man are good. But if the essence is good, the nature as such must also be good, because it is nothing else than the vital energy springing from the essence and the tendency toward the attainment of the end which the Creator destines for the being in question.

If, then, the essence and substance are indestructibly

[2] Cf. Alticoti, *De antiquis et novis Manichaeis* [Lamertius Alticotius (Alticozzi), S.J., *Dissertatio historico-critica de antiquis novisque Manichaeis*, Romae; 1763]. The author shows how the Jansenists tried to find in St. Augustine's treatises against the Pelagians the defense of the very doctrine which he had so vigorously and victoriously combated in sixty books against the Manichaeans.

good, the nature as such must also be indestructibly good. Therefore its natural goodness cannot be lost any more than nature itself can, since it is based on the goodness of the essence and proceeds therefrom. Consequently the powers given for the pursuit of natural goods and the inner, necessary striving for such goods cannot be lost. This is so true that even when sin becomes like a second nature in the will, nature continues to resist, and the keenest torment among the devils and the damned themselves consists in this conflict between nature that strives irresistibly for good and the will that is turned against good. And I maintain, furthermore, that such is the case with nature that is burdened with original sin as well as with nature that is not afflicted with original sin. As man's substance remains the same after sin, nature too is the same.

Because the substance is good, therefore, the vital energy proceeding from it and the tendency toward a destined end must also be good. The proposition that a power striving for development necessarily arises from the essence in every substance, especially in every living and spiritual substance, is, I do not hesitate to say, so firmly established philosophically, that the opposite is thoroughly unphilosophical and incomprehensible. Many philosophers even describe the essence itself as a power that is ever active.

This truth is even more certain in the dogmatic field, for the Church chose this principle as the decisive criterion in its conflict against the Eutychians, Monergetes, and Monotheletes. The Church insistently discerned the resuscitation of Eutychianism in the latter two heresies, because the human nature of Christ, if it really existed, could not be conceived and represented as bereft of power and a tendency toward its own proper activity. And therefore the Church drew from the teaching of those heretics the conclusion that, if Christ's human nature were completely inactive and motionless, it would cease to be a real nature and a real, existing essence.

Consequently, if every being has a power and inclination for activity, and indeed for good activity, since the power and inclination come from the Creator of the essence and are given by Him, we can say with full right that they who, like the Jansenists, deny every power and inclination toward good in fallen nature, are no less Manichaean than are those Lutherans who often asserted, to the discredit of creation, that man's substance had become evil. We can say this with the same right as that with which the Church said to the Monergetes and Monotheletes that, by denying all power and energy in the human essence of the Savior, they had relapsed into the Monophysitism of the Eutychians.

This principle, which is so clear in itself and is recognized by every sound philosophy (incidentally, it is the one truth found in rationalism), must uncompromisingly be maintained: every being, whatever its state may be, has in it an active power and tendency to strive for its own good, to realize that good in itself, even though not without external help, and thus gradually to grow up to its perfection, to reach this goal, and to move toward the last end commensurate with it. In particular we must maintain that nature as such remains in rational beings, in spite of any derangement and disorder of the faculties resulting from abuse. Reason in such beings is no mere passive capacity to receive ideas infused or imposed from without, no mere possible intellect (*intellectus possibilis*, in the scholastic sense) that is reducible to act, but is at the same time an active intellect (*intellectus agens*), reducing itself to act, hence an active power of forming ideas for itself. And this power must not be thought of as dormant; it is endowed with a permanent inclination and aspiration to develop itself and to exercise its activity as soon as an object is presented and incidental obstacles are removed. Lastly, we must hold that the will's power for good is never abolished, even by the greatest moral depravity, and that it is not a passive but an active faculty; far from slumbering, it remains ever a power striving after its object, a power to will what is good.

Although this philosophical conception is so simple, we have to be insistent in emphasizing it. The unphilosophical view (as it is proudly called, while reason, the source of philosophy, is boastfully spurned and trodden under foot) does not cease, up to the present day, to emerge again and again in subtler form and with every appearance of elegance; its specious refinement, though flattering and deluding the imagination, grossly affronts reason. Its adherents were soon compelled to abandon the error in its crudest form, with its patent contradiction and absurdity that man's substance was evil or had become evil or had even been partly annihilated (thus Luther at various epochs). They then retreated to the position that the substance remained but that its powers were destroyed or had become thoroughly evil (thus moderate Lutherans and Baius), or else that the powers of nature were in themselves completely passive, and therefore in reality non-existent. And when this modification was perceived to be still too crude, the more subtle Jansenism came on the scene, devised sharper distinctions, and taught that the powers were indeed there but were lacking in the energy needed for development, as though they were in a dormant state and had no inclination to good. What Jansenism taught mainly about the will was later taken up by traditionalism, which is related to Jansenism, and went more deeply into the question, and applied to the cognitive power underlying the will: that the intellect never had or at any rate does not now have any aspiration and energy by which it seeks to develop itself and can by itself grasp and elaborate the objects presented to it.

All such views pervert the concept of nature itself or at least the concept of a good nature. For nature is nothing but the essence regarded as striving by its active powers for its end, which is good and has been foreordained by the Creator.

Therefore we must unconditionally hold fast to the simple proposition that every being has a nature which as such is good under all circumstances and relations (human nature in particular remains good even after falling into sin, by which it lost its original goodness), and preserves its active powers and its aspiration toward a good which it can and ought to attain by the development of those powers.

Here we may pass to the second principle mentioned above with reference to the order of nature, namely that there is a definite goal for nature as such.

That good which interiorly perfects and completes a being and thus terminates its development and progress, we call the being's internal end. The external end is the position it occupies relative to other beings, especially higher beings; this end is to be reached by the being's movement and activity. The internal end is the perfection inherent in a being (among rational beings it is beatitude); the external end is the relationship established with other beings (which among all creatures in general consists in the fact that by their interior goodness they make known the glory of God, are subject to Him, and serve Him). We are immediately concerned with nature in its progress toward interior perfection and completion.

Two questions can here be proposed: (1) What perfection is nature capable of? (2) What perfection must nature have in order not to miss its absolutely necessary end and thus avoid appearing faulty and defective?

The first question is inherently ambiguous, as was remarked before, and can have a double meaning. If the first question is not distinguished, the second question cannot be answered; if a distinction is duly made, the second question is answered in advance.

Nature can be capable of a perfection either in such a way as to acquire it, or in such a way that it can receive the perfection; that is, nature can come into possession of the perfection either by its own efforts, although perhaps with the stimulation and support of other beings, or by receiving it as a gift from another being, although not without its own cooperation. Evidently, to avoid missing its goal positively, nature does not necessarily have to become as perfect as it absolutely can become; it has only to become as perfect as is consistent with the range of the power conferred on it. For this power does not outreach itself, but aims only at the development that lies within its competence. It does not aspire to become a power of a higher sort, but tries to bring out and unfold what is contained in it. Thus the necessary perfection of a plant is not what can in any way be imparted to it, for instance, by the grafting of a higher species or even of a higher variety, but is only what can be attained by the full development of the power latent within its seed. This power aims at nothing else than its own growth, and needs nothing else than air and nourishment to display its activity. The plant is certainly capable of being improved by grafting so as to receive a new, higher power and thus rise to a higher perfection; but it does not require such a perfection. Hence it is perfect in its kind and does not absolutely miss its end if it does not, by a process of engrafting, reach the higher perfection of which it is basically capable.

The perfection which nature must attain by itself and which is therefore natural (it is thus called because it is so bound up with nature that nature would not reach its end without it), cannot be gauged from the simple fact that nature is capable of it, but only from the fact that nature has in itself the active capacity and power for it and, having the power, strives to realize it. But if we wish to designate as natural the highest perfection which nature can attain in any way at all, on the ground that it has some sort of capacity for the perfection (through its obediential potency), we may do so, assuming that everyone knows the sense in which the word is being employed.

This point has to be considered in the inquiry whether the beatific vision of God, which is proper for His children, must be the unique end and natural consummation of the created spirit. The occasion of this question confronts the history of dogma with the difficulty that the holy Fathers, especially St. Augustine, and even St. Thomas, who is noted for his accuracy, seem to connect the destiny for the beatific vision directly with the rational, intellectual nature of the soul. However, they do not intend to assign reasons why the soul must have received such a destiny; their purpose is to show why spiritual creatures could receive it. And if they say that that end is the unique last end of man, the reason is that it alone actually is the highest and last end which man can attain, whereas the natural end is much lower and, in a certain sense, is but a first step toward it. That this represents their real mind is clear from the fact that those Fathers require for the vision of God a new power, a new light, a transformation and elevation of the natural intellect; they bring this out when they play on the Psalmist's words: "In Thy light (the divine light, received from God, not our human light) we shall see light" (Ps. 35:10). But elevation of a faculty is not necessary to its perfection and does not pertain to its due development, which takes place within its own sphere.

Here, too, we have a clear, simple, and certain principle which only delusion, party spirit, or gross prejudice can obscure. We can never wonder enough how certain theologians [3] could deny the principle and thus uncover a hybrid lying between the Jansenist and the Catholic teaching about man's natural end. They confounded the active striving for a good that is involved in the power to procure it, with a sort of passive aspiration that is nothing but a receptivity for the good if it should be given. Only the former, evidently, can imply a necessity for reaching the good; the latter implies only an indifferent capacity which awaits the free decision of the giver and is not the basis for any claim to the good that may be desired.

Accordingly we have gained two general principles: first, nature as such is good in every being and has a power and

[3] Such are especially Cardinal H. Noris, L. Berti, F. Bellelli, and in general the so-called "Augustinian School" that attached itself to Gregory of Rimini. Their esteem for St. Augustine and in part their interpretation of him were the source of much good. But by departing from the common and better kind of Scholasticism, which also adhered closely to St. Augustine, and by going astray in their analysis of his teaching, they lost the clue to a sober understanding of him. Their entire interpretation of the learned Father runs somewhat parallel with that of the Jansenists, although we do not wish to identify the two tendencies. A close historical connection between the teachings of Gregory, the *tortor infantium* [the appellation comes from his doctrine about the sufferings endured in the next life by children who die without baptism] and the errors of Luther is easily recognizable.

tendency for a certain development; secondly, the necessary and natural sphere of a being's development and perfection is that alone which corresponds to the active powers found in nature.

In the interest of further clarification, we add to these two a third principle, that the faculties of nature, like nature itself, are based on the thing's essence, flow from it, and depend on it; or, what comes to the same, that the powers of nature are to be measured by the material and formal principles of nature, as St. Thomas says. In view of the definition of nature given above, we can assume this principle as philosophically evident; hence we are ready for our task and can turn attention to a consideration of human nature.

Manifestly the fullness of treatment and the argumentation underlying the various propositions cannot be given in the detailed way that may seem to be required. A more ample presentation is not needed for certitude, but may seem advisable for the sake of coming to an understanding with certain readers about some words and concepts that have become vague and indefinite in these latter times. I hope that a plain and simple exposition will suffice to carry us to our goal.

CHAPTER IV

MAN'S COMPLETE NATURE

WE BEGIN by considering man's complete nature. We shall study the principles of that nature, or man's essence in its component parts, to which the nature itself and all that belongs to it are adjusted.

Man is made up of body and soul. More precisely and metaphysically we may say: Man is a being consisting of a potential and an actual principle, a material (determinable) and a formal (determining) principle. But the formal element in this composition is not engulfed in the material element (as in purely material beings), or dependent on matter for its activity (as in plants), or bound to matter as the support and organ of its functions (as in animals). The form is so autonomous (since it is a form that not merely inheres in something else but subsists in itself) that it can exercise a completely independent activity which is even hampered by materiality; this activity is intellectual cognition. Yet this one principle in man represents all the functions which other formal principles in their various gradations represent in lower natures. Thus an extremely rich and manifold life and the most varied kinds of activity unfold in man. All the degrees of the scale of being in the spiritual and material world are concentrated in him, but in such a way that by their encounter they are mutually modified in their activity and relations.

Spirit and matter, high and low, are wonderfully united in man; and this gives rise to the difficulty of understanding man's nature in all its wealth of meaning. But in general we may say that all the perfection of this nature comes from the side of the spirit, i.e., of the informing, determining, higher principle, while all imperfection and weakness come from the side of the sensible, hence the material, determinable element. The perfection of the spirit is based on the fact that it does not include matter in its being, precisely because matter is a purely potential element. These two opposed elements enter into a certain unity, in which they reciprocally affect and modify each other. The material body, which in itself is a mass without unity, life, or movement, is held together in coherence, endowed with life, and moved by the spirit as the principle that unifies, animates, and moves. But by its union with matter the spirit forfeits its purely spiritual independence to a certain extent, and even incurs a sort of slavery to matter. Matter prevents the spirit from beholding itself in its spiritual essence, and in general from enjoying the intuition of purely spiritual things. It forces the spirit to direct its spiritual activity to objects on hand within the realm of matter, to things of sense, yet does not thereby upset the independence and spirituality of this activity.

Thus the union of the two elements with each other does not turn to the advantage of the higher of them; it causes the higher element to become somewhat estranged from itself, in the sense that this element does not possess itself as perfectly as it would if it were alone. Furthermore, the resulting union is not perfect, as this would imply the complete subjection of the lower element to the higher. The essential opposition between matter and spirit gives rise to a certain cleavage and opposition in man, which cannot be overcome by the spirit's inherent power. This dissension does not only manifest itself in an occasional clash between the higher and the lower life in man; since matter irresistibly proceeds in the direction of dissolution, the tension eventually becomes so taut that it rends man's whole nature asunder. The spirit is then thrown back on itself and goes on to develop its own life more freely, while matter loses its form and its life.

This opposition between matter and spirit may give the impression that the spirit is thwarted, persecuted, and shackled by matter, and that freedom has to await the death of the body. It also keeps human nature from achieving perfect unity. From ancient times, therefore, this has been the reason why many thinkers regarded matter itself as evil, or the union of spirit with matter as unnatural, and as punishment for some sin committed by the spirit.

But the union is in fact natural. The spirit fashions matter into its own body and pervades it with its own life. Matter, which is not evil in itself but only imperfect and potential, yields submissively to the spirit. However, since matter and spirit are so immensely different, a completely harmonious union cannot be wrought by the spirit's own power; the spirit cannot wholly conform matter to itself any more than matter can wholly immerse the spirit in itself. Matter cannot draw the spirit down to its own level in such a way that the entire life and activity of the spirit is organic and bound to matter, as is the case with the formal principle in the purely animal and vegetable life of beasts and plants. On the other hand, the spirit cannot draw matter and corporality up to itself and rule them in such a way that their entire activity and aspirations join forces with the spirit's functions, and that the life which the spirit imparts to matter becomes as indestructible and imperishable as its own spiritual life.

As long as the cleavage is not overcome, we have no unified and no perfect nature; and therefore some thought that they had to maintain that in the normal, natural state, the spirit must have power to produce such unity, that is, the power to subject sense life to the life of the spirit, to make it conformable to the spirit, and to hug the body to itself in indissoluble life. No doubt the ideal picture we paint of human nature includes this thoroughgoing "spiritualization" of matter, by which matter is fully subjected and conformed to the animating spirit. More than this, it even implies that the spirit, notwithstanding its enduring union with matter, retains complete control of itself, so that it is able to develop its own activity as spiritually and freely as though it were not united to matter at all.

Yet who does not perceive how far beyond the natural power and ability of the spirit is the demand that it should be thus intimately united with matter and still not be tied down by matter? Who does not see that matter would then be not only animated by the spirit but in a sense spiritualized, so that the spontaneous development of its own properties would be quite inhibited? Surely such a power is no more natural for the spirit than the present union (in which human nature is now situated) of the spirit with the body is unnatural. Accordingly the spirit lacks the power to mend the cleavage and to concentrate the whole nature within itself in a higher unity. On the other hand, matter does not permit its own spontaneous development, such as it is, to be thwarted. Consequently man's nature has neither the power nor the need to repair the dissension by producing such unity.

Is the cleavage, then, to remain forever? And if so, where is the unity that is unconditionally necessary for the perfection of nature? But why, I ask in turn, must human nature remain forever? The contrary principles of which this nature is composed cannot be held together eternally by natural force. Nature harbors within itself the principle of its dissolution; this is a sign that it has no claim to permanent duration. If that is so, the dissension prevalent in nature does not have to be repaired in such a way that the lower part is conformed to the higher part by an elevation and transfiguration of its natural essence; release can be procured by the progress of the lower part toward the death it carries within itself. It will be separated from the higher part, and the latter can develop its life freely and without restraint in untroubled unity, and thus more easily realize its own perfection.

But does not the union of the spirit with the body turn out to be unnatural if it is only transitory, if it is not to endure forever but must come to an end just when the spirit is at the point of attaining its full perfection? No, it is not unnatural, because spirit and matter are united to form one nature, as I explained above. In a certain sense it is unnatural for the spirit, which finds its activity hampered by the union; and therefore, if the spirit cannot be freed in any other way, it must attain its natural perfection by the dissolution of the composite nature. We may state the case thus: Although human nature as such lacks the power to endure permanently as a whole and to adjust the opposites found in it, it is truly a nature and a good nature; but, while it exists in its totality, it has no more right to achieve a stable, permanent, and unified development than other purely animal natures. Only its superior, spiritual part, which is endowed with power to live an indissoluble, unified life, can and must aspire to arrive at such a goal.

In its vegetative and animal life, human nature is on a par with lower natures, and has no stable and permanent end assigned to the individual. In its spiritual life it is on a par with purely spiritual natures, and does have a permanent, enduring end destined for the individual. Since the lower and higher life are united in it, no reason is apparent why it should be either wholly immortal or wholly mortal. Its spiritual life follows the laws governing spirits, and its sense life follows the laws governing things of sense. Consequently the opposition that endures throughout the union of both elements is resolved, not by the victory of one of them over the other, but by their eventual separation.

Thus we are confronted with a truly remarkable prodigy, but one that arises from the peculiar relations of this nature. The problem calls for a solution; the challenge has to be met, yet reluctance to take it up is understandable. Although human nature is truly one nature, it cannot in totality achieve a unified development and reach a permanently enduring end, because elements so diametrically opposed as spirit and matter are combined in it; power to compose the differences is lacking. Full development and attainment of the end are possible in only one of the elements—the higher. Accordingly the seeming paradox must really be true: the unified development and enduring perfection of man's composite nature must be something supernatural. The material nature of the lower part and its tendency toward material multiplicity and dissolution cannot be modified or completely surmounted unless the lower part is raised above its nature so as to be conformed and subjected to the higher nature of the spirit that is united to it; it must in some way be spiritualized. In other words, the perfect and enduring unity of man's total nature is supernatural, because human nature virtually contains two natures whose opposition cannot be reconciled unless the lower one loses its own disposition and limitation and is made conformable to the higher one by being drawn up to its level. The higher nature has to pervade and rule the lower nature with a power it does not possess of itself and can receive only from some superior nature.

No wonder, then, that that which in one respect seems to be the most natural thing in the world and, in purely spiritual natures, actually is natural in every respect, turns out to be supernatural in human nature. The unified and stable development of composite human nature, involving immortality and subordination of the flesh to the spirit, is natural, if by that we mean a highly fitting and desirable perfection of nature. But it is not natural in the sense that it is necessary for nature and is required by nature. In the first place, the perpetual endurance of the whole nature is not natural, for nature has the power of immortality only in its spiritual component. It is certainly desirable for the spirit to preserve the body (especially if the spirit were not kept from its inner fulfillment by the body); but the spirit has no more right to permanent possession of the body than it has power to secure it. In the second place, freedom from the rebellion of sensuality and of the flesh against the spirit is natural to the extent that it effects a desirable unity among the various tendencies. Indeed, we may say that it is necessary to the extent that the spirit in its perfect state must be freed from this opposition by complete victory or by complete separation, if it is to enjoy peace; just as now it must constantly strive to rule and dominate the rebel. But such freedom is not natural in the sense that the conflict does not necessarily arise from the components of nature and may not exist during the time of nature's development and progress toward its end. The spiritual will is hampered in its striving by the flesh, but it is not destroyed, any more than reason is destroyed by the activity of sense and imagination. On the contrary, the will may be reinforced by sense appetite, just as reason may be assisted by phantasms.

I remarked in passing that the spirit does not in all circumstances find it desirable to remain forever united with matter, for the reason that its own full development, particularly in interior and superior knowledge, is obstructed by the body. This is especially true when the spirit is left in its natural power and its purely natural relations with the body. Even then its activity is spiritual, although it is chiefly and directly concerned with material things, as the spirit is in some measure bound to matter. To develop its own activity freely and vigorously and thus attain its end, it must be equipped with a spiritual power of a higher order that will enable it to preserve its independence of the matter united with it, and to raise this matter to its own level without in any way being pulled down in the process; or else, if it is to have nothing but its natural power, it must be completely separated from matter before it can reach the state of full perfection. Therefore, if we consider man's lower component we find it not unnatural, and if we consider his higher component we find it even natural that the higher part of nature, the spirit, on which personality and all man's special powers and prerogatives depend, should be able by itself to reach and hence to require an unruffled, immortal life. But the same cannot be said of human nature regarded as a whole; if it is left with nothing but its own powers, which is undoubtedly possible, such a life is beyond its grasp.[1]

[1] Here we have an opportunity of describing and justifying in greater detail a point of dogma that is firmly settled, namely, that the immortality of the body and the unimpeded efficiency of the soul's faculties, or more exactly the complete subjection of sense appetite to the guidance of reason, are supernatural. Such perfections do not arise from the principles of nature; in fact, as is clear from the principle established above, they need not even be conferred on nature by a higher nature and power. Nature is capable of existing in the integrity and perfection that are absolutely necessary for it without them.

But these truths are secondary in this work; besides, they have often been treated. They can be reconsidered here only so far as they are needed for grasping our main thesis and for rounding out our exposition when it comes into contact with them. The chief object of our investigation is nature and supernature in man with respect to his spiritual life, insofar as man himself is of spiritual nature. For it is only by the elevation of the spirit, the highest and most excellent part of nature, that man advances beyond his nature and is brought closer to a nature above him. In this way alone a new sphere of life and activity that really belong to another, higher nature opens up for him. A supernatural relation between spirit and matter in man is possible only if the lower part is made more conformable and subject to the higher part than it would be if left to itself. By this means man can reach a position of eminence that is proper to a higher nature, for example, that of the angels, and in this respect his state can and must be called supernatural.

But such a state is not supernature. In the first place, no new, higher system of life is established by it. Secondly, man's nature is not raised above its highest component. Yet the relation mentioned above does, to some extent, raise the lower part of nature to the level of the higher part and, although it does not flow from the principles of nature, it enters into the domain of those principles, since it intervenes between the two extremes that compose nature. This is the reason why many scholastic theologians number the gifts of integrity and immortality among goods included in the order of nature as constituting an integrity of nature, in opposition to a certain disorganization and infirmity that are inherent in nature. They contrast a natural original justice or rectitude with the gratuitous original justice that is the effect of supernatural grace. Thirdly, these gifts merely accompany and follow the state we have called supernature in the strict sense. When the spirit arrives at the higher state of supernature and thus comes closer to God, source of all spiritual power, it is filled with a vital energy that enables it to pervade the entire nature belonging to it, to make this nature conformable and similar to itself, and in a certain way to spiritualize it. If we focus our gaze on what is properly supernature, that is, the elevation of the spirit

This investigation of man's complete nature shows that if the composing and constituting principles of nature are left to their own resources, nature in its totality is not capable of a uniform and enduring (that is, immortal) perfection. Not even the higher part, which is naturally capable of such perfection, can reach that goal as long as it remains a component element of the complete nature.

---

to a share in the divine nature, we can spare no more than a passing glance for the supernatural in man's composite nature.

Chapter V

SPIRITUAL NATURE OF MAN

Since we are considering man's nature in its striving for a stable and unified perfection as its end, we must devote less attention to the composite nature and concentrate on the nature of the higher, formal, and spiritual principle in man. Besides, the composite nature of a being is mainly determined by the principle that raises it above all the other beings of the same category (genus) and gives it its distinctive excellence (the specific difference) by which it occupies a definite place in the hierarchy of beings. The proper end of a being depends chiefly on this principle, and all the other principles and powers in the being are directed and subordinated by it to this one end. A being's true, genuine, positive perfection and development are realized in the higher, formal element of nature, especially if that element, as in man, is essentially independent of the lower element. All the lower powers and dispositions serve the higher part and, if no other alternative is possible, must even be sacrified to the perfection and development of the higher part whenever they happen to impede and obstruct its progress.

Accordingly the real, positive perfection of human nature is a thing of the spirit; from now on the nature of the spirit will be the direct object of our study. We shall first inquire how the spirit, in its own right and as separated from the body, is capable of solid development and full perfection such as it ought to attain. Secondly, we shall examine how it can and ought to strive for this absolute perfection in an imperfect way while it is still united to the body.

Man's spiritual nature consists in the power of vital activity arising from the immaterial, and hence simple, unmixed, noble substance and essence of the soul, along with a tendency to perfect itself up to a certain point by the actualization of a potency inherent in its faculties, and thus to repose in the fullness of its richly developed life as in its end. The two faculties of knowledge and love emanate from this immaterial nature; and love in turn is based on knowledge and directed by it. Other faculties are often included, such as emotion, freedom, and the like; but they are only consequences or modifications of these two powers. If anything else is to be added, it must be a power to move or affect some outside being, a power that has no immanent act, although it is put into operation by the immanent acts of the other two powers.

The interior perfection, and consequently the interior end of man, so far as his spiritual nature is concerned, consists in the full development of these powers, that is, in knowledge of the supreme truth that lies within the orbit of the natural intellect and in union through love with the supreme good to which the will by itself can attain, along with a peaceful, uninterrupted, joyous possession of such truth and good.[1]

---

[1] I beg leave at this point to express my mind about a philosophical conception of the relation between eudaemonics [theory of the happiness resulting from a life of activity in accord with reason] and ethics. Knowledge of this relation can help considerably toward an understanding of the exposition to be given later.

Two aspects must be carefully distinguished in the activity of the powers

Simultaneously with the growth of this inner life, the spirit enters into an orderly relation with the beings that are around it, under it, and over it, especially with God its Creator. The spirit must acknowledge and maintain this relationship by appropriate action in order to reach its external end.

---

mentioned above. First, the true life of the soul consists in its activities, for by its actions the soul is united with the good it strives for and thus reaches its interior end and perfection. Secondly, by its actions the soul measures up to the relations and obligations it has to other beings or to parts of its own being, and thus realizes its external end, that is, its due position and order with respect to other beings. In the completely developed life of the soul the knowledge of God with which the soul is filled and perfected, and the love of God by which the soul is united to God in blissful joy and reposes in Him, make up the interior perfection of the soul which the older Scholasticism called beatitude in the proper sense (hence not the experience of happiness, but the repletion of the soul's inner life which is the cause of the experience of happiness). Conversely, the knowledge of God by which God's majesty is acknowledged, glorified, and praised, and the love of God, especially the surrender, subjection, and esteem of God connected with it (*devotio* and *religio*), constitute the external fulfillment of the soul in its external relations. The activity of the soul can be called properly moral only in this second aspect. For moral activity as such is always an activity that is performed on account of an end, as due to an end and suitable for reaching an end; it must always be in conformity with a person's relations to something else; it is activity that is in accord with order. Only when love and knowledge are regarded as actions which we direct to an end in accord with the order of reason, can they be called moral actions; they truly are moral actions, and therefore pertain to the rectitude of the mind, whereby the mind is rightly related to something. In themselves, as knowledge and love, they procure union with their object; by this union they establish, not a rectitude of the mind, but the spirit's supreme vital activity, and hence beatitude.

The two aspects of spiritual activity are interconnected, as they flow from the same source; frequently they intermingle, although the formal distinction resulting from their different relationships is not suppressed. Even prescinding from the fact that the same act, for example that of love, belongs to the first category according to one relation and to the second category according to the other relation, they reciprocally support each other. For instance, a true union with God or the desire for such union induces us to adopt a fitting attitude of subordination and subjection to Him. Conversely, subordination to God imposes on us the

The created spirit which, like the angels, is not held down by bodily ties, can develop the entire energy of its spiritual power right from the beginning; it can and must attain its internal and external perfection in an instant. This is no nebulous hypothesis. The full flowering of intellectual cognition can accompany the gift of nature; the will, with all the energy of its pure, simple power and inclination

---

duty to unite ourselves with Him in the degree He requires of us, and to honor Him by our love to the best of our ability.

The realization of our moral relationship to God is the natural manifestation and outcome of our already consummated or inchoative union and oneness with Him by love. This is a normal relation, in which action for the sake of an end proceeds from union with the end. But if union with the end does not flow from the natural development of life, it can be based on an abnormal relation and be brought about by a will that is stimulated by fear of punishment to satisfy its relations and its indebtedness toward the Judge, and thus to appease and propitiate Him by love and desire for reconciliation.

Moral motivation in the strict sense is found in the end that demands an action of us and induces us by obligation or invitation to perform it. Love as such can underlie all moral motives, but in itself is not a motive, because love moves us by the pleasure it gives us, not by obligation. Therefore love is properly a eudaemonistic motive, in the sense that it incites us to do good to the beloved object by the pleasure and joy it takes in that object (not on account of the desire for joy). Morality is exalted, not degraded, by such eudaemonism.

The doctrine outlined in this note must be applied later to gain a correct conception of the distinction between moral and theological virtues and to avoid misunderstandings. A superficial consideration of the terms can result in the notion that the moral virtues are all natural and that the theological virtues are so supernatural as to have no corresponding analogon in the natural order. But that is not true. The formal, distinctive character of the two classes of virtues, as specified by us, does not cause them to belong to different orders, natural or supernatural. Moral virtues are those that are directed to the establishment or the fulfillment of a relation to others, and hence both parts, subject and object, are contrasted and distinct. Theological virtues refer to the possession of another Being and union with Him; both subject and object meet to become one. Moral virtues in this sense are found also in the supernatural order, although moral virtues are often distinguished from supernatural virtues as such. Conversely, knowledge and love of God are found in the natural order as the basis of moral aspirations and as analogon for the corresponding theological virtues.

to good which lie in the very nature of the spirit, has only to join and follow the intellect and decide once for all to love what is good and acknowledge the order in which the Creator has placed it. If this is done, nothing required for natural perfection is wanting. All the powers of the spirit have matured and remain in a secure, permanent state, without desire for anything further. According to the teaching of St. Thomas, the will's inflexible constancy in good is not an effect of perfect natural knowledge, as is the case with supernatural, intuitive knowledge of God's goodness, but is a natural result of the decision the will makes with all its energy.

In the same way the obduracy with which spirits that have turned to evil unfailingly and with a certain consequent necessity harden themselves in malice without any possibility of conversion, is not the effect of natural necessity or of a supernatural influence coming from God, who does not cooperate with evil any more than He withdraws natural powers for good, or of the condition of their knowledge. This situation can arise for no other reason than that the simple spirit, with undivided and unrestrained force, turns away from its true end and reverts upon itself. We must likewise admit that without God's supernatural influence and apart from any reason based on knowledge of the good, the will of the pure spirit is permanently confirmed in good by its unreserved, undivided decision in favor of good and its subordination to its true end.

Accordingly the pure spirit's natural perfection can be achieved in an instant; by deciding to love the good which it knows, it enters into complete and secure possession of that good and reposes in it. A gradual, slowly progressing development does not take place. In a similar way the human spirit, as soon as it begins to exist like a pure spirit, can reach its goal, the full development of its native powers and its untroubled, definitive perfection.

But as long as the soul is united with the body in a natural way, as I said above, it cannot fully develop the powers it possesses. Intellect and will are both hemmed in. The mind can have only a defective knowledge of objects akin to it, the higher, spiritual objects by which it is to be perfected. The will, partly because of the dullness and inconsistency of the intellect, partly because of involvement in so many other, lower appetites, cannot decide irrevocably either for good or for evil, and so cannot enter into a peaceful, secure possession of its good estate. A healthy though gradual progress and growth may occur; the somewhat restricted and latent faculties that require development begin to turn toward their goal and to pursue it. Yet their full maturity in the state of beatitude is not precisely the result of their activity, in the way the tree grows from the root, the bud from the tree, the blossom from the bud, and the fruit from the blossom. By striving for its perfection and realizing it to the degree now open to it, the faculty is made ready to pass from the present state to another in which its full, free, sudden flowering becomes possible.

While the soul is in the body, it must use its faculties as best it can and aspire after that knowledge and love of good which will eventually make it happy. It must also acknowledge the relations it has to other beings in this state, especially to the Creator, and must warily keep on guard in difficult circumstances, that it may become worthy of one day finding itself, to its joy and happiness, in better and more secure relationships. During the present preparatory period, which is a time of striving for a goal, love for the good predominates; the blessed state of perfection has to be merited by action. Knowledge of the good to be possessed may be somewhat less energetically pursued. It need not be cultivated so intensively; whether it is more or less cultivated during the preliminary period is of less importance, or of no importance at all, for arriving at full maturity of knowledge in the higher state.

Thus the human soul has a perfect, final end, namely, the culmination of growth it reaches in the state of its full freedom and repose. It has also an imperfect, proximate end, namely, the orderly development of its powers in the direction of the last end, the consummation of all desire.

Up to this point we have been speaking of the end and the growth of spiritual life in the abstract and in general. Let us now see in what the end consists concretely and in particular, and how the detailed development proceeds. At the same time this investigation will disclose the limits possible for natural progress.

The internal goal of the spirit, as we have said, is union with the highest good, or possession of the highest good that can be reached by knowledge and love. The external end is the spirit's harmonious and orderly relation to all other beings.

The highest good with which the created spirit can enter into union by knowledge and love is undoubtedly God, the nature exalted above all other natures and the supreme, absolute cause of the spirit's own nature. Consequently the latter is meant to be united with the divine nature by knowledge and love. It is meant to be thus united, because it has the capacity for this union in its own natural powers. If, as we are taught by Sacred Scripture, we can come to a knowledge of God's majesty, glory, and beauty by contemplating the great beauty of material creatures, how much more readily can the spirit know God and marvel at His beauty by contemplating its own essence, which is so like to God! This is the knowledge of God that matches the spirit's natural power; the spirit knows God, not as He is in Himself, but as He appears in His works, which contain traces of His glory, like an image that is reflected in the mirror of creation, though only in rough outline and in faded colors. The proposition that a creature, even a spirit released from the shackles of the body, cannot with its natural powers behold God immediately in His own essence, is a truth so firmly established by the teaching of Sacred Scripture, the unanimous voice of tradition, and the declaration of the Church itself, that it excludes all doubt.[2] The same truth can be cogently demonstrated on solid philosophical grounds.[3]

The following proof seems to be quite clear. As power to know depends on the immaterial nature of the knowing subject, this nature is the most immediate and natural object to which it is referred, and also regulates the measure of knowledge. Therefore the spirit can know inferior things as well as it knows itself; but it can know higher objects less perfectly than it knows itself. The highest object of all, the spirit's transcendent, infinite cause, it can know least perfectly, that is, only as reflected in the spirit's own nature and in other creatures; these give forth a weakly mirrored image in which the rays of the infinite sun are, as it were, infinitely broken up. Thus the most perfect knowledge of

[2] Among the propositions condemned by the Council of Vienne under Clement V was the following: "The soul does not have to be elevated by the light of glory in order to see God and enjoy Him in beatitude." Cf. Denz., 475.

[3] A detailed discussion of these reasons may be found in St. Thomas, *Contra Gentiles*, III, cc. 49, 51–54, along with the masterly commentary of Francis Ferrariensis, a true Thomist, in whom the spirit of the great doctor is not stifled by a profusion of subtleties or deprived of its freshness by rigid formalism. [This commentary is reprinted in the Leonine edition of the *Contra Gentiles*].

God obtainable by the natural powers of the created spirit is a knowledge of God in His works, a knowledge in which God is seen as in a mirror, "through a glass in a dark manner" (I Cor. 13:12). This mirror reflects only those rays which reach it, that is, those emitted from the surface of the mirrored object that is turned toward the mirror. But the mirror does not receive any rays from the hidden interior or from the reverse side of the object, and therefore does not reflect them. In a similar way, knowledge about God derived from His works can be perfect in its kind, without being absolutely perfect or disclosing the depths of the divinity. When the power inherent in nature achieves its full development, this is enough to perfect such knowledge in its kind and to bring nature to the maturity suitable for it.

Let us advert to this principle: as long as the created spirit is left to its own powers and needs, its knowledge is no more than a knowledge of God derived from His creatures. More clearly, the created spirit's natural knowledge, the knowledge proportionate to its nature, is no more than a knowledge of God derived from created nature, that is, the nature that is proper to the spirit and is found in all other creatures. Nature, as the subject of knowledge, is also the proximate object of knowledge, and therefore regulates the measure of knowledge objectively as well as subjectively.

Consequently nature knows only so much about God as is externally revealed in nature, and has no idea about God's essence and properties beyond what it can gather from their influence on creation and the government of the world.

God's nature or essence, as it is in itself and transcends

all union with created nature, lies above the creature's natural knowledge and is therefore inaccessible and hidden—a mystery.

Nevertheless the spirit, by the natural light within it, knows from its study of creatures that God, as the ultimate and highest cause of all being, must be one and infinitely perfect, that He must combine in Himself, in a more eminent way and in supreme unity and purity, all the perfections found in creatures; that He is eternal and omnipresent, all-powerful, all-wise, and all-good. From the greatness and beauty of creatures, so closely related to one another in spite of their variety, the spirit gains some idea of the infinite beauty which must arise from the association of all those splendors in the harmonious divine unity. It knows God as its benevolent Creator, whose love has given it existence, life, light, and, in addition, so many images of His infinitely magnificent beauty. All this the spirit knows, and experiences joy and happiness in this knowledge. Having this, it possesses everything that it can and may require according to its nature.

Nothing else is due to the spirit as a creature; indeed, perhaps it cannot even suspect that anything better is possible for it. How is it to suppose that it could in some way be made capable of immediately touching and seeing the infinite God, and thus embracing Him in His essence as a whole (*totum*), though not wholly (*totaliter*)? Would not the desire to draw near to that inaccessible light, in which the immortal God alone dwells, imply boundless temerity? How can the spirit dare to aspire after a knowledge which belongs solely to the divine nature, which is due to God alone, for which He alone has capacity, which the Father has by His essence, which He communicates to the Son as the latter's glorious and distinctive inheritance ("neither doth any one know the Father but the Son" [Matt. 11:27]), which only the Holy Ghost, who proceeds from the Father and the Son and reposes in them, can fathom? "For what man knoweth the things of a man but the spirit of a man that is in him? So the things also that are of God no man knoweth but the Spirit of God" (I Cor. 2:11).

Only they who blindly persist in error can deny the principle that was established above and is so clear in itself, that the aspirations and rights of nature cannot reach beyond the horizon of their active power. That was the mistake of the Jansenists and of some theologians who unfortunately sided with them. They admitted that nature did not have the resources to see God's essence as it is in itself, but maintained that nature had a positive desire and title to the beatific vision as its natural end. This contention seems to us to be not only false but to involve a *contradictio in terminis,* an intrinsic contradiction, as we pointed out when explaining the principle.

God is the supreme object of knowledge and hence the goal of the development of the natural intellect. He is also the supreme object of love, and consequently the goal of the will's development. Love of the good, which is inherent in the will, can and must rise toward the good and repose in that Good which is the good of every good. All the love which the spirit naturally has for itself leads back, under nature's guidance, to its Author. The spirit loves God as its Creator to whom it belongs; it loves God as the infinite beauty reflected in a thousand images, but most of all in the spirit's own essence; it loves God as its greatest Benefactor and loving Protector. It must experience happiness and blessedness in this love, by which it is united with the highest good. And as the spirit loves God, its Creator, to whom it subordinates the love it has for itself, so it subordinates all the love it has for its own equals to this higher love, and thus reduces love to its higher unity.

This love which nature has for its Creator and Author is pure and noble. It is sometimes called love of God as our Father. It could more appropriately be called the love of a servant for his kind and generous master. For nature as such does not stand in filial relation to God; the creature as such is God's servant and menial. Only because the creature has its origin from God (though not by generation or quasi-generation) and is loved by God and loaded with benefits (though not with fatherly love or a son's inheritance), can it with some sense call God its father and love Him as such. But the creature cannot love God in the fullest and best sense of the word, with the intimacy and tenderness with which real or adopted children embrace their father. This natural love always implies great reverence. It does not effect, but rather forbids, the inception of a union between the spirit and God resembling the union of friend with friend or of father with son. The union resulting from natural love has more of respectful retirement in it than intimate association.

The spirit achieves its internal end by knowledge and love of God. The case is similar with the actions that proceed from knowledge and love of God, maintain the spirit's relationship to God, and constitute its external end. The spirit that was created by God, not because of any need but out of overflowing kindness, had to be appointed by God to be a witness of His glory; the spirit has the duty of glorifying and serving God. This is done in the measure in which the spirit knows and therefore manifests the glory of God, as well as in the way in which it loves God and therefore carries out His will in all things out of love for Him.

By these means the spirit also enters into correct relationship with all other spirits. It loves them because they have the same nature as it has and because they too are to know God, love Him, glorify Him, and serve Him. It esteems them because they have a dignity and personality equal to its own.

Thus we have come to a detailed knowledge of the natural end and the natural perfection of the created spirit. The internal end would consist in knowledge of the highest truth attainable for the spirit by its own nature. This is knowledge of God, the creating nature; a knowledge derived from created natures, mostly from the spirit's own nature, plus love of the highest good with which it is united through its own nature, that is, love of God as the Creator and supreme Lord of its nature, and as the infinite Beauty known through its own and all other created natures. The external end would be the establishment of orderly relationships to God and other spirits: to God, by venerating and adoring Him as the absolute principle of the spirit's nature, and by praising and glorifying Him to the best of its ability; to created spirits, by loving them and respecting their personality and by living with them in intimate fellowship in the enjoyment and service of God.

This is the perfect end attainable by the spirit, if it is left merely in its own existence and powers. All that has been said applies to the human soul after its separation from the body, as well as to the angels.

If we regard the human soul in its union with the body, i.e., in the state of its growth, its relations, powers, and activities are substantially the same. But they are less perfect, and their development does not proceed along so straight a line.

In this state, too, knowledge and love of God are the proximate end and the proximate interior culmination to be achieved by the spirit. But the knowledge is less perfect, because the spiritual intellect is directly concerned with the material elements to which the soul is united. Things of sense are its proximate and natural objects, and the soul is not able immediately to apprehend itself in its spiritual nature that is united with matter. Consequently the knowledge of God that it can and ought to obtain in this state is predominantly a knowledge of God derived from the beauty and greatness of sensible nature. This is the way the human mind, including that of pagan philosophers, ordinarily comes to a knowledge of God, and Sacred Scripture itself teaches that man is impelled by nature to know God by this process (Cf. Wisd., chap. 13; Rom. 1:17 ff.). Natural love of God corresponds to this knowledge; however, love of the spiritual in general and of God in particular is considerably more hampered in its development by union with sensibility than intellectual knowledge is.

I repeat, a natural love corresponds to this knowledge; for the soul's relations with God and spiritual things are not negated by its union with the body. This is a love whose power and tendency reside in the nature of the soul itself, as was taught by most of the Fathers who were not driven by their conflict with the Pelagians to introduce a different terminology under pain of misunderstanding. The Church, too, took official measures against the contention of Baius that such love, proceeding from natural, philosophical knowledge and the powers of nature, was prejudicial to the merits of Christ's Cross.[4] But I have pointed out that

[4] Cf. the condemnation of Proposition 36, Denz., 1036.

the progress of this love is incomparably more handicapped by sensuality than intellectual knowledge is. The reason is that sense knowledge is not directly opposed to intellectual knowledge, whereas sensuous love is often directly opposed to spiritual love which has to struggle to escape its clutches. The flesh lusts against the spirit, and the spirit has longings that are opposed to the flesh (Cf. Rom., chap. 7). Moreover, although the yearning of the spirit is the higher, it is the weaker. Sensuality has its object directly before it, and the object exerts all its charm and attraction, whereas the spirit does not thus have its proper objects presented to it directly in their vitality and spiritual beauty, but only in the mirror of the sensible. And this weakness of the spirit in conflict with the flesh is so great that if God did not come to its aid and support with special help and strength, it would inevitably succumb to the flesh (Rom., chap. 7). Therefore it is difficult, if not morally impossible, for the spirit by its natural power and inclination to love God, really to love Him above all else, not merely in estimation, by esteeming Him above all, but effectively, by overcoming everything for the sake of God and resisting all temptations.[5] But we should note well that this is a moral, not a physical impossibility, since this kind of love of God does not surpass the physical power or tendency of the spirit, but is quite in accord with it; if the love cannot go into action, the reason is found in the obstacles that thwart it.

Even during the period of its union with sensibility, the soul can and ought to know and love God. As a natural growth and orientation toward interior perfection open up

[5] It is evident that God can and must assist this natural weakness with special help without overstepping the order of nature. This special help would not be the supernatural grace merited by Christ, but would be what some theologians call a grace pertaining to the natural order.

before it in this state, it also has an orientation and inclination toward a natural external perfection, consisting in activity of the moral order which it must observe conformably with its nature. It has the same relation to God as that we specified for pure spirits, and it can live up to this relation in the same way as it can elicit love of God. Moreover, it enters into a special relationship of dependence on God. Because it requires God's special assistance to grow in goodness and to avoid evil, it must also in a special way honor God, thank Him, and pray to Him.

The spirits that are close to it are, in the first instance, those that share in human nature with it, and are therefore likewise subject to a gradual growth in goodness and are in need of mutual assistance. Consequently the general social relationship among spirits, mentioned previously, is modified to the extent that it exacts mutual esteem and love, particularly mutual support and help in spiritual and corporal needs, and checks all disorder in the legitimate pursuit of the end. Finally, a quite special moral relationship, that of the soul to the sense appetites inseparable from man, is added to the two already mentioned; the soul must safeguard its own dignity in the face of sensuality and secure dominion over it.

All these moral relationships are normal for the human soul and constitute a natural system of morality. The relationships are naturally knowable, because they have their foundation in nature. Thus we have a natural moral philosophy, in which a pagan, such as Aristotle could advance to astonishing lengths by his keen analysis of human nature. In nature, too, are found the physical powers to love spiritual things and the supreme creative Spirit, as well as to live in accord with known moral relationships in the manner described: powers that can go into full action under God's natural cooperation and instigation, whether general or special. Consequently there is a natural moral life and a natural moral activity. The powers of the spirit, as contained in its nature, are somewhat hampered in their operation, and require frequent exercise, energetic striving, and unremitting pursuit of the good before they can develop their activity easily, quickly, and efficiently. Their inclination must be tempered and strengthened, particularly in situations where sensuality directly or indirectly tends to withdraw them from what is good. The power that is thus tempered, strengthened, and made fit, is really virtue (*virtus*, perfected *vis*), which arises from the gradually crystallizing habit of the faculty owing to its good activity. The powers receive their perfect inclination to good in consequence of frequent effort and practice; but in themselves they already have a radical tendency toward good, to which the tendency acquired by habit has to be added. Thus the seed of the true virtues (*semina virtutum*) are buried in the natural faculties, and the seed grows in them. The presence of these natural seeds of virtue in nature accounts for the existence of natural virtues that have God, our neighbor, and ourselves for their objects.

To summarize what has been said, we are confronted with an order based on man's spiritual nature, known by this nature, and to be carried out by its powers; an order that is meant to lead to a definite natural perfection, interiorly by knowledge and love of God, exteriorly by observance of its moral relationships. Briefly, in addition to the supernatural order of human development established, revealed, and inaugurated by Christ, man has a natural order, based on his nature. This would be the permanent order destined for man if God had not decreed something better, and, in a tenable view of many theologians,[6] would even now be the established order subsequent to original sin, if God had canceled all our relations to a higher, supernatural end.

This means that a purely natural state would be possible, that is, a state without any genuine supernatural elements. At the same time, it indicates the correct middle ground between two contrary, false conceptions.

The Jansenists, like all the Gnostic and Manichaean sects, denied the possibility of any other good state of nature than that in which man, endowed with supernatural powers and virtues, would be truly a child of God with the beatific vision as his inheritance. They turned what is really the supernatural state into a natural one, and thereby made it the only good state. Other heretics, on the contrary, turned what is really the natural state into a supernatural one. They refused to admit that nature as such has any active powers tending to natural goods, for example, love and knowledge of God as explained above (somewhat as we say that nature has only a receptivity for the supernatural, but no active tendency and power for it). To realize such objectives they required as absolutely necessary those aids which in reality are not needed except to attain supernatural goods, such as belief in divine revelation and the Christian grace of justification. According to the first group, nature as such cannot be good without divine holiness; according to the second group, nature is, if not evil, at any rate blind and helpless. But according to the true doctrine, nature of itself possesses, not indeed the higher, divine goodness, but a human, natural goodness. But it truly does

[6] Cf. A. Berlage on original sin, in his *System der katholischen Dogmatik* (Münster: 1856), V, 193–391.

possess such goodness in its own right, and is therefore the basis of a definite, well-rounded order of life.

Since the second of these two errors is common among many who either do not know what "supernatural" really means or destroy nature, we desire to dwell a little longer on this point. We must unconditionally reject all views according to which the soul, in any state of human nature (spiritual monstrosities in the individual need not be considered here) loses all spiritual power, or at least lacks energy or inclination to go into action. Owing to confused ideas about the present state that is the result of original sin, many believe they must hold this sort of position. In their opinion, the human soul no longer has the ability to know what is purely spiritual, or at any rate higher spiritual, divine things. In any case such power would be so dormant and sluggish that it would have to be awakened from its sleep by the word of another spirit, and ultimately of God, before it would be sufficiently aroused to acquire an intellectual knowledge of sensible things, or at least of supersensible things. Many seem to fear that any admission of spontaneous development of higher knowledge in man would be not only rational but rationalistic. But just as the doctrine that nature of itself can will something good and can even love God without strictly supernatural grace is not Pelagian, so the contention that nature has the ability of itself to know some truth even about divine things is not rationalistic. Rather, the denial of the first assertion would lead to Jansenism, and that of the second would lead to the traditionalism which, in this application at least, has been rejected by the Church.[7]

[7] L. Bautain's traditionalism was condemned in 1840 by Gregory XVI, and that of A. Bonnetty in 1855 under Pius IX. Cf. Denz., 1622–27; 1649–52.

The truth lies in the middle. The spiritual power of knowledge and love in the state of nature, in which the spiritual faculties are not completely free and independent because of their union with matter and the lower faculties, is indeed somewhat impeded and restricted. But it is not so chained down that it is deprived of all force and energy, still less that the faculties themselves are completely suppressed and consequently are intrinsically and physically (through lack of necessary vitality) unable to know and love spiritual things and God Himself. No, the power remains. Some inclination for activity also remains, so that up to a certain point knowledge and love of God can always develop spontaneously; without such a tendency no natural vitality can be conceived. But the full, easy, speedy, and flourishing development of the powers is restricted. That such wholesome progress may take place, they require outside assistance, not by the addition of a new, higher power, but by aids that will stimulate and support them.

Therefore it is rationalistic to maintain that the development of reason is not hampered by any restrictions, and that reason can mature quickly, easily, securely, and completely without any outside help, which in the last instance must be traced back to God. Further, it is Pelagian to maintain that the natural power and tendency of the soul to desire good and love God are not somewhat impaired by the downward pull of sense appetite, and are not so weakened that God does not have to come to their aid with special external and internal stimulation and strengthening influence, to assure their uninterrupted, continuous pursuit and attainment of their end.

Yet the truth remains that man, even in his purely natural condition without supernatural revelation and divine grace, can know and love God in a fitting way and so can prepare himself for his natural destiny. The external help we have mentioned can at best be called supernatural because it comes to nature from outside. But it is not simply supernatural, since it is an aid intended for nature and is necessary. It confers no new, inner vitality, and conduces to no exalted, supernatural good transcending the powers supplied by nature. Coming as it does from outside, from another being, it is a mere external stimulation of the interior, natural power, designed to facilitate the removal of obstacles and to bring the object of activity closer.

Thus plants, for example, may require assistance from outside to be able to develop all the energy stored in the seed and to reach their natural growth. Ordinary cultivation is not always enough; sometimes extraordinary measures are required. Yet the outside aid confers no new power on the plants, but only supplies the existing power with material, and facilitates the exercise of their activity by removing impediments. If the plant should die or at least were to lose all aptitude for growth, all the outside helps in the world could avail nothing. But if the seed is still alive, it has some chance of growing, and whatever else is needed cannot be supplied by conferring a new power, such as engrafting another seed, for in that case the existing power would not develop but a new one would take its place. The external help consists in providing stimulation, material, and aid in the overcoming of obstacles.

In somewhat the same way, the help which God would impart to man's nature as such would suppose that its vitality and energy are not dead. It would further suppose that the vital acts to which aid is given are not essentially beyond the spirit's capacity, and hence are not physically impossible. If such acts cannot be performed, the reason is the presence of various obstacles in the way; therefore they are only morally impossible. This so-called moral impossibility is not in itself foreign to the will regarded as a morally free faculty; it simply means that the will, which by virtue of its freedom is often able to make a decision, is almost certain not to make the decision because of an urgent inclination toward the opposite. In a wider sense we also speak of a moral impossibility with regard to natural knowledge, for example, of all the perfections of God, when the cause is not a lack of the physical power to know, but a deficiency in the requisite resources or in intellectual formation.

More specifically, the help needed by pure nature is neither supernatural revelation nor supernatural grace. It is not supernatural revelation, because aid can be given in various other ways than by God's direct speech to us men, for instance, by a strengthening of reason in individual people, by calling into existence a number of exceptionally brilliant men, or by a widespread dissemination of good education under the guidance of a wise providence. It is not supernatural grace, because an intensified inclination of the will to good and a vivid, frequently renewed incitement to fear and love of God, resulting from His exterior and interior influence, are quite sufficient for gaining control of the passions. Briefly, nothing more would be needed than the sort of revelation admitted by many rationalists and deists, and the kind of grace allowed by some Pelagians, Semipelagians, and, in more recent times, by Hermes. This is revelation in the widest sense, by which truth is made known in any way at all; and the grace is likewise taken in the widest sense, that is, it is any special gift of the good God.

But a revelation in which God Himself speaks to us, to link our minds with His, to base our knowledge on His, and to introduce us to His mysteries, a revelation such as God has given in the Christian dispensation, and a grace that confers a higher heavenly value on our actions, making them meritorious for heavenly beatitude, and unites us with God by a true filial love, can by no means be needed as assistance in the natural order. And the more moderate rationalists and Pelagians, such as those we just mentioned, do not offend against Christian revelation and grace by admitting what they do; they err by remaining on this level and by refusing to grant a higher reason for the necessity of revelation and grace than weak nature's need of some help. They deny the real existence of a higher order and a higher life that are inaugurated by such revelation and grace.

In reality, the present order is not natural but supernatural. This is the reason why we seldom or never view natural life in its full power, independently of the supernatural life that rests on supernatural revelation and grace. But we may not forget that they who reject and scorn the supernatural order confronting them, also violate their natural relationship to God. They make themselves unworthy of natural help if they refuse to accept the supernatural help offered to them. The naturally good activity of those who loyally and thankfully receive revelation and grace, blends with their supernatural activity, and therefore does not stand out prominently. Yet the natural life of those who may still be ignorant of revelation can and in fact does develop. In the present economy of the world, however, natural life is often raised somewhat above the natural level because of the revelation that was made at the beginning, or the revelation which God can impart interiorly to man. Usually, indeed, all the activity men now perform is directed by God in one way or another to a supernatural end;

just as, inversely, a sort of supernaturally evil power, that of the fallen angels, draws man from natural good to evil.[8]

We are now in a position to gather together what we have said about the capacity for the true and the good possessed by the human soul conformably with its essence and nature. By virtue of its essence, the human soul has the power, and with it the inclination, to know the true and to love the good, and thus to aspire after perfect knowledge and love of the highest truth and good. But this power, constricted and hampered by other, lower, and partly opposed powers, must in a suitable way be supported and fostered from without, especially by God.

The certitude we have about this whole doctrine concerning man's nature, powers, and activities results from the simplicity and truth of the principles on which it rests. This teaching can and ought to be known by unaided reason, its source, because it refers exclusively to nature. But it is also supported by revelation and the infallible teaching of the Church, which is a secure guide even in natural truths that are connected with revelation.

The Church necessarily supposes that there is a natural goal and end; for it teaches that the end now appointed for nature, consisting as it does in the beatific vision of God, is absolutely supernatural, and is to be communicated to us by a special grace. And yet there must be a necessary end for nature.

That man in the present state, considered only according to his natural powers, can know and love God in his own way, is clear from the condemnation of many propositions contained in the works of Baius and the Jansenists. For

[8] The actual relation of purely natural life in the present supernatural economy of the world would require a more protracted discussion, which must be reserved for another occasion.

these heretics attacked the doctrine as it is here reported and as it was maintained in substance by almost all the theological schools of that time.

After the conflict with the Pelagians, the Latin Fathers either did not consider the nature of man at all, or treated it casually when they had occasion to speak of its capacity for true good, especially for love of God. This now strikes us as very strange. Even most of the Scholastics, when they discourse about the good works which nature of itself is able to perform, mention only external actions, such as building houses, planting trees, and the like. Particularly Augustine and Prosper, as the Jansenists were quick to notice, ordinarily based their proofs of the absolute necessity of grace, not on the nobility of supernatural acts, but on the grounds of nature's tendency to evil, which to their mind was so strong that nature was unable by itself to rise to anything good or divine; all naturally good knowledge and love that had nothing to do with grace seemed to be excluded.

But is it not also surprising, as the same Jansenists shrewdly perceived, that these were mainly views of the Latin Fathers, not of the Greek Fathers? The latter were accordingly denounced by the Jansenists as "calumniators of grace" because they ascribed to nature so pronounced an inclination toward good and even to the love of God, and were summarily refused a hearing as being untrustworthy witnesses for the nature of grace. And why did the Latin Fathers hold the views they did? Because they had to wage battle against the Pelagians, and in this conflict concentrated their efforts on showing what nature could not do. Besides, they considered these questions only in their polemic bearing and practical application; they made no attempt to treat them comprehensively from the speculative point of view or to break them down into their component parts and connect them with other doctrines.

Against haughty Pelagianism the Fathers taught that not even one spark remained in us of that good we are accustomed to speak of in Christian circles, namely, the supernatural good that is profitable for eternal life. They pointed out rather that an evil mass of combustible debris was contained in us, and that we were not able, by our own inherent powers, to prevent it from bursting forth into a fearful conflagration. On the one hand, therefore, they dispossessed nature even of the germ and the slightest seed of true good; on the other hand they contended that a rank cancer of corruption was festering in nature. What nature was capable of doing without reference to salvation was simply omitted; this was "beside the point," as Augustine often expressed it. Yet nature's ability to do good was occasionally acknowledged: "that power of God's image by which it naturally does some good," in Augustine's words.

Indeed, the question could hardly have been touched by the Fathers, whereas it appeared to be the main difficulty to the opposite camp. For the erring teachers, particularly the well-meaning Semipelagians, thought they were contradicting Augustine's doctrine when they ascribed to nature some power for good. But this was not where the error lay. Had they ascribed to the nature created by God a power and inclination to good placed in it by the Creator, acknowledging that free will can strive for good in free cooperation with this God-given tendency, in accordance with our present conception of the power of nature, their opinion on this point would have been correct, and Augustine would have had to go more deeply into the question and show that the absolute incompetency of nature referred only to a higher order. But they taught a freedom that could give to itself the first impulse to good, without dependence on any antecedent impulse, even a natural one, in the way the first man, still free from any tendency to evil, gave himself an impulse to sin to which nothing drew him.

This was a freedom that contradicts the natural as well as the supernatural order; to refute it the Fathers, strictly speaking, did not have to go into the distinction between the two orders. We may wish that they had done so; but since they did not do so, or only rarely did so, the cardinal point of the question could not receive adequate illumination. Yet the truth itself was firmly held by the Fathers. Even Augustine, in his controversy with the Manichaeans, defended the rights of nature brilliantly when he taught than man's substance and essence were always good, and that consequently his essential powers were always good and remained capable of good, so that the freedom of the will could not be lost.

But what was lacking in the Latin Fathers was clearly and distinctly brought out by the more scientific Greek Fathers; and even the Greek Fathers who were interested in practical affairs often exhibit a more serene and comprehensive speculation than the fiery Augustine, who was ever in search of a solution to the burning questions of his day. And from the Greek Fathers the doctrine of nature and grace later passed over in all its clarity, through the first Scholastics, to the Latin Church. We can gather this even from the Jansenists, who condemned and reviled the Greek Fathers and the Scholastics equally as defamers of grace and eulogizers of nature. We can also show convincingly that the doctrine of a self-enclosed order of nature and a superior sphere of grace, which reached its full development not long after the beginning of Scholasticism, can be found in the ancient Greek Fathers in all its details and ideas, including even the very terms of its formulation.[9]

The Scholastics ordinarily taught without hesitation that nature as such was capable, by its own powers, of a natural knowledge and a love of God that, in its way, is a love of God above all else.[10] God's help, of the kind mentioned above, is needed for this; but, we may remark in passing, divine assistance seems to be required, not for the purpose of loving God above all, but for the effectiveness of this love and its constancy in the face of strong temptation. Nevertheless the examples the Scholastics give of nature's competency in this area are such as we have listed; they refer merely to some external activity that is conformable to reason, such as building houses, planting gardens, and the like.

But these are only examples; nature is fully equipped for such works, and no higher influence can come into consideration; at the very first glance we see that they involve nothing supernatural. I do not deny that a number of theologians, even such as agree with the principles established above, quite illogically restrict the powers of nature to external good works of this sort, on the grounds that they are purely human. But man's nature, precisely as human nature, contains something godlike because of the soul, by which it is the image of God, and because of its spiritual faculties, by which it can know and love God. If godlikeness is completely extinguished in man, his nature ceases to be a true human nature. It is the rational soul, by which man can know and love God, that accounts for what is truly human in man; this is what raises man above the beasts. Let no one say that nature, though good in itself, is made

[9] Cf. Isaac Habert, *Patrum Graecorum theologia de divina gratia*, especially Part III, *De gratia habituali*.
[10] See St. Thomas, *Summa theol.*, Ia IIae, q. 109, a. 3.

incapable of anything divine through sin. However shocking sin may be, whatever diabolical obduracy it may engender, good nature and the power and exercise of natural knowledge of God, as well as the power and tendency for natural love of God, are not destroyed by the evil will that resists them. Much less can such destruction be wrought by original sin which, according to Jansenist teaching, involves an evil will on the part of the person encumbered with it, or by any personal sin of man, who, so long as he is a man, can never turn to evil with such obstinacy and decisiveness as completely to suppress the element of good within him.

But we wish to bring this discussion to a close, and erect the structure envisioned by us on the foundation that has been established.

PART THREE

GRACE AND THE SUPERNATURAL ORDER

Chapter VI

THE FOUNDATION OF SUPERNATURAL LIFE

THus far we have considered nature, which is better known than grace and can be investigated by philosophy. We have learned that the essence of a spirit in general and that of the human soul in particular gives rise to a disposition having the character of a substratum for powers that possess a definite tendency for a certain degree of activity, by which they can reach their full development and thus attain the necessary goal of their endeavors. We have further learned that the natural order, that is, the order of nature having its own end, consists in the basic power and direction of life proceeding from the spirit's essence; and this basic power and direction of life, together with the various pertinent faculties and the resulting activities aiming at the goal necessarily to be attained, we have called nature. We have also discovered something about the limits surrounding the natural order of the created spirit. Since the latter is circumscribed in its essence and therefore in its powers, it can develop its life only within a definite and closed sphere. Consequently the spirit must recognize that its Creator has an essence infinitely superior to its own, with an infinitely higher nature, higher powers, and a higher sphere and order of life. The spirit must acknowledge that this higher nature has a natural life of which creatures can have no clear, distinct idea.

101

Much less can the created spirit receive from nature an intimation that God wishes in some way to share the life that is natural to Him with the created nature which is so immeasurably inferior to His own nature and which has not the slightest seed of the higher life within it. The creature cannot possibly suspect that God intends to inundate the finite with the fullness of His infinity. Here we behold the greatest marvel of God's omnipotence and love; a marvel that is the center, the summit, and the goal of all that God has wrought in Christianity; a marvel that fills all souls that have duly appreciated it with deepest reverence and highest rapture; a marvel that transports the two princes of the Apostles into holy ecstasy whenever they touch on it in their epistles. It is something immeasurably greater than all miraculous cures of bodily illnesses, even greater than the awakening of a dead man to natural life. Some theologians rightly add that in a certain respect it surpasses creation itself.

For the gift of divine life requires an act that is beyond and above all created principles and causes, an act that excels all created powers; indeed, a new creation erected on the substructure of the first creation; a new establishment and foundation of a new, immensely higher life, for which no germ or seed was found in nature. It requires the communication of a sort of new, second nature, as the source and center of the new life. This new nature does not draw two finite creatures together, but brings the finite creature close to the infinite Creator, to receive from Him a share in His nature and life: "That by these [promises] you may be made partakers of the divine nature" (II Pet. 1:4). It requires a communication which, much more than creation, resembles that inconceivable, heavenly production and generation by which God the Father communicates

His entire nature and essence to His only-begotten Son. For man, previously begotten as flesh from flesh and man from man, is now more nobly born of the Spirit of God into a higher, more godlike spiritual life (Cf. John 3:6). By the grace flooding his soul he becomes a son of the heavenly Father and a brother of the only-begotten Son, that, like the latter, he may embrace the Father with filial love, reposing with the Son on the heart of the Father, see Him face to face, and be initiated into all His secrets; that in most intimate fellowship with those persons who essentially possess the divine nature, as son of the Father, brother of the Son, temple of the Holy Ghost, wholly glorified in God, pervaded by His light, fired with His love, he may enjoy divine bliss and beatitude, and be immersed in the ocean of God's happiness.

What can be greater than this miracle of God's omnipotence, which raises the helpless creature to so magnificent and heavenly a life? What can be greater than this miracle of God's love, by which He opens up His fatherly heart to us strangers and servants, and bestows on us the life and inheritance of His only-begotten Son? This miracle explains that other miracle of love, the incarnation of God's only-begotten Son who assumed our nature. *Ideo Deus factus est homo, ut homo fieret Deus,* God became man that man might become God, in the frequently recurring phrase of the ancient Fathers. "God sent His Son, made of a woman . . . that we might receive the adoption of sons" (Gal. 4:4 f.).

Here we feel impelled to cry out gratefully with the Apostle: "Blessed be the God and Father of our Lord Jesus Christ, who hath blessed us with spiritual blessings in heavenly places, in Christ: as He chose us in Him before the foundation of the world, that we should be holy and un-

spotted in His sight in charity; who hath predestinated us
unto the adoption of children through Jesus Christ unto
Himself, according to the purpose of His will; unto the
praise of the glory of His grace, in which He hath graced
us in His beloved Son" (Eph. 1:3–6). These are the ines-
timable riches of Christ (Eph. 3:8), riches of infinite value,
as the blood with which they were acquired is of infinite
value. The blood and the death of God's Son could not purchase for us a mere natural and human life, spiritual and
moral though it may be; they had to purchase for us a divine life.

The Apostle says: "To me, the least of all the saints, is
given this grace, to preach among the Gentiles the un-
searchable riches of Christ" (Eph. 3:8). And in fact he has
made known the wealth of Christ with exquisite delicacy.
Following his teaching and that of the other apostles, especially St. Peter and St. John, each of whom treats of the
same theme in his own way but with like heavenly wisdom,
I shall try to describe these riches of Christ in their untarnished supernatural splendor. And wherever occasion war-
rants, I shall introduce appropriate comments from the
holy Fathers.

When we were speaking of nature, we were able to perceive and prove nearly all the points by reason. But now,
when we are dealing with the supernatural and supra-
rational order, we must give ourselves over to the revelation
of God, who will admit us into His secrets. External revelation, however, is not enough; an interior illumination must
accompany it.

The Apostle teaches us to pray for this grace when he
himself falls on his knees and beseeches the God of our
Lord Jesus Christ, the Father of glory, to give us the Spirit
of wisdom and revelation that we may know Him, and to

enlighten the eyes of our heart that we may perceive "what the hope is of His calling, and what are the riches of the glory of His inheritance in the saints, and what is the exceeding greatness of His power towards us who believe" (Eph. 1:17 ff.).

My intention is to set forth the supernatural order in all its implications and to bring out the supernatural character of all its phases. I believe I can adopt no better procedure than to take as my point of departure the foundation of the supernatural life regarded as a sort of second, higher nature or as supernature. Starting with this basic concept, I shall try to throw light on all the aspects of the supernatural order and explain in detail its supernatural character. At the same time I shall not hesitate to bring in other reasons of a special kind and to treat them in similar detail, with a view to defining the basic concept more accurately.

I could begin by postulating this basic idea as a hypothesis, and then substantiate it by showing that the inferences derived from it provide the best key both for a more penetrating and satisfactory explanation of passages from Sacred Scripture and the Fathers that will be adduced, and for the reconciliation of the apparent and otherwise insoluble antitheses found in the teaching of the Church, as mentioned in the Introduction. However, to avoid giving an excessively hypothetical cast to the subject, I prefer briefly to establish the fundamental principle itself from the data of revelation.

Nature in general means the disposition of a thing arising from its essence, the principle of its proper activity, especially its vital activity, and, in our question, the vital principle rooted in the created spirit's essence regarded as a power and tendency for vital activity. Similarly supernature, taken in the narrower sense as explained in the chapter on preliminary notions, means a principle of life that does not arise from the essence and substance of the created spirit and is not due to the created spirit, but is proper to the uncreated Spirit as springing from His essence. If, therefore, it is found in the created spirit, it comes from without and has to be communicated by God.

The existence of such a higher principle of life in man, raising him above his nature to the divine nature and inaugurating a divine life in him, can be apprehended clearly and unmistakably from that sublime passage of St. Peter in which he assigns as the epitome of all the promises and precious gifts of God to us the fact that we are "made partakers of the divine nature" (II Pet. 1:4). The full sense of these words can be only this: we who have been elevated above our nature receive a sort of higher nature by which we are drawn so close to God that we become like Him in divine prerogatives that are proper to Him to the exclusion of all that is created, and thus are made capable and worthy of a life that in itself belongs to God alone. This is the way various Fathers explain the text.[1] If the passage stood alone without parallel, a cold, cheerless rationalistic exegesis could regard it as nothing more than an emphatic expression of our similarity and union with God as attainable by our own nature and commensurate with it. A rationalist

[1] This interpretation was rather common among the Fathers, especially the Greeks. They touch on the subject when they demonstrate the divinity of the Holy Spirit from the fact that sanctification is ascribed to Him. They say in effect that the Holy Spirit must be God by nature because He has the power to make us sharers in the divine nature, to divinize us. Moreover, they often relate this participation in the divine nature to the union into which we enter with the divine nature through the Incarnation or the Eucharist. But this union is external; its purpose is not achieved unless we are interiorly united with God. The Son of God has assumed our nature to make us sharers in His nature, and the Eucharist is the channel through which He imparts to us the divine life He has received from the Father. Cf. John 6:57 f.

could say that we do not share in the divine nature by receiving from God a sort of new nature like His or a new
vital principle resembling His, but that we draw close to
God by the powers of our own nature which in its way is
vaguely similar to the divine nature and can know and love
God, and even in some measure enjoy and possess Him.

But such an interpretation cannot satisfy. Our partaking
and possession of the divine nature are exhibited in Sacred
Scripture, not as a result or development of powers found
in us, but as a new perfection of life coming to us from
without, from God, a new creation which, erected on the
foundation of the old, calls forth a life entirely beyond the
capacity of nature; a true begetting that imparts to us a
new life resembling that of the begetter, since it places in
us a new seed, a new root of the higher life (I John 3:1 f.,
9, 24). In all truth, we are not only called, but are the sons
of God (I John 3:1). And as proof that we are truly God's
children, Sacred Scripture points out that we are made to
share in that life, glory, and beatitude which the only-
begotten Son of God receives from the Father along with
the divine essence. All such passages throw a clear light
on the profound meaning of St. Peter's words and indicate
that we can scarcely do justice to their depth and vitality.
The teaching that emerges is this: we are born of God and
become like Him through an accidental form and nature,
as the only-begotten Son is born of the Father and is like
Him through the substantial and essential communication
of the Father's nature to Him.[2]

This truth gains in light when we reflect on the express
teaching of Sacred Scripture and the Church about the
existence of certain kinds of vital acts, indeed a whole cir-

[2] Pertinent texts of Scripture will be cited and further discussed in the
course of this book.

cle of vital acts, namely, those that are meritorious of the
eternal life promised by Christ or that are preliminary to
such merit, and the acts of eternal life itself. In this domain
nature is completely powerless. Such activity requires
much more than a stimulation and intensification of our
inherent vital powers; it needs an entirely new, higher vital
power, an elevation of the existing basic power to a higher
sphere. So for the time being we may conclude that a vital
power, supernaturally infused, must be given to us. Nothing stands in the way of this conclusion; rather, everything
impels us to interpret St. Peter's words in the sense declared, which is also the obvious sense. At the same time
the truth itself is demonstrated by the argument just outlined, even though we may be slow to admit that the doctrine stands out clearly in the text.[3]

Accordingly we have settled our starting point. Let us
now endeavor to learn more about the subject, and especially to bring forward some of the main teachings of the
Fathers. This will enable us to define the concept more
clearly from the outset, even though we may have to come
back to it later.

[3] It is no easy matter to present the many arguments that can be drawn
from a thousand passages in Sacred Scripture to prove this doctrine
in so conclusive a fashion as not only to obviate the possibility of contradiction, but also to dispel all obscurity that may result from precon-
ceived notions and confused ideas; such an attitude constitutes the chief
stumbling-block. A bare enumeration of texts, even though accompanied
by the usual exegesis, is not enough. They must be grasped in their
mutual interconnections and be combined into one great argument, in
order that the spirit pervading them may manifest all its power. We
must avow that the ordinary processes of demonstration used by theologians
of the past two centuries against the Jansenists leave much to be desired. What is lacking in them has been brilliantly supplied by Kleutgen
in the second volume of his *Theologie der Vorzeit*, especially in the third
chapter, where the absolutely supernatural character of the fellowship
with God brought about by Christianity is proved with considerable skill
and originality.

The kind of higher nature or essential form or vital principle we have been speaking of is related to what stands beneath it, that is, nature, in the following way.

1. Its primary purpose is not to round out man's nature in itself; it presupposes nature as complete, and is added to it. "After this creature, man, was fully constituted in his own nature by the divine Creator, he forthwith received also a likeness to God. The Holy Spirit was breathed into him and thereby the image of the divine nature was imprinted in him." Such is the teaching of St. Cyril of Alexandria [4] who, along with several others, Basil, Athanasius, and generally those Greeks who went more deeply into the dogmas of the Trinity and the Incarnation, developed this whole doctrine in a masterly way.

2. This image of the divine nature, in its function of principle of a divine life, presupposes in nature another image and likeness of God pertaining to the nature of man. In the words of the same ecclesiastical teacher, this is "the rational soul with its natural desire and knowledge of all [natural] good . . . and with a longing for goodness and uprightness . . . so that we may say that man is by nature a good and upright creature. But that man . . . might bear in himself more brilliant traits of the divine nature, God breathed into him the Spirit of life . . . by which the creature was refashioned according to the highest form, the divine." [5]

3. Because this principle presupposes that nature exists and is complete in its species, it does not belong to nature as a necessary element. Furthermore it is not a vital faculty emanating from the essence of nature, like the natural faculties, but comes from without. Although it is called

---

[4] *De adoratione in spiritu et veritate*, lib. I [*PG*, LXVIII, 145].
[5] *Adversus anthropomorphitas*, cap. 2 [*PG*, LXXVI, 1079 f.].

holiness, it must be carefully distinguished, as is evident from number 2 above, from the natural striving for rectitude that proceeds from man's nature.

Thus St. John Damascene says: "The very angels received holiness from the Holy Spirit as something that is outside their essence." [6] Since this holiness is infused by the Holy Spirit, it is more external to nature than the good decision made by the free will in its activity. This latter goodness of the will is not, indeed, directly imparted to man along with nature; if it is present, however, it is only an outgrowth of a power contained in nature. It is not a new power, but a definite orientation given to a previously existing power. [7]

4. As the supernatural vital faculty is not an ingredient of nature but is outside nature and above all that is natural, it is superior to nature, an elevation of nature. It confers a "supercosmic beauty" and an excellence transcending creation. [8] "We are refashioned by it to newness of evangelical life in Christ and mount up to likeness with Him in the Holy Spirit, so that we appear to be quite different men." [9] "They who are called to the sonship of Christ by faith in Christ, lay aside the lowliness of their own nature and

[6] De fide orthodoxa, II, 3 [PG, XCIV, 869].

[7] St. Basil says in his homily on Psalm 32, no. 4 [PG, XXIX, 333]: "The Holy Spirit imparted sanctity to the angels at their creation. For they were not created as infants who would gradually become perfect by exercise and would then be made worthy to receive the Spirit; but as soon as they were created, holiness was infused into them by the Holy Spirit as though it were mingled in with their substance." St. Ambrose, De Spiritu Sancto, I, 7 [PL, XVI, 724], clearly distinguishes the spiritual holiness that is proper to the Holy Ghost and also the holiness which is received from Him, from the holiness which the angels can have in virtue of their nature.

[8] St. Cyril of Alexandria, De adoratione in spiritu et veritate, lib. I [PG, LXVIII, 141].

[9] St. Cyril of Alexandria, In Isaiam commentarius, V, 54 [PG, LXX, 1200].

are raised by God's ennobling grace to a supernatural dignity." [10]

5. By elevating nature, this principle gives to nature the
highest perfection it is capable or susceptible of. It does not
bestow new basic faculties of a natural kind, but so elevates the faculties possessed by nature that they are united
with God, the object of their desires, not in some low degree, but in the highest and most intimate way possible.
This perfection is what the Greek Fathers call holiness.

6. This is not ordinary holiness, implying a well-ordered
love of what is good and right, but is understood in a far
higher and fuller sense. It is a higher consecration by which
nature receives a more excellent and noble dignity, such
as only the divine nature by right possesses. It makes nature
capable of a lofty and intimate, a pure and secure union
with the divine goodness and excellence by love, such as we
do not find in the most perfect of created natures, a union
which, as St. Basil says, is natural only to the Spirit of God,
who is the very love and holiness of God.

The notion that supernature, regarded as holiness, affects
nothing but the will, must be resolutely excluded. No, it
gives a higher consecration to the whole being and pervades all the faculties. The spiritual life of knowledge is no
less elevated and transformed by it than the spiritual life
of love. Holiness may refer chiefly to the will, and in a state
in which the entire glory and splendor of the higher life
have not yet dawned for us, it is manifested mainly in love.
But actually it is found in knowledge as well as in love, because it is nothing else than the fullness of divine life communicated to us by the adorable, holy, divine nature, as we
shall point out presently. The divine nature abides in us as

[10] St. Cyril of Alexandria, *In Ioannem commentarius*, I, 9 [*PG*, LXXIII, 153].

in a temple which it fills with all its majesty and which it glorifies, consecrates, and sanctifies by its presence.

In its relation to what lies beneath it, therefore, the vital principle we are speaking of presupposes nature as complete in itself and, indeed, as good and godlike. It is added to nature, raises nature above itself, carries nature to its supernatural perfection, and confers on it a higher consecration.

Let us now examine this principle in its relation to what is above it, in its origin and positive value.

1. As we have seen, it is represented as an image of the divine nature and goodness. But it is not an image of the kind in which God is communicated to creatures as such and is mirrored in them. For God gives to creatures as such only their own limited nature, in which the rays of the infinite sun peer forth in dark shadows. It is rather an image in the way wisdom issuing from the mouth of God is an image of His goodness (Wisdom 7:26). It is an image of the divine goodness somewhat as the only-begotten Son is the perfect image and mirror of the Father, but with this difference, that in the latter case the divine essence is communicated, whereas in our case an effect of divine power is produced. Therefore it is an image in which God is reflected and mirrored not in the ordinary way, but in the perfections that characterize Him as distinct from all other beings. "Through this image," St. Cyril says in a passage quoted above, "man reflects more brilliant traits and attributes of the divine nature" than he can through the spiritual nature of his own soul. He thereby acquires a higher spirituality, in the presence of which his natural spirituality, however perfected and cultivated it may be, may almost be said to vanish and to seem material and animal. Later we shall explain this point more fully and shall also

specify in detail the properties that are reflected in this image.

2. Because this principle is so excellent an image of the Godhead and, in its capacity of vital faculty, imparts divine life to us, it raises us to an inconceivable nearness and relationship to God. The higher we mount above our own nature, the closer we come to the highest nature of all, the divine nature. We draw so close to it and become so like to it that we may be said to be divinized and actually are. "From the Holy Spirit there comes forth a joy that will never cease . . . likeness to God; to become God—that is the acme of man's desires," says St. Basil.[11]

3. This relationship can be made more definite. Through the power of the divine nature we receive, in a way we cannot comprehend, a life that belongs to God to the exclusion of all other beings. Therefore we are born to a new, higher life. God becomes our Father, not in the absolute sense, but in a very true and sublime sense; and we are not only called but are His children. Hence we also become brothers of the only-begotten Son who possesses the divine life essentially and substantially.

4. Since this principle is not found in nature and does not belong to nature, which consequently has no right to claim it from God, it is a pure grace and a wholly gratuitous gift of God. But since our entire nature is elevated, adorned, and made like to God by it, it is the effect of a unique kindness and grace of God; it is in some measure the seal and pledge by which we in turn are made and remain worthy

[11] *De Spiritu Sancto*, c. 9, no. 23: "Hinc gaudium numquam finiendum . . . similitudo cum Deo, et, quo nihil sublimius expeti potest, hinc est ut deus fias" [*PG*, XXXII, 109]. Cf. Gregory of Nazianzus, *Or. 38 in Theophania*, no. 7 [*PG*, XXXVI, 317]: "He draws us to Himself . . . and makes us godlike, and then treats us as His familiar friends . . . as God united to gods."

of His kindness and grace. That is why this gift is called pre-eminently the grace of God; it places us in a state in which the full love of God is poured forth over us. God floods us with the same love with which He embraces His only-begotten Son; He loves us with a truly fatherly love, in which He communicates to us his whole being, so far as that is possible, and consequently gives us the greatest good within His power.

5. We do not exist in this state of grace by nature, and cannot transport ourselves to it; we can mount up to it only if God freely and graciously places us in it. Grace must confer a new worth on us, not only in name but in fact. It must be the foundation of our new relation to God. This relation cannot be real unless something real is given and infused into us by God; it must also be real because God's love and favor cannot remain without effect, for God loves nothing without making it good and lovable.

At the first glance we perceive clearly that all the characteristic properties of supernature, as we remarked previously, are concentrated in the single idea that by grace God adopts us as His children in a proper sense of the word, and that we become by grace what the only-begotten Son of God is by nature. When we are adopted by God as His children and are spiritually begotten, we receive God's nature in its faithful image which we call supernature. Thus it is clear from every point of view that supernature really transcends nature and that nature itself is elevated and sanctified; supernature does not arise from our essence, but bestows on us a sort of new existence, a higher nature. From all this we can perceive how and why supernature must reflect the beauty and sublimity of the divine goodness; how and why it makes us like God our Father and imparts His life to us; and finally, why it is a gift of God's grace and at the same time transfers us to the state of divine grace and love.

Our next step will be an endeavor to develop this idea of divine sonship in all its implications.

Chapter VII

SUPERNATURE AND THE GRACE
OF DIVINE SONSHIP

St. John, the Apostle of love, gives us as the best proof of God's love for us and the bedrock of our love for God, the fact that we have been made children of God through Jesus Christ. "Behold what manner of charity the Father hath bestowed upon us, that we should be called and should be the sons of God" (I John 3:1).

Let us be on our guard against belittling and underrating this infinite benefit of God's love, this marvel of His charity. It is true that in Sacred Scripture God is sometimes called the Father of all beings, particularly of the living. He gave them their natural existence and life by creation, and constantly preserves them in being. He proves His love and care for them, as a father does for the children that have issued from him, by bringing them to their last end. He even supplies food for the most insignificant worm and keeps it alive.

But He is Father of spiritual and rational creatures in a stricter sense. And on their side such beings are called children of God, which is not the case with irrational creatures. For they have personality, are capable of reaching beatitude, and receive a higher, spiritual life from God. In their existence and life they resemble God in a special way, even by their nature. They may be called God's children more

116

justifiably still if they live in conformity with the dignity they have as likenesses of God and thus prove worthy of their exalted relation to God.

This is the kind of sonship to which a superficial, rationalist philosophy and theology usually restrict our relationship to God; they regard the beautiful expressions and teachings of Sacred Scripture as exaggerations and vivid figures, which contain nothing but a meager kernel of truth. To the minds of such men the sublime intimacy with God so often mentioned in Sacred Scripture and the Fathers is nothing more than the nearness, not indeed to be despised, by which God fills the soul with natural light, according to the words of St. Paul: "In Him we live and move and are" (Acts 17:28). They think that our close union or even unity with God is nothing more than the sort of union man is able to establish by a knowledge and love, respectful rather than confiding, such as nature can produce. This is no doubt a true relation; even pagan philosophers, like Aristotle and particularly Plato, discovered in man's soul a godlikeness and therefore, since the soul comes from God and gravitates back to Him, a certain relationship to Him. This is a true relationship, but not the highest and noblest; it is not the relationship that Christianity sets before us as the reality; it does not exhaust the full wealth of meaning contained in the idea of sonship.

It lacks precisely the highest and most significant element of a child's relationship to his father. The son resembles his father in some respect. As he receives nature from his father, he is in some measure one with him and shares in everything the father has, rank, life, and property. The child is like the father not only in a vague way, but in all the features and traits that distinguish the father. The child's association with his father is of the most intimate and trustful kind. The most affectionate friendship reigns between the two; it withholds no secrets and admits no fear. The spirits of both almost seem to blend into one.[1] In a word, the son is completely one with the father in nature, life, possessions, and love.

No created being, no created spirit is a son of God in this way by nature. The eternal Word alone is the Son of God by nature and is consequently the Only-begotten of the Father. No created being has any sort of equality with the Father by nature. Only the Word who is in the bosom of the

---

[1] The threefold analogy between the creature's divine sonship and that of the eternal Word is expressed with incomparable beauty by St. Thomas, *Summa theol.*, IIIa, q.23, a.3. Our adoptive sonship is an imitation of natural sonship in God. The Son of God proceeds naturally from the Father as His intellectual Word who is one with the Father. Some similarity with the Word can be achieved in three ways. First, according to the idea of form (so far as it is a word, that is, the expression of a specific form), although not according to the idea of the form's intelligibility. Thus the form of a house built outside the mind resembles its mental word in its specific form, but not in its intellectuality. In this way every creature (and its origin) is like the Word (and His generation).

In a second way the creature is like the Word, not only with reference to the form (or in general, the expression, the image), but also with reference to its intellectuality. Thus the knowledge engendered in the mind of a pupil is similar to the word in the mind of the teacher. In this way the rational creature alone, and by its very nature, is like the Word.

In yet a third way a creature resembles the Word with reference to the oneness (of nature and love) he has with the Father; and this is brought about by grace (participation in the divine nature) and by charity (filial love). For this purpose our Lord prays: "That they may be one, as We also are one" (John 17:22).

This resemblance with the Word is completed by the idea of adoption; an eternal inheritance (eternal life, not only life that is never-ending, but the life that is proper to the eternal Father) is reserved for those who are thus made like the Son. Therefore adoption does not befit all creatures, but only rational creatures; and it is not actually granted to all but only to those who have charity (*caritas,* filial love) and actually enter into the relationship of oneness with God.

In the second article of the same question, St. Thomas says: "Although adoption is common to the whole Trinity, it is appropriated to the Father as author, to the Son as exemplar, and to the Holy Spirit as imprinting the likeness of this exemplar on us."

Father and receives His entire nature from Him has such equality and unity with the Father: a unity in which He proceeds immediately from the nature of the Father and by which all that belongs to the Father is His; a unity by which He returns to the Father in an inexpressible way in the spiration of the Spirit of love. This Son alone is literally begotten by the Father in a spiritual generation; for He, the image of the Father's essence, the impress and figure (character) of His substance, the untarnished mirror of His glory, the expression and Word of His knowledge, proceeds as light from light, God from God, and is one God with the Father. This begetting, this sonship and fatherhood, is the ideal of all begetting, of all sonship, of all fatherhood in heaven and on earth, whence "all paternity in heaven and earth is named" (Eph. 3:15), containing all perfections and excluding all imperfections.

Because this sonship is the ideal, it cannot even approximately be attained by any other nature that is left to its own resources. Such a relation to God is impossible for all other natures because they do not proceed from the Father's nature within the divinity by generation, but are summoned forth from nothing by God's almighty will, and exist outside God as the works of His hands. What has the only-begotten Son in common with God's works, with those paltry creatures that were made by Him? The Son is inseparable from the Father and reposes in His bosom; but they are outside God, remote from Him. The Son is equal to the Father and is His perfect image; but they are infinitely inferior to God and bear in themselves only a dim and feeble outline of His image. The Son is the Father's heir and receives as His inheritance all the Father's wealth, all the treasures of His omnipotence, wisdom, and knowledge, by reason of which He alone sees the Father face to

face: "No man hath seen God at any time; the only-begotten Son who is in the bosom of the Father, He hath declared
Him" (John 1:18); but the creature, as left to himself, must
be excluded from that inheritance. For he cannot claim
the same rights as the Son of the house. The creature belongs to the household as servant, and, as we have shown,
has no claim to behold the Father face to face: "Christ as
the Son in His own house" [that is, in creatures], "and
Moses was . . . in all His house as a servant" (Heb. 3:5 f.).
The Son is one with the Father in the most intimate and
ineffable love and unity, and is united with the Father by
the Holy Spirit as the inexpressible kiss of an indescribable
embrace, as St. Bernard puts it; but the creature must humbly stay afar off. The creature can and must love his Creator and Lord, as the servant loves his master; but he cannot
hope or expect to receive a kiss from the Father's mouth
and to embrace Him with the freedom of a child.[2]

No creature, therefore, can by his nature be a son of God
in the full sense of the word, precisely because he is a creature. For the creature was not begotten of God's nature,
but was called into being from nothing by God's will, and
consequently has a nature that is infinitely different from
the divine nature.

This truth can be corroborated by the teaching of the
very heretics who deny it. In ancient times the Gnostics
and Manichaeans, in the Middle Ages the Beghards and
Fraticelli [3] who were condemned by Clement V, taught
that some spirits were children of God in the full sense by
their nature and were accordingly endowed with divine
holiness that is incompatible with sin, as well as with a
faculty of cognition to which the immediate intuition of

---

[2] Cf. St. Bernard, *In cantica*, serm. 8 [*PL*, CLXXXIII, 810–14].
[3] Cf. Denz., 471, 475.

God was due; thus they possessed the dignity and inheritance belonging to children of God. The heretics had to establish or assume as the principle or consequence of their doctrine that the created spirit was a part or a member or an emanation of the divine Spirit. St. Augustine, with his keen insight, had observed that the Manichaeans knew nothing about grace because they taught that God had been obliged to give to souls, His members, all that, according to Catholic teaching, He has given as grace.[4] That is one reason why he insisted that the creature, whether man or spirit, as portrayed in Catholic teaching, was made a son of God by grace, yet was not such by nature.[5]

Nature does, indeed, give us a relationship to God that by vague analogy, as we remarked above, can be described as a sort of sonship. But this relationship does not deserve that beautiful and exalted name in the full sense of the word; absolutely speaking, it can and ought to be called a state of servitude rather than sonship. The reason we dare to use the name signifying the higher and more affectionate kinship is to tone down the harshness and oppressiveness that the state of servitude implies among us men. As works of God, we are created for His honor, to serve Him, glorify Him, and adore Him in deepest reverence. We are His slaves and servants. But the master we serve is not a tyrant. He is our kind and considerate Lord who overwhelms us with benefits, who has given us all that we have and wishes us to be happy in His service in a way that is suitable for us; we ought to love Him and not only fear Him. This is a

---

[4] *Contra duas epistulas Pelagianorum*, II, 2 [*PL*, XLIV, 573].

[5] This is the most important clue in St. Augustine's doctrine for solving the objection that he paid relatively little attention to that which is ontologically supernatural, and never fully developed it. But the force of the traditional doctrine, which was always held, though not always carefully and accurately formulated, is manifest in this cardinal point, which he often stresses.

relationship like that of the Jews in the Old Law. In that Law the supernatural sonship brought to us by the Son of God was not yet clearly known, and as far as the nature of the Law is concerned was not present; it was not explicitly presumed in the Law itself; it was, however, present by anticipation, although the Jews were not fully conscious of it. As outwardly formulated, the Old Law was largely natural in content; it was a type of the true supernatural Law only in spirit. The supernatural Law was not revealed in its definitive form until its foundation, namely, the supernatural relation of sonship to God, was revealed and inaugurated in man's life; this took place in the New Testament when the Son of God came.[6]

By nature, therefore (not by sin, surely, for by sin we become enemies rather than servants of God, galley-slaves rather than domestics of the household), we are, as St. Cyril says, not children of the house, but only menials and servants of God, our Creator, in His great house, the earthly, created world that He has made for His glory.[7] By nature we are subjects of God, the great King who rules this world, not children of the royal palace, reigning with the Father. As such we are far from God and are strangers in the house: "You were afar off," not "domestics of God" (Eph. 2:17, 19). This, too, is not the effect of sin but the condition of our nature, by reason of which we dare not abide in the royal castle, in the halls of the Father of the house, much less in His bosom. We dare not come in to tarry in His immediate presence and converse with Him face to face, sit at table with Him, enjoy His happiness, reign with Him, possess all

---

[6] "The law [of servants] was given by Moses [because he was a servant]; grace and truth [of the sons of God] came by Jesus Christ [because He was the Son]" (John 1:17).

[7] *In Ioan.*, X, 2 [*PG*, LXXIV, 384].

that belongs to Him, and thus receive the inheritance of the royal Prince.

How could the creature presume to address the Creator, the King of heaven and earth, as Father, with that confidence, ardor, and affection the Apostle talks about? How could mortal man presume to say "Father" to the King of immortality who dwells in inaccessible light? How could the son of earth venture to greet as his Father Him who is purest and most perfect Spirit? How could he boldly and with childlike trust appear in the presence of God as Father, before whom even the seraphim fall down in adoration and veil their countenances? And here another consideration comes in. The only-begotten Son of God alone is eternally and indescribably born from the Father's bosom; He alone is the likeness of the Father's essence, He alone has divine life from the Father and shares it with Him, He alone is one with the Father and creates, rules, and governs with Him. Is it not a sacrilegious encroachment on the Son's rights and privileges to place at His side a creature that was summoned from nothing by this very Son and, if not supported by the might of His will, would again fall back into nothing? Shall such a one join the Son in sharing the Father's heart, inheritance, and love, and become one with the Father as the Son is one with Him?

"Behold," exclaims St. John, "what manner of charity the Father hath bestowed upon us, that we should be called and should be the sons of God" (I John 3:1). God has extended to us men, as also to the angels, the love with which He loves His only-begotten Son, the Son of His love (begotten with infinite love, though not by way of love), to make us like to His Son.[8] By His love He has made us

---

[8] "Who hath predestinated us unto the adoption of children through

what we were not before. He has raised us poor creatures
to the condition of children, and thus placed us at the side
of His own, true, only-begotten Son, making Him the firstborn among many brethren.

So great was the love the Son of God had for us that He
did not wish to remain alone in the Father's heart and reign
over us miserable creatures as His servants. He Himself
took over the great task of acquiring for us the life of the
children of God, and He did so at the price of His divine
blood. He assumed our nature to share His own nature with
us. He became our Brother in human form to make us His
brothers in His divine glory.[9] He, the only-begotten, regards it as a matter of honor "that He might be the firstborn amongst many brethren" whom "He also glorified"
(Rom. 8:29 f.). Therefore He is the first to say that His
Father is also our Father: "I ascend to My Father and to
your Father" (John 20:17). He tells us that He has come
into this world to give us the same eternal life He has received from the Father. He prays for us to the Father that
we may be one with Him as He is one with the Father, in
a unity which St. Cyril does not hesitate to call physical as
opposed to moral [10] (in a sense we shall examine later).
Hence He wishes us to share with Him the heart and love
of the Father, and also to have part in His inheritance. He
wishes us to be co-heirs of that glory which He Himself re-
quested for His humanity at the Last Supper, of that glory
which He has with the Father before the beginning of the
world when, in the resplendence of holiness, He proceeded

Jesus Christ unto Himself . . . unto the praise of the glory of His grace,
in which He hath graced us in His beloved Son" (Eph. 1:5 f.).

[9] "Grant that we may be made partakers in the divinity of Him who
has deigned to become partaker of our humanity" (Prayer at the Offertory
of the Mass).

[10] *In Ioan.*, XI, 11 [*PG*, LXXIV, 557].

SUPERNATURE AND DIVINE SONSHIP   125

from the Father before the rise of the morning star, as His Word and the mirror of His infinite knowledge and beatitude.

What the Father's love has destined for us and the Son's love has gained for us, is applied to us by the Holy Ghost, who is the very love which the Father has for the Son and the Son has for the Father. The Father sent the Holy Spirit to be the witness of His love in our hearts, and the Son sent Him to bring us into filial relationship with the Father and to teach us to lisp His name. The Father has sealed our hearts with Him (II Cor. 1:22); by Him the Father has raised us to the condition of His adopted children; and therefore He is called pre-eminently the Spirit of sonship (the Spirit of the Son is also the Spirit of the adoption of sons), in the natural as well as in the supernatural order.

Since we do not become God's children and sons by our own nature which we receive from God, our sonship is not natural or the product of literal generation, but is an elevation to the status of sonship imparted by God out of free and overflowing love. This grace cannot make us children of God in the same way as the Son of God is, that is, by natural generation, any more than adoption among us men makes a person the natural son of the one who adopts. It has only the effect of placing the person who receives grace in relations such as result from true generation. That is the reason why the Fathers commonly teach that the sonship brought about by grace is entirely different in nature from that which belongs to the truly begotten Son of God. The Latin Fathers generally use the juridical term "adoption," the main implication of which is that the adopted person is drawn closer to the adopting person and receives a title to the latter's inheritance along with the natural children. The Greek Fathers use expressions signifying "adopted son," "son according to, or by, adoption," that is, a person who is made a son by the decision of the adopting father; such a one is an adopted son by grace. St. Gregory of Nyssa says that those who are adopted are sons, but only by a supplementary and acquired title; the name "son" is acquired and received by them, but does not belong to them by nature.[11]

Adoption among men implies no more than that a moral act takes the place of physical generation. Such an act, of course, does not communicate a new nature or life, but merely extends the father's love to the son, raises the latter to the external rank of the father, and confers on him a right to the father's inheritance. Whatever is positive in this act is verified in the act by which God adopts us as His children, but in a much fuller measure. Adoption by God differs greatly from adoption among men. When we are adopted by God we are not only called but actually are His children. We are not only morally elevated but in a certain sense are reborn and receive a kind of new nature and new life. We acquire not only an external right to an inheritance, but are interiorly equipped and empowered to receive it, since the inheritance does not consist in external goods but is a most exalted life of knowledge and love of God.

St. John says that through God's love we are not only called but are His children. God's love is not like man's love, which presupposes lovableness in the object but cannot confer a new lovableness. God's love makes a thing good by embracing it. It is necessarily operative; and we can say that God loves a person only to the extent that He makes him good and communicates goodness to him. How could this high love of God, this love that is called simply

[11] *Contra Eunomium*, III [*PG*, XLV, 605].

and pre-eminently God's love, be an idle affection for created nature? How could it confer on men the new name, God's children, which even from the juridical point of view means so much even though it is empty, without at the same time imparting to them a new, higher goodness and perfection? No, God's love, with which He loves us in His only-begotten Son, gives us not only a new external dignity, but a new internal goodness and beauty. It is so powerful that it makes us conformable to the image of His Son, inaugurates in us a new, higher man, and, in a certain sense, establishes in us the beginning of a new substance (if we take Hebrews 3:14 literally, as seems best). "For whom He foreknew [or chose as His children, the saints, about whom the Apostle is speaking throughout the chapter] He also predestinated to be made conformable to the image of His Son" (Rom. 8:29).

Accordingly this love, being divine, is not unfruitful; it imparts to us a new existence and a higher life, and begets us anew. The Savior told Nicodemus that what was born of the flesh cannot be born again in the flesh, but that what was born in the flesh can "be born again of water and the Holy Ghost" (John 3:5), so as to become spiritual and rise to a spiritual life. Nature cannot be born a second time to the life that it already has and is contained in it; but it can be born again to a higher life. St. Peter says that we are "born again not of corruptible seed but incorruptible, by the word of God who liveth and reigneth forever" (I Pet. 1:23). St. James adds: "Every best gift and every perfect gift is from . . . the Father of lights. . . . For of His own will hath He begotten us by the word of truth" (Jas. 1:17 f.). God has planted a seed in nature, from which a new life springs up: "Whosoever is born of God committeth not sin; for His seed abideth in him" (I John 3:9). God planted the seed by giving us the Spirit, and this Spirit in us becomes a rich source that gushes forth unto everlasting life, as the Savior told the Samaritan woman.

St. John often says that we are born of God, and he calls us children of God. Although divine adoption is the effect of God's love, it is more like generation and birth than the simple moral relationship implied by human adoption. The reason is easily perceived. Divine adoption communicates to us a new, incomparably higher life, a life for which no seed is produced by us, but has to be planted in us. As the new life is divine, the seed that is planted in us must likewise be divine. This seed is the Spirit of divine life,[12] given to us by the Father, as St. John says. How this is to be understood, we shall see later.

The life into which we are thus born is not any sort of life; it is the divine life that God Himself possesses and has communicated in its fullness to His only-begotten Son. And that is required, in order to verify the analogy of generation as fully as possible. For generation, in effect, is the origin of a living being from a living being in similarity and likeness of nature (*generatio est origo viventis a vivente in similitudinem naturae*). In generation understood according to its stricter sense, the life that is communicated must be the same as that of the begetter. We have referred to this truth repeatedly. We find the best proof of our assertion in Sacred Scripture, according to which God's own

[12] Concerning the way in which we are reborn of God the Father in the Holy Spirit, we should not overlook Matt. 3:11: "He shall baptize you in the Holy Ghost and fire," or in the fire of the Holy Ghost. Baptism is the sacrament of our rebirth as children of God. This rebirth is here represented as an interior, spiritual baptism, that is, an immersion of our spirit in the fire of the divine Spirit. Pervaded by the Holy Ghost's divine ardor and spirituality, the soul takes on a beauty, splendor, and life resembling corresponding perfections in the divine nature, and thus is truly born as a child similar to the Father in His glory.

life is communicated to us in our supernatural generation. This truth is wonderfully expressed in the beautiful comparison of the vine, in which God's Son represents Himself as the trunk from which life flows and spreads into all the branches. It occurs again and again in another heavenly figure, which indicates our relation to the Son of God so forcefully and truly that it can scarcely be called a figure. I am referring to the comparison of the human body, in which we are likened to the members and the Son of God is likened to the head that concentrates in itself all the vital powers of the body and sends them forth from itself. As the life of the head and that of the members are of the same kind, the life which the Son of God communicates to us must be like His life and, so far as that is possible, of the same kind. Does not God's Son promise us that we shall live by Him, as He lives by the Father? [13] Does He not desire that we should eat at the same table with Him and dwell in the same house with Him? The Apostle had that unity and life in mind when he exclaimed: "I live, now not I, but Christ liveth in me" (Gal. 2:20). That is the only reason why he could say that the Spirit of divine life is also the Spirit that moves our life,[14] and maintain that we are filled with all the fullness of God.[15]

This consideration leads us to another point that is often brought out in connection with generation and can contribute to further clarification. The nature of generation requires that it should be the origin of a living being from a conjoined living being, so that an intimate union and relation exist between the begetter and the begotten. This link consists in the fact that the very substance of the begetter

[13] John 6:58.
[14] Rom., chap. 8.
[15] Eph. 3:20.

passes over to the begotten either entirely (as in the generation of the Word in God), or partly (as in animal generation). Such unity is distinct from the mere specific unity of life found in the begetter and the begotten. In this sense, a unity between God and the spirit that is raised to divine life by His love is unthinkable, and would lead to open pantheism, and would even do away with the idea of generation by way of freely bestowed love. Hence our generation is infinitely inferior to that of the eternal Word. But in a certain respect the union of the soul with God resulting from grace is far higher and more perfect than that which takes place between the begetter and the begotten in animal generation. It is a spiritual generation; furthermore, it contains in higher degree the perfection peculiar to generation, since it links the begetter with the begotten in a far more intimate and stable union that is never to be broken off. In communicating divine life to the created spirit, God draws the spirit closer to Himself, pervades it with His divine power as with fire or an ointment, and endows it with an energy that does not arise from the created essence but comes immediately from the divine essence by which it is continually supported and sustained. The spirit is thus raised up to God in a way we cannot fully understand, and receives from Him the power to lead a divine life, that is, a life resembling God's life; what the spirit receives is not, of course, a substance, but a new quality modifying its own substance. The soul is simultaneously wedded to God and born of God. It is wedded to God by receiving from Him a sort of seed for the new life it is to develop and build up (and also by becoming one spirit with Him; St. Paul says that he who cleaves to God is one spirit with Him, much as the man who cleaves to a woman becomes one body with her); and it is conceived and born of God, since the seed of life it receives is the seed of its own life that makes it a child of God.

Although the sonship we receive from God by His freely given love is not natural, as it does not come to us from our own nature, it is not a mere juridical adoption, because it communicates to us a new existence and life by an act that implies a kind of generation. This generation imparts to us a second, higher, godlike nature, which is an image of the divine nature; it is a vital power and tendency enabling us to lead and attain a life that in itself belongs to the divine nature alone. Therefore the relation of sonship effected by grace, by which man is united to God, has an analogy not only with adoption, but with natural sonship among men.

The knowledge of the intimate nature of this sonship we have gained prepares us to pass to a consideration of all the other relations that are based on it. Here we may, and even must, take as our norm a principle which, if it were not explicitly and emphatically expressed in divine revelation and laid down as a proof of God's wonderful love, would strike us as rash and blasphemous. But now that it has been revealed, neglect of it would imply ingratitude and lack of interest in the deeper truths of our faith. The principle is that our relations to God are to be measured and judged according to those which the only-begotten and natural Son of God has to His Father. The most important of these relations and the one that sums up all the others is the unity of the Son with the Father.

In general, a natural son is one with his father in two ways: first, by unity of similarity, which means that the form or nature which the begetter and the begotten have in common is the same (specifically or even numerically), because of the unity of likeness in nature by which they are not only united but are simply one (that is, one thing, not one person—*unum sunt, licet non unus*); secondly, by one-ness of union, by which the two are not simply one but only have one thing in common. The first is in itself unity and therefore also union; the second is in itself unification and union, and is unity only in this sense. This union is two-fold in God: the procession of the Son from the Father who communicates Himself to the Son and generates Him, and the return of the Son to the Father through the infinite, substantial love with which the Son embraces the Father and the fruit of which, as St. Bernard says, is the Holy Spirit. These three different kinds of unity are really one in God and mutually imply one another. The Son possesses the nature of the Father because He is begotten by the Father; and He is begotten by the Father because He re-ceives the Father's nature, and can embrace the Father with unutterable love, penetrate into His heart, and be perfectly one with Him in love, because He is one with Him in nature and by generation. This oneness must be called natural in every respect, because it is either formally a unity in nature, or a unity by which nature is communi-cated, or a unity that is based on the oneness and communi-cation of nature. Therefore unity in love, considered formally in itself, cannot simply be called moral unity; it must rather be called natural unity or, if the term "moral" is to be used, it must be given a higher signification than it ordinarily has.[16]

---

[16] The supernatural union of love between the creature and God would likewise have to be called physical rather than moral, because it reposes on a certain unity of nature, especially if the good are to be distinguished from the wicked by it. The wicked are not merely wanting in the moral development of a vital faculty; they lack the supernatural vital faculty itself, which can exist only in those who accept it freely and put no obstacle in the way. However, if the union of love is conceived in op-position to union of nature, it can be called moral.

In the usage of the Greek Fathers, physical unity is not only the unity

According to these preliminary conceptions we can see how much our union with God surpasses the dualism and separation from God found in creatures as such, and how it can imitate and approach the inexpressible oneness of the Son with the Father. As we have said, divine revelation teaches us with certainty that the oneness of God the Father with His natural Son is the model of the unity to be established between us and God. The Savior prays to the Father that we may be one, as He is one with the Father. This passage is thus understood by many of the Fathers, particularly St. Cyril.[17] If we were to say that the Savior prays that we may be one among ourselves, we would not give to the text its full sense and would not do justice to the comparison. In any case we can be perfectly one among ourselves only to the extent that we are one with God. Some of the holy Fathers affirm that this unity with God is natural. The assertion makes good sense if God communicates to us a sort of new, higher nature by spiritual generation, a nature that is, so to speak, specifically similar to His, since

---

of two things that join to form one nature, but in general any real union, especially a union of two things according to nature (*secundum naturam*), even though they do not constitute one nature (*non in naturam unam*), in which one thing shares in the nature of the other or becomes similar to it. Nature itself and what constitutes it are called physical in the first instance. In an eminent sense, the term "physical" is applied to the faculty of knowledge in a spirit, because a spiritual conception or birth is wrought by it, and the spiritual nature reproduces itself by it. We can and should say that any naturally operative faculty and any naturally performed action are natural, so far as nature's necessary mode of operation is opposed to the will's free mode of operation toward an end known beforehand. Since free actions as such proceed from an ordination to an end and therefore tend to preserve necessary orders and relations, the view was gradually formed that everything having real existence in the proper sense, as nature, or power or act of nature, can be called physical, and that, on the contrary, whatever consists in mere external relations can be called moral.

[17] Cf. *In Ioan.*, XI, 9 [*PG*, LXXIV, 512–17].

it receives and shares in prerogatives that in themselves belong to God alone, to the exclusion of all creatures. This natural oneness can be considered according to the three lines of thought we mentioned above. Our union with God is natural and not merely moral, first, because it is a kind of oneness in nature, secondly because it is a unity of union between God and us brought about by His love, with a view to effecting this oneness in nature, and thirdly because it is a unity of union between our souls and God, not by some indefinite sort of love, but by the love that is based on oneness in nature with Him.

As God the Son is one with the Father, that is, is like Him because He has the same nature, we too are one with God, that is, we are like Him and conformable to Him in nature, because we receive, so to speak, the same nature, to the extent that we are capable of it. The difference is this: the Son of God possesses the fullness of divine nature substantially and in numerical identity, whereas we do not possess the fullness of the divine nature but only participate in it; moreover, it does not exist in us as a substance but only as a quality that imitates this substance and as a power of activity; and we do not have it in numerical identity but only by specific resemblance. We become like God, the Father of light, when He enkindles in us a light similar to His own. As we shall see more clearly later, our resemblance with the Father is caused by the fact that He communicates to us a divine power of knowledge by which we, knowing the divine essence and reflecting it and expressing it in ourselves in imitation of God's only-begotten Son who proceeds from Him as His Word and likeness, receive His image and so are "made conformable to the image of His Son" (Rom. 8:29).

Thus we are made one with God when we "are trans-

formed into the same image from glory to glory" (II Cor.
3:18) by His Spirit who shines in us. The splendor of the
divine sun becomes the splendor of our souls in which it is
concentrated as in a crystal globe in such a way that its
pure rays are not broken up into various colors; the beauty
of the soul becomes the same in kind as that of God. Because of this unity and similarity between the soul in grace
and God, we are even called gods in Sacred Scripture. This
designation occurs in a passage that expresses the special
nobility man receives when he is given a share in a particular divine good, and in a certain sense represents this nobility. Yet the Fathers are fond of applying the expression to
the state of soul we are speaking of. In this state the soul
has so great a resemblance with God that it even seems to
be God. The Fathers, especially the Greeks, often speak
of a divinization of the spirit, although they carefully guard
against giving the impression that the soul becomes identical with God. They assert clearly and distinctly that nothing more than a unique kind of resemblance can be understood, a resemblance that implies a very close union with
God.

Pseudo-Dionysius the Areopagite, in particular, is ad-
dicted to very striking expressions. In general he is extra-
ordinarily bold in his language and thoughts. On the other
hand, he has an exquisite skill in saving the most audacious
concepts and terms from misunderstanding by giving them
an appropriate and characteristic turn; his facility in this
respect is remarkable. Unfortunately this fact is often overlooked by those who consult his works.

"Divinization is the closest possible assimilation to God
and union with Him." [18] But it is not the result of the great-

[18] Pseudo-Dionysius, *De ecclesiastica hierarchia*, c. 1, no. 3 [*PG*, III,
371].

est union with God that is possible for our nature by itself, that is, it is not brought about by the development and growth of the godlikeness that is natural to us. In the first place, the latter is not the greatest possible assimilation, and further, it does not establish man in a state enabling him to appear to be something more than man. But the most salient feature in divinization is precisely man's reception of a higher dignity and quasi-nature, and the consequent capacity for a higher development and activity. The godlikeness that is added to nature consists not only in an activity promoting union with God, but also in the bestowal of a new divine principle of activity. Activity is properly divinizing if it proceeds from the divine nature and power elevating and transforming it, but not if it proceeds from created nature's own powers. This remark is directed against Staudenmaier who, with great success and acumen, if it can be called that, tried to reduce all the expressions found in the Fathers and Sacred Scripture about man's divinization and rebirth, to the activity of mind and will uniting us with God. But he failed to perceive that, if a new nature and power likening us to God did not underlie these activities, all the noble and exalted teaching of the Fathers and Scripture degenerates into a pretentious bombast that has little or no meaning.

The first effect of supernature, therefore, is to make us one with God. We are made similar to Him, in existence as well as in activity, in nature as well as in life itself. Such a state surpasses our nature and befits His. Accordingly we have, I repeat, a nature that in a certain way is like His, and become naturally (in the sense explained) one with Him.

This unity brings with it, as we have said, two other unities of union that likewise surpass every union of creatures with God, and approaches that oneness which the natural Son of God has with the Father. Like the first unity, in its own way it may be called a natural rather than a moral unity with God. All creatures are similar to God, although so imperfectly that they are more unlike Him than like Him and do not let the effulgence of His Godhead pass through them clearly but break it up into many rays and obscure it. Furthermore, all creatures are united with God in such a way that, as St. Augustine says, God is the deepest root of their being and their life, the root from which they draw all power and fullness of life, to which they return, and for which they live and work. By our very nature we live, move, and are in God; and God is the King for whom everything lives that lives (*regem cui omnia vivunt*), the good that everything desires. God lovingly bends down over the creature to give it what is good, and the creature in turn is drawn up to God by love to complete the circulatory movement of love.

Thus God is all in all in created nature. He is present in all things by His activity and His power (*per potentiam*), by which He gives them existence; and since His activity and power are His essence, He is also present in them by His essence. He is more perfectly in them the more He acts in them and the more He allows them to share in His essence, that is, to imitate Him in their degree. At the same time He remains above them as their supreme Lord and King; He gives them their essences and natures that are similar to His, but in their way and not in His. As their Creator, therefore, God does not unite Himself with them eternally in the way the Begetter gives Himself to the Begotten in eternal oneness. This intimate union belongs exclusively to God the Father and His only-begotten Son; the Father bears the Son alone in His bosom and His heart, as the trunk holds the branch united to itself to communi-

cate to it its own life. But the Father's gracious love reaches
out to us, too. As we have seen, He communicates His own
nature to us, breathes His love into us, and begets us spiritually, yet truly and really. He embraces us along with the
Only-begotten and presses us to His fatherly heart, becoming one with us as He is one with His Son. "The glory which
Thou hast given Me, I have given to them; that they may
be one, as We also are one; I in them and Thou in Me; that
they may be made perfect in one, and the world may know
that Thou has sent Me and hast loved them as Thou hast
also loved Me" (John 17:22 f.).

God is one with created natures in the sense that His
power calls into existence essences and substances from
which the vital faculties these beings possess naturally
flow. But in the supernatural order He endows the creature
with vital faculties that do not emanate from its essence
and therefore have the divine essence as their immediate
source, so that these powers in the creature are related to
the divine essence somewhat as the creature's faculties are
related to its own essence. To some extent God's essence
takes the place of the creature's essence, in the sense that
the creature's supernatural faculties are radicated immediately in it. When the regenerated soul is reborn its union
with God is so close that it is raised above all creatures and,
somewhat like God's Son, who receives the Father's essence not only as the foundation of His powers but also in
its substance, is immediately united with the Father.

To this union and unity of God's essence with the spirit
that is supernaturally transformed when it receives its
higher life and nature at its birth from God's love, there
correspond a union and unity of the elevated spirit with
God consisting in the activity of the powers communicated
to it so that it may turn to God by knowing and loving Him.

Even the mere created powers can and must have God as the ultimate goal of their activity and striving; to some extent this is their immediate goal, in the sense that created goods and objects can arouse desire only because of the uncreated goodness that shines forth in them. However, as the faculty is rooted in a created essence and does not come from God except in the sense that it accompanies this essence, its activity is immediately directed to this essence and mounts up to God through it; such is the case even if the creature is completely subordinated to God. Consequently the union that is thereby established with the divine goodness is not very close and is certainly not direct. That is true of all creatures within their spheres, but particularly of the activity of intellectual creatures. They know and love God through their knowledge and love of created beings, by knowing and loving Him as the Creator of nature. God's Son alone, who is one with the Father in nature (as form) and by nature (as generation), can by nature direct His activity immediately to the Father, so as immediately to see Him in His essence and to embrace Him with the most intimate love, the same love as that with which the Father loves Himself.

The lover is perfectly and truly one with the beloved only if he loves the latter with the same love as that with which he is loved. But this is impossible unless both are already united to each other in a different way. In other words, the love that truly makes them one must be based on a previous relationship of unity; the closer this relationship is, the more intimate will the unity of love be. This principle may be applied to the unity between adopted children and God. Since a higher unity with God already exists in them, a like higher unity and union with God can also be attained by the activity they direct to God, especially by love. As their higher faculties are immediately rooted in the divine essence and are an imitation of God's vital power, they are so free and are raised so high that, tied down to no creature, they can make the divine essence the immediate object of their activity. Consequently the creature can know the Father's essence immediately; can savor and love its goodness and sweetness immediately; can be intimately united to it by love, and, we may say, can sink into its depths. Thus the creature loves the Father with the same love as that with which His Son loves Him and with which He loves Himself, with the love which terminates in the Holy Spirit and is infused by Him into our hearts.

In this way the child of grace is made mystically and supernaturally one with the Father in a relation that should be called physical rather than moral, and that in itself pertains to no creature but to God's only-begotten, natural Son alone.

This discloses to us the depth and insight that led St. Thomas to place the characteristic trait of true, supernatural sonship of God in the fact that it makes us one with the Father as His natural Son is one with Him.

We are also made one with God by resemblance or unity (*unitas*) of nature and by union (*unio*). This union is twofold. There is a union by which God unites Himself with us when He takes us immediately to His essence and heart to communicate His life to us; and there is a union by which we make God's essence the immediate object of our activity and love in order to unite ourselves with Him and to cling to Him. In a way, we share with the Son the nature, the heart, and the love of the Father.

The relation of personal unity between the natural Son of God and the Father establishes the Son's right to the

Father's inheritance. This right is nothing else than the community of goods between Father and Son that is inseparable from their personal unity. The only-begotten Son of God has everything the Father has. "All My things are Thine, and Thine are Mine" (John 17:10; cf. 16:15). For that matter, the inheritance coincides perfectly with the sonship itself. In God, being and property, person and nature, potency and act are indivisibly identical, and the basic oneness of the divine being virtually unites in itself all the relationships that in creatures are opposed. In the same way, the Son of God is not otherwise Son than God, and is not otherwise Son than heir. Even the divine nature which He receives from the Father in richest plenitude, in infinite actuality with its entire life of immeasurable beatitude, including His procession as the reflection and Word of the Father, as the image of His light and essence, is His inheritance, His superabundant heritage.

The Father's wealth does not, as with us men, consist so much in the possession of external goods as in the infinitely rich and happy life He has in Himself. Among us men, a father's natural life is not enough to procure his happiness; he needs external goods to sustain his life and to make it happy. Accordingly, he does not impart to his son, along with life, all that is needed for the latter's well-being and happiness, but has to leave him external goods for this purpose. Because life and goods are so different, there can be a sonship that consists in a mere right to an inheritance, without an interior communication of life. Although our supernatural sonship with regard to God is an image of that of God's Son, the concepts of sonship and inheritance are to some extent distinct; yet they are associated. Hence they are not completely different, as in human sonship. The concepts are distinct because the life of the adopted children is not, like that of God's natural Son, given to them once and for all in its complete fullness and maturity, but exists in an inchoative and elementary way; they must cherish and cultivate what they have received and make themselves worthy of its full flowering. The initial stage of this life invests them with a sort of dignity belonging to the children of God; the perfect culmination of this life is held out to them as the inheritance to which they have a title and which they are to merit. But the concepts of sonship and inheritance are associated, since what is reserved for the children of God is not an external good, but is the culmination of the vital power of growth that is in them. They will be fully children of God and perfectly begotten of Him when they come into their inheritance.

This explains why Sacred Scripture teaches at times that we are already God's children, at other times that we will be God's children, and that we are still "waiting for the adoption of the sons of God" (Rom. 8:23). St. John combines the two: "We are now the sons of God; and it hath not yet appeared what we shall be" (I John 3:2). At present we bear within us the seed that will later burst into full flower. At present we are still like small children clasped to God's heart and clinging to Him with childlike love; but later we shall be perfect sons and grown men, displaying in ourselves all the majesty of our Father.

Consequently our attainment of sonship is separate from our reception of the inheritance, because we have a two-fold generation and birth. We are already begotten and born of God in the Holy Spirit by the bath of regeneration, and yet we still await our better rebirth (*regeneratio*), of which the first is no more than a pledge and preparation. Christ the Son of God already lives in us and shares His

life with us in the most intimate way; nevertheless Christ
our life has not yet appeared, and therefore we do not yet
appear with Him in glory (Cf. Col. 3:4). We already bear
within us the image of the Son; but it has not yet been
formed "unto a perfect man, unto the measure of the age
of the fullness of Christ" (Eph. 4:13), who was perfect
from the beginning. We already enjoy some measure of
the freedom and glory of the children of God, but we are
still longing for its perfection. We have already put on
Christ in baptism and in a sense have become Christ Himself as members of His body; He already dwells in our
hearts by faith and has risen in us like the morning star;
but He has not yet risen as the sun of beatitude and glory,
to transfigure us wholly into His image and to fill us with
all His glory and beatitude. God has already regenerated
us, but only "unto a lively hope . . . unto an inheritance
incorruptible and undefiled and that cannot fade, reserved
in heaven for you, who by the power of God are kept by
faith unto salvation, ready to be revealed in the last time
. . . at the appearing of Jesus Christ" (I Pet. 1:3-7).

Therefore our inheritance is nothing else than the full
flowering of the seed of divine life already planted in us.
This is the same life as that which the Son receives from
the Father for His glory and beatitude and which we are
to share with Him. Does He not tell us Himself that we are
to sit with Him on His throne, as He sits on the Father's
throne; that He prepares for us a kingdom as the Father
prepares one for Him; that we are to be where He is; that
we are to eat and drink with Him at His table? And what
does that mean if not that we are to have part in His glory,
power, and beatitude?

"The glory which Thou hast given Me," says the Son to
the Father, "I have given to them. . . . I in them and

Thou in Me, that they may be made perfect in one, and the world may know that Thou hast sent Me and hast loved them as Thou hast also loved Me" (John 17:22 f.). As He is in the Father, we are to be in Him, and as He receives eternal life from the Father, He will give us eternal life (John, chap. 6).

What is that glory the Son had from the Father before the world was (John 17:5), when, in the brightness of the saints (or the splendor of holiness, according to the Hebrew), He was begotten of the Father before the day star (Ps. 109:3), living with the Father in inaccessible light? What else than the glory of His procession from the Father as light of light, as mirror of the Father's majesty, as effluence of the glory of almighty God, image of His goodness, full expression of His essence, Word and likeness of the infinite intuition with which the Father beholds Himself (Wisd. 7:26; cf. Heb. 1:3)? And what else is the eternal and blessed life of the Son of God than that He alone, reposing in the Father's bosom, sees Him face to face, embraces Him entirely and reflects Him in Himself, and in this vision enjoys a beatitude and rapture which no mortal ear has heard, no eye has seen, and no man's heart has divined? And why do I say, "no man's heart," since even the highest angels, the cherubim and seraphim, blinded by the brilliance of that light, veil their countenances in deepest reverence? Only the Spirit who is in God, who proceeds from the Father and the Son and searches "the deep things of God" (I Cor. 2:10 f.), is by nature a witness of the inexpressible beatitude the Son enjoys in the vision of His Father. This glory and this happy, eternal life are the inheritance of the Son of God, because he receives it by His very generation. He is begotten of the Father as the likeness of His contemplation and the word of His knowledge; hence He receives the Father's glory and eternal life precisely by His generation.

Therefore we too are to receive the Father's glory and eternal life by our spiritual generation. Our glory likewise consists in the fact that we receive the image of God and are made like to Him. To speak first of our perfect generation, we become like God and receive His image in us when we see Him as He is, in St. John's words (I John 3:2); when He fills us with His divine light (the light of glory, *lumen gloriae*) which makes us capable of reflecting God's essence in its true divine beauty and splendor, and are transformed into His likeness. And in what does our eternal life consist if not, as God's Son Himself teaches us, in our knowledge of the Father, the one true God, and of Him whom the Father has sent as the Mediator of this knowledge, Jesus Christ?

The inheritance the Son of God receives at His generation is communicated to us in a new birth by which God imparts to us His light to transform us into His image, and bestows on us His knowledge and love that we, His children, may have eternal life in the beatific vision.

Let us try to gain a clearer idea of this teaching about the true connection of sonship with inheritance in our supernatural union with God. By this means we shall not only penetrate more deeply into the mysteries God has revealed to us through the Beloved Disciple, but shall acquire a firm and sure foundation for our further development.

In Sacred Scripture, St. John usually assigns, as the distinguishing property setting God's Son incomparably above all created natures, the fact that He, the Word proceeding from the Father's intellect and mouth, begotten of Him spiritually, the perfect Son, like and equal to the Father in all things, has His eminent life and inheritance in the immediate vision of the Father. And he says explicitly that the Son alone has seen the Father, because He is in the bosom of the Father. He does not, of course, exclude the Holy Spirit who, as St. Paul remarked, dwells with the Son in the Godhead and searches out the deep things in it. But the vision of the Father is not attributed to the Holy Spirit as a characteristic property, because He does not proceed from the intellect of the Father and therefore is not thought of as reposing in the Father's bosom. In his own words, which are also those of the Savior, St. John, who characterizes the Son's relation to the Father as just described, signalizes our relationship of adoptive sonship in a similar manner and says that the Son of God has come into the world to give to all who believe in Him the power to be made the sons of God.[19]

The Only-begotten was sent into the world to make us His brothers by extending to us the fullness of His grace (here regarded as His love of the Father), His life, and His truth which He receives from the Father, and by sharing with us the same love as that with which the Father loves Him (John 17:26), the same life (John, chap. 6), and the same truth the Father has given Him: "All things whatsoever I have heard of My Father I have made known to you" (John 15:15). Entering more deeply into the effect of the Father's love for us, into the object of the life of God's children and the wealth of truth He reveals to us, He says: "No man hath seen God at any time; the only-begotten Son

---

[19] John 1:12, 18. Cf. also chaps. 6 and 17. In these three chapters, especially, the Evangelist describes the precious goods brought to us by the Son of God at His Incarnation.—On this subject see the masterly works of Dom Columba Marmion, O.S.B., *Christ the Life of the Soul* (St. Louis: Herder, 1923) and *Christ in His Mysteries* (St. Louis: Herder, 1939).

who is in the bosom of the Father, He hath declared Him"
(John 1:18), obviously because the Son has seen Him.
Here the Son's relationship with the Father is character-
ized, and our relationship is therefore clearly indicated.
The grace of divine sonship and the life of the children of
God consist mainly in their reception of truth and light by
which the Word is the natural Son of God.

This truth and this light, comprised in the vision of God,
are the proper prerogative of the Son who is in the bosom of
the Father, whereas the servant stands without, and cannot enjoy the rapturous sight of the fatherly countenance.
By nature we were servants of this kind, because we were
not in the bosom of the Father; by nature we did not know
the Father and could not know Him, because He dwells
in inaccessible light. We did not even know that there was
in God a Father who begets a Son as the image of His countenance. We had no idea of a Father in God in the proper
and higher sense of the term, and therefore had no notion
that we ourselves could be made children of God in a
proper sense and thus see Him face to face. The only-begotten Son alone, dwelling in the bosom of the Father,
knew His sweet name; He alone knew Him as His own
Father and rejoiced in the sight of Him.

Hence the Son alone could make known the Father's
name; He alone could lead us to the beatific vision. And He
revealed to us His Father's name to let us know that we too
are His children who are to share in His fatherly love, and
are called, like the Son, to see the Father face to face and
thus to receive His glory and life. "I have made known Thy
name to them," says the Son to the Father, "and will make
it known, that the love wherewith Thou hast loved Me may
be in them and I in them" (John 17:26). He revealed the
Father's name to us when He taught us to know Him by

faith and to love Him. He will further reveal the Father to us in the beatific vision into which our faith will be changed. We are to share it with the Son, and by this vision of the majesty of God we shall express the same majesty in ourselves, thus to be begotten into the full likeness and life of the Father. "We shall be like to Him, because we shall see Him as He is" (I John 3:2).

But before it is revealed what we shall be, before the likeness of our heavenly Father is generated in us in its full splendor and Christ our life appears, our life is hidden with Christ in God. Yet we live and carry His likeness in us and are therefore already born of God. The Savior says that He has already revealed the Father's name to us in some degree; the Apostle says that Christ already dwells in our hearts by faith. Faith is already a light lowered down into our souls by the Father of light. It is a dim and veiled light. Basically, however, it streams forth as immediately from the source of eternal light and is as much a participation in the knowledge of the eternal Word as the clear beatific vision of God in the Word Himself. Through this faith we already know God as our Father and in faith are already begotten by Him as His children that resemble Him. The knowledge of faith, dim as it is, fills our souls with so great a light and splendor that even now we are transformed into the image of the Lord (II Cor. 3:18); by faith we are even now "light in the Lord" (Eph. 5:8), who has led us out of darkness into His wonderful light. The knowledge of faith is not excluded from the Apostle's words: "But we all beholding the glory of the Lord with open face [that is, not covered with a veil, as when we see God merely through a creature as a cloudy mirror], are transformed into the same image from glory to glory, as by the Spirit of the Lord" (II Cor. 3:18).

By the light of faith, therefore, we have an anticipation of the glory and life we are to receive as brothers of the Son, in the vision of the Father, when we come into our inheritance. And since we are made children of God in fullest measure by that inheritance, our first begetting imparts to us, along with the life of the children of God, an earnest of our future heritage.

On the basis of our generation that is effected by grace, we have shown that the most important relations existing between a son and father are present in our relations of sonship to God. And these relations are incomparably more perfect, not only than those found in adoption among men, but even than those found in natural sonship among men.

We have also made it clear that we cannot possess or attain these relations by virtue of our own nature. They raise us above our nature and enable us to enter into union with the only-begotten Son of God.

Chapter VIII

METAPHYSICS OF SUPERNATURE

Our next endeavor will be to examine in greater detail the so-called higher divine nature that is ours as God's children. We shall study it in itself, its faculties, its life, and its activities. Our purpose is to formulate the doctrine in a more scientific way, and also to profit by the clarification it can contribute toward acquiring a more profound and lofty conception of many passages in Sacred Scripture, the Fathers, and the mystics. By carefully marking the boundaries of the sphere of discussion, we shall preclude all misunderstandings. A few repetitions of ideas already considered cannot be avoided, because the various phases influence one another; besides, a review of some of the points will safeguard us against overlooking anything of importance.

In our investigation of the supernatural, divine life, we must begin by distinguishing two things: its activity (*actus secundus*, for example, the vision of God), and the principle of this activity (*actus primus*, as it was called by the ancient Scholastics). The former is the act *which* is performed (*actus qui agitur*), the latter is the act *by which* the agent acts (*actus quo agitur*). The latter, being an active potency and virtually containing the former, cannot be an empty potency, and therefore has a certain actuality that is called act. The former is an operation, the latter is a principle. This is to be kept in mind especially when a living nature is in question; for both the vital activity and the vital principle, the *actus vitae* and the *principium vitae*, are called life. The latter is properly nature.[1] The distinction must be insisted on, to avoid a gross misunderstanding that can obscure all that has gone before as well as all that is to follow. Thus we can say that the generation we spoke of in previous chapters may be understood as a communication of life in a wider sense, a moral sense, as when we use the name "father" of a person who has not really laid the foundation of our spiritual life but has promoted its growth or given it a new direction. In this sense the Apostle tells the Corinthians that he has begotten them in Christ by his Gospel (I Cor. 4:15).

I do not deny that in some passages of Sacred Scripture this sense can also be applied to God, if the passage is considered in itself alone, for example in the text: "Of His own will hath He [God] begotten us by the word of truth" (Jas. 1:18). In itself, this sentence could be understood of a mere awakening of our own spiritual powers by the preaching of God's word. But from other texts we learn that exterior revelation is powerless without interior revelation; that all knowledge must result from a new illumination God produces in our souls by a light enkindled to dispel its darkness; that we are quite dead and incapable of any acts of proper union with Him and therefore need a kind of new creation (Eph. 2:10); that in general such acts of knowledge and love far exceed the powers of our nature and can be natural to God alone.

In view of such texts we see that communication of life and generation in the supernatural order are not a mere stimulation to activity for slumberers or a new direction given to perverted faculties, but must be a new establish-

[1] Cf. St. Thomas, *Summa theol.*, Ia, q. 18, a. 1.

ing of a new vital principle such as nature of itself does not possess. Although the light that transforms us into the likeness of God reaches its climax in the act in which we shall actually see God, it must also imply a new faculty that is actively revealed in this knowledge, and of which the act is a sort of reflection. In the same way the light of reason is revealed in the act of knowledge, but in itself is not an act of knowledge.

Since all the excellence and elevation, all the similarity and union with God that are involved in supernatural acts have their basis in the supernatural principle of life implanted in the soul, all their perfections must primarily be referred to this principle. In fact we know this principle, as we know all other faculties and principles, mainly from its acts; consequently in any analytical procedure, treatment of this principle would have to come last in the series. However, we have already said a good deal about natural acts; and supernatural acts are no less hidden from reason than their principle, and are knowable only by faith through revelation. Accordingly we prefer a synthetic procedure, particularly as it is best adapted to a scientific, systematic exposition. We shall speak first of the supernatural principle of life and later more in detail of the faculties and acts springing from it.

The principle of our supernatural life must be related to its acts in the way the nature of the soul is related to natural acts. This principle has the power and tendency to perform acts, although an external stimulus coming from God and the presence of an object are needed. In the same way a power and tendency for natural acts are found in the nature of the soul. The difference is that the supernatural principle is not really a new substance, but inheres in a substance, is linked with the essential, basic faculties belonging to this substance, and makes them capable of a higher domain of activity. It is present in the natural substance and faculties as a form determining them to a new existence, power, and activity. Therefore it is called a habit, whereby the soul exists in a definite way, especially with regard to a certain end and to acts of life.

Yet it must be carefully distinguished from those external habits by which the soul receives exteriorly a higher station and relation but does not receive interiorly a higher existence. It is likewise distinct from those interior habits in the faculties of the soul which do not equip them for acts of a higher kind, and so do not elevate them intrinsically, but leave a faculty in its native condition and bestow on it no more than a strong ordination and decisive inclination to its own proper acts, with the result that these acts may be performed more easily, quickly, and efficiently.

The supernatural habit, too, confers a certain facility, chiefly by supporting nature in its struggle with sensuality and generally in the conflict against temptations and inducements to evil. But this is a secondary matter and a consequence, owing to the fact that the higher power which is bestowed includes a tendency toward its proper object. Thus it can readily happen that a man endowed with a high degree of grace experiences extreme difficulty in the practice of virtue. The main thing is that the faculty itself is elevated so that it can elicit acts of a higher kind and order, which it would not have the slightest ability to perform if left to itself. The supernatural habit agrees with the ordinary, natural habit only in the fact that both signify a quality modifying the substance of the soul and its faculties, but do not signify the soul itself. In modern languages, words such as "state" or "condition" may be used to designate a supernatural habit; but they have the disadvantage of being too indefinite. Other terms, like "custom," which often correspond to the Latin *habitus*, cannot be employed in this connection, since the habit we are speaking of is not acquired (*acquisitus*) by repeated acts, but is divinely infused. St. Thomas well defines the nature of the supernatural principle of life when he teaches that it is a state by which the soul enters into such a relation with a higher nature as to share in its life.[2]

This state is accidental to the creature, and in this respect is less excellent than the creature's substantial, natural perfection. But in the sense that it elevates nature to the plane of the supreme, divine nature, it is more excellent and confers an incomparably greater perfection than all natural gifts. Since it is accidental, the soul remains substantially unchanged; that is altogether clear. Hence the soul does not become divine, that is, a divine substance, but becomes godlike in its condition.

The supernatural principle of life, or supernature, does not have quite the same relation to its acts as the nature of things has to its acts, as though it were a substance; for it is not a substance. Yet if we consider it minutely, we can say with St. Thomas that it shares with substance the function of being a single, common substratum of the various supernatural faculties and acts. It is not one of these faculties or all of them taken together; it is their common substructure. Some theologians are unwilling to regard this as a real distinction; yet it may be regarded as such. In any case the distinction may be made in conception; and this has to be done, if clear ideas are desired. The objection may be raised that this is only a subtlety invented by St. Thomas, and that it has no meaning other than providing an opportunity for disputations. In point of fact, however,

[2] Cf. *Summa theol.*, Ia IIae, q.110, a.4.

as we shall soon see, no great subtlety is needed to draw up a system of the supernatural order that is intelligible from all angles and quite consistent. For the distinction is intended merely to supply a solid, definite foundation for the whole order, without which it can never acquire an assured, scientific structure.

In concept we represent the essence and substance of a thing, along with its specific nature, as being logically prior to its activity. The activity that is natural and suitable for a thing is judged according to the thing's substance and specific nature, and the faculties are the potency, inherent in the specific nature of the substance, to pass over into activity. Thus we conceive the thing's substance as first and absolute, and the faculties as secondary and relative, with reference to the activity that is to be performed. Moreover, the faculties can be different and manifold. But if they are to be truly unified and are to function as a thing's necessary faculties, some unifying principle must underlie them, to determine which and how many faculties are required for a being's development. The faculties themselves do not, in the last instance, determine the entire measure of the being's activity; they are only a potency for activity, which, as has just been pointed out, is based on the perfection and specific nature of the being itself.

When, therefore, the philosopher contemplates any whole, he does not merely seek out the conglomeration of qualities pertaining to it; scientific knowledge demands more than this. It searches for the substructure of all these various qualities, and this substructure can be sought only in the specific nature of the essence underlying the qualities or of the substance of the thing. As long as this is not discovered or at least approximately ascertained, science is not content; all the separate data cannot be rightly illuminated and their intrinsic value cannot be appraised; and so science runs the risk of losing even what it possessed before.

In the supernatural order the situation is similar. A theologian cannot afford to go astray in this matter. Scotus with his school, for example, and Bellarmine admitted supernatural acts, a supernatural end, and supernatural virtues and faculties; but they had no stable, general norm for bringing all these elements together, clarifying them by one another, and hence for explaining each element more accurately. There are some who deny that grace is formally anything else than the supernatural virtue of love, and who consequently remove every common, unifying substratum of the supernatural faculties. They deprive themselves of any norm for defining the sphere of supernatural activity and for establishing a clear distinction between supernatural and natural acts. They never advance beyond a negative definition of the supernatural, and a uniform, scientific synthesis of all the pertinent doctrines is no more possible for them, as has just been remarked, than a unified explanation of all the factors belonging to a thing is possible in the natural order without going into the thing's basic nature.

Accordingly, we cannot help marveling at the great scientific acumen of St. Thomas when we observe how he, proceeding from a knowledge of natural things, transferred the notion of a single, essential form underlying all the various faculties to the supernatural order. He did this with the same right and the same utility as that with which we justify that conception in the case of natural things. The above-mentioned factors, which determine this conception in the natural order, retain their value in the supernatural order. The sole difference, as we have remarked, is that the substratum of the natural faculties is the substance and essence of the thing itself, whereas the substratum of the supernatural faculties can be no more than a quality modifying the substance of the thing, a quality caused by a higher substance and essence with which it is united.

This difference is the reason why a single supernatural faculty can be infused without the substratum which would bring all the other faculties along with it. The supernatural principle of life can be possessed in greater or lesser measure because it is not an indivisible, substantial essence, but is a participated quality. Moreover, the supernatural faculties have their cause, not in the subject to which they belong, but in God; besides, they have a quasi-material substratum in the basic faculties of nature. Although a separation of the supernatural faculties from their substratum or from one another is not natural, it is not intrinsically contradictory and hence impossible, as is the case with the natural faculties. Such a separation in the natural faculties is impossible because without their natural substratum, the substance, every material and causal substratum vanishes, and therefore a separation is not even conceivable.

To clarify this point, let us suppose, for example, that the fire in the sun is a substance which has power to illuminate and to warm. This fire can first cause a responsive body to shed light; it can further cause the body to be warmed and to give off heat. But the light and warmth are in a sense external to the body, and are not connatural to it unless it heats up and glows and becomes a fiery body. The fire itself is neither light nor warmth but is their cause, the single nature underlying them both. In some such way as this, the soul is related to the Godhead. The latter is like a substantial fire and heat; its nature is the sheerest, purest heat, which is light as well as warmth. From its own riches it has given existence to other beings and has enkindled a fire in them. Spiritual natures, with their higher power, reason, and love, are in themselves an image of the divine fire. But their fire is wholly different in kind from the divine fire and is infinitely inferior to it (just as no substance on earth has in it a fire like the sun), and therefore contains no divine light or fire.

Yet God wishes His own light to shine in us and to pervade us with His own warmth. He can transmit to us light alone; many bodies diffuse light but give off no warmth. But then the light is in a condition of unnatural separation. God can bestow on us His light along with His warmth; but as long as our nature itself does not become fire in its own way, the light and warmth in us remain foreign to us and are not natural to us. This very perception that the separation of light and warmth is not natural, that is, conformable to nature, supposes that we have an idea of a nature that is neither the one nor the other, but underlies and connects both. If we feel that light and warmth alone would be foreign to us and would have no firm support in us, we are led to the thought that there must be a sort of new nature in us by which both in their union become natural and proper to us, that is, that we ourselves according to our capacity receive the nature of divine fire, so as to be not only illuminated and warmed by it, but to be, in a way, fired to white heat and thoroughly pervaded by it. This comparison of the Godhead with fire that pervades and heats another body is often used by the holy Fathers in this subject matter, although it is not always carried out in detail.

If we prefer to dispense with figurative language, we can present the doctrine as follows. It is certain that God imparts to us knowledge and love of the kind that belongs to Him alone, and that in consequence He gives us the powers needed to elicit these acts. But why does He give us these acts and powers? Why both together, so that their separation is unnatural? We find the answer in Sacred Scripture. We must have such knowledge and love of our Father because we are born of God and, as His children, are made to share in His divine nature. By reason of the new nature we have received, this knowledge and love are natural, whereas a separation of love from knowledge is unnatural. What does this mean except that some common substratum underlies the distinct faculties of supernatural knowledge and love, something that qualifies and sustains them? What does this mean except that in the supernatural order we must receive, as the ultimate principle on which in the last analysis everything depends, something corresponding to what, in the natural order, is called a thing's nature in the strict sense, and which in consequence may rightly be designated as a sort of second, higher nature or supernature? Thus we can no more conceive the supernatural in its unity and essence without a supernature, than we can conceive the natural without the nature in which it is rooted and has its substratum.

Supernature can be nothing else than a participation or share in the higher, divine nature as such, conferred on the created spirit as a sort of nature. This involves the necessity we are under of conceiving, on the analogy of created things, that God's nature in the strict sense is the substratum underlying His own power and activity. Although God's power and activity are identical with His substance, we can and must think of this supremely simple but eminently rich substance primarily as existence, as purest existence and most perfect nature. That is the only way we have of representing it as the principle and object of the activities of knowledge and love elicited in it. We can say that

God has, and must have, so sublime a knowledge and love of Himself because He is so perfect a Being and so exalted a spiritual nature. Obviously no likeness and participation found in creation can imitate God's being in its innermost perfection of self-existence. However, we can speak as we do if nature signifies the positive perfection of the divine existence, a characteristic proper to His being, the eminent spirituality which is His, that is, supreme freedom from all the bonds of matter and all inner potentiality that resembles matter.[3]

The activity of thinking is directly proportioned to the simplicity and purity of existence or being. All things are either thinking or thought; all bear in themselves a thinking or a thought image, their form, their specific nature. In material things this form is in a sense renounced, as it is bound to crass matter; the more it disengages itself from the restraint of matter, the closer its activity comes to true thinking. To be able to think really and truly, the form must be completely free of the shackles of matter and must exclude matter from itself. But even the spirit that is free from literal matter always retains something that is similar to matter, which does not indeed prevent it from thinking, but obstructs the full perfection of thinking and keeps it from such perfection, somewhat as matter does with regard to the form united to it. This is the intrinsic potentiality

[3] A definition of spiritual nature that goes no deeper than the assertion that it is a thinking being betrays a very defective philosophy. Such a definition is true; but it describes the being only according to its activity. To conceive the activity itself, we must define the essence more accurately, as activity depends on essence, not vice versa. Since St. Thomas, in treating of the philosophy of the soul, insists so strongly that the intellectuality of the soul is based on its immateriality, and accordingly defines the soul as an immaterial or subsistent form (that is, a form not inhering in matter as though dependent on it), he has to pursue a similar path in his philosophy of grace.—Cf. *Summa theol.*, Ia, q. 75, a. 2; *De veritate*, q. 2, a. 2.

which in all created spirits is the source of an opposition like that between matter and form, and keeps them from eliciting the supreme intellectual act, the direct intuition of the pure, simple essence of God. God alone has in His infinitely pure, simple essence (which stands at the summit of all spirituality and in comparison with which created spirits may be said to be material rather than simple and spiritual) the resources and power to know Himself immediately and to love Himself with a perfection proportionate to this knowledge.

God's eminent spirituality, that is, complete freedom from all contradiction and all ties with matter, as well as from the potentiality resembling matter, is His proper nature, as we are now considering it in opposition to created natures. This spirituality is the reason why God has a power and activity such as belong to no created being.

Therefore, when we say that, besides participating in the divine power and activity of knowledge and love to a degree surpassing the knowledge and love proper to created natures, we also share in the divine nature itself, regarded as the substratum of God's power and activity, we mean that God has given to our souls something that is to be the substratum on which our titles to that higher activity are based (a quality of the essence that involves such powers and activity). We mean further that God has enriched us with a spirituality, that is, a purity and freedom from material elements and other restrictive elements resembling matter, that renders our nature spiritual in a higher sense than it is by itself; it becomes spiritual in the way God Himself is spiritual. This does not imply that the potentiality and finiteness necessarily accompanying the created spirit are annihilated; they are only, so to speak, covered over and repressed. When the soul is drawn into the immediate presence of God and is thoroughly pervaded with His power, it becomes like fire, and in this state of glory takes on the appearance of a new, higher spirit, a higher nature. When pure fire penetrates a pure metal with its heat, the metal loses its massiveness and hardness, and at the same time gives forth light and warmth, without forfeiting its own essence. In some such way the substantial fire of the divinity penetrates the soul with a heat it irradiates, owing to which the soul loses, not its own nature, but its natural lowliness and ponderousness and is drawn up to God, to receive light and warmth resembling the divine heat. We shall have more to say about this new spirituality.

If we have understood that we have been admitted to fellowship with the divine nature by the grace of divine sonship, and therefore participate in its spirituality, we have found the reason why we are to share in the knowledge and love characteristic of the divine nature. Consequently we are able to assign the order of these two activities and to indicate the relation existing between them. This is a point of great importance. If we unduly stress love and the moral element, we take a stand that is incompatible with the substratum that has just been established and have to relinquish it. And that is the reason why those theologians who identify grace with the supernatural habit of charity usually refuse to regard grace as a nature in the narrower sense. In general all who consider the supernatural life as nothing more than a higher moral life must banish from it all that is physical along with all that is intellectual. But then they must abandon any specific distinction between the supernatural and the natural that has a physical basis; at least they cannot maintain and justify the distinction scientifically. The battle waged by many theologians against the Jansenists was not conducted with all the scientific advantage they could have enjoyed, because they failed to dislodge the enemy from the ethical domain on which he chose to fight and to draw him over to the intellectual and physical sphere. How can anyone solidly uphold a supernatural, ethical order if he does not admit that our supernatural love is founded on a new, supernatural kinship with God and our fellow man, and does not recognize new relationships existing between us, God, and our neighbor?

It is more reasonable to place emphasis on the intellectual element. The intellect is a primary faculty that does not, like the will, suppose another faculty guiding it. In fact that element comes into prominence if, as I have said, we admit that a basic form which is like a second nature underlies the supernatural faculties. We do not define a spiritual nature according to its characteristic activity by saying that it can love and will; we have said enough if we designate it as an intellectual nature. The reason is that the activity of love and desire is included, according to a general law, in knowledge. For example, we do not say that man is a being capable of loving; we say that he is a living, rational being (*animal rationale*). The faculty of knowledge is the spirit's fundamental faculty; it is based immediately on the essence and nature, which it characterizes clearly and properly. This is so true that, as we saw above, we may even be tempted to shun the labor of penetrating more deeply into the nature of the spirit. In that case, spirituality is identified with the faculty of pure, intellectual knowledge, although, strictly speaking, this faculty is only a manifestation of spirituality, that is, of immateriality. That is why some theologians have tried to place God's essence in infinite intellectuality. Such a view is not wrong, if thereby we wish to indicate, not the deepest property we can find in God, but that which most clearly distinguishes His nature from others. For in point of fact nature is revealed in the activity of thinking, by which it grasps itself, in a sense fashions and develops itself, perfectly expresses its species and form, conceives itself anew, and gives testimony of itself in the image it forms of itself.

We may transfer this to our present subject and say that supernature, which is essentially a participation in the immateriality of the divine nature, is also, considered from the viewpoint of a faculty, a participation in the divine intellectuality proceeding from the divine nature. When the created spirit is transfigured, it is raised by this participation to the spirituality and intellectuality of the divine nature.

This significance of the intellectual factor is most clearly perceived if we consider the state of supernature in its ultimate culmination, that of beatitude in heaven, where all the factors enter a condition of repose in equilibrium and thus come together in their natural, final relationship. Supernature consists in the intrinsic quality by which we are born children of God according to the image of God. We said above that we appear as perfect children of God when we have the beatific vision by which we see God as He is; eternal life consists chiefly in this vision, which transforms us most perfectly into the likeness of God. This is so emphatically taught in Sacred Scripture (especially in I John 3:1 f.), that at first sight the impression could be given that we are children of God by the act of vision alone. But that is not so; the difficulty vanishes if we regard the act of knowledge of God as the most characteristic manifestation of supernature, which is an intellectual nature. Strictly and formally, we are made children of God by receiving in our nature the likeness of His intellectual nature and thus becoming like to Him. Through this similarity with His intellectual nature we are made capable of engendering in ourselves, by way of knowledge, the same image it engenders in itself, the image of the divine essence.

Our first similarity is with the divine nature as such; this is brought about by the light of glory, which transfigures our nature. Hence, like the Son of God, we are begotten light of Light. Secondly, we receive a likeness with the divine intellect, in the sense in which we may speak of a cognitive faculty in God, by the same light of glory, which gives us the power to behold God. Thirdly, a resemblance of the divine knowledge is imparted to us by the act of knowledge through which we reflect in ourselves the divine essence. And how about our love of God, the virtue of charity? Is it something subordinate in the character and dignity of the children of God, hardly worthy of consideration? Even if the true value of charity is acknowledged, it must retire to the background for the present. It does not blossom forth until after its seed has been planted and its foundation laid. Many theologians believe they can say nothing finer than that we become children of God by filial love, and that consequently everything supernatural, being related to the grace of sonship, has only a moral hue and character (for what is physical belongs to the intellectual realm).

I perceive quite well that our filial relation to the Father is made manifest and must be made manifest by filial love, and that it must be safeguarded. But who can comprehend that if we are not already children of God, we are made such by filial love? Indeed, how can we picture a truly childlike love that does not rest on some pre-existing filial relationship, that does not presuppose a natural or juridical kinship with the Father? [4] For my part I am unable to understand it, although I can well conceive, and can produce a long series of examples in support, that such theologians, if they were orthodox, must have had a more or less vague idea of the supernatural in general; and that is all they could have, as they have lost all basis for distinguishing between supernatural and natural love. I also see why precisely the Jansenists and all those theologians who through bad faith, or by yielding to the seductive spirit of the times were more or less contaminated with Jansenist errors, proclaimed so loudly that man is made a child of God by love. Their fundamental stand was nothing else than that man was, or ought to have been a child of God by nature, but that by disloyalty he turned his back on his Father and became God's enemy, so that to recover the formal relation of sonship, all he had to do was to return to filial love.

To tell the truth, filial charity is the sign of a filial relationship; and this relation is maintained by love, so far as it involves a friendly, reciprocal interchange. Since filial love must proceed from that relationship, which is morally violated if love is not present, the moral relationship of love is taken for sonship itself. Thus a man can say that such and such an individual is no longer his son if the relation of love has ceased, although the sonship itself is not dissolved. But more than this is contained in our sonship with regard to God. Filial love is not connected with the grace of sonship by mere moral necessity, but is bound up with it by physical necessity; where there is divine sonship, there love is also

---

[4] At least we must be called to such a relationship, as happens when a sinner, hoping to receive the grace of sonship that is destined for him, begins to love God with filial love.

found; and where love is found, there divine sonship exists. For he who is born of God does not sin (as long as he remains God's son) because (and as long as) God's seed remains in him; and he cannot sin, because he is born of God.[5] A person cannot be so intimately related to God as His child without cleaving to Him, and he cannot fulfill the conditions laid down for his adoption to the state of son without at once sharing in this grace. Accordingly filial love of God is an infallible sign that one stands in the relation of son to God, even though the existence of this sign is not infallibly known. But for the very reason that it is a sign of this relationship, it is not this relationship itself; love is based on this relationship and presupposes it, and with such necessity that without it we cannot conceive why love should be called filial.

To attribute to charity its rightful place and importance, we must first consider its foundation, that which really makes us kin to God as His children. We saw that this kinship is brought about by our participation in the divine nature, the supremely pure and spiritual nature. Since the characteristic excellence of this participation is primarily disclosed in the knowledge of God it involves, and moreover, since knowledge is a preliminary condition of love, knowledge must take its place as the second main factor. After that comes love, regarded as union with God arising from our kinship with Him and knowledge of Him, a union corresponding to these two foundations and based on them.

This exposition presents no difficulties if, as I said above, we think of these factors in the equilibrium of the state of consummation and repose. But great difficulties appear

[5] Cf. I John 3:9: "Whosoever is born of God, committeth not sin . . . and he cannot sin, because he is born of God."

when we consider them in *statu viae,* in the state of progress and striving after their full development. In this state knowledge seems to lose its close relationship with supernature (which is here seen to be sanctifying grace), since faith can be completely separated from sanctifying grace. On the other hand, love (habitual charity) enters into closest union with supernature, with which it has so intimate a reciprocal action that the two seem to be identical. And this is the solution many theologians come to; they regard the state of charity as identical with the state of God's grace, by which we are children of God, are like to Him, and have a title to the divine inheritance.

Here we must note at once that the period of growth cannot provide a norm for discerning the intrinsic value and absolute significance of the various factors. The separability of faith from grace and charity is not owing to the fact that faith is supernatural knowledge, but to the fact that the supernatural knowledge it involves is imperfect and obscure. This imperfection is the reason why it can exist without love; the perfect and clear knowledge possessed in the beatific vision necessarily includes love. And because faith can exist without charity, it can also be separated from the grace of sonship. This grace, being a sort of new nature, is necessarily accompanied by its full retinue of faculties and can exist only if they are all present together.

But charity cannot be infused without the grace of sonship. In the first place, it always presupposes knowledge; therefore, if it is granted in addition to knowledge, nothing is lacking for the reception of supernature. Furthermore, the distinction between the charity of this life and the charity of heaven is not so great as that between faith and vision. Lastly, in the state of striving and progress toward the end, knowledge is of less consequence than effort and desire for the end. As supernature is at present in a state of growth and development, in which it must be constantly perfected by contact with its source, the divine nature, that element must be especially prominent by which we cleave to God and unite ourselves with Him. This element is charity, filial love for the Father of light, who transforms and spiritualizes us in proportion to our efforts to cleave to Him. Accordingly the chief activity of supernature during the period of progress is exercised in charity, which therefore is also the surest sign of the presence of supernature in us.

Yet this does not mean that charity is the fundamental activity. The fundamental activity remains always faith, supernatural knowledge, which is the substructure of charity, since faith manifests our kinship with the Father of light on which charity is based. Faith is also the deepest revelation of the divine sonship in us, for it fashions and expresses in us the image of the Father of light which we, His children, bear because of our new nature. That is why the Apostle, speaking of the knowledge of faith, said that by this knowledge we "are transformed into the same image [that of the Lord] from glory to glory" (II Cor. 3:18).

Our kinship with the Father of light begins by faith, the divine light in us. For, since the divine nature is purest light, we are made akin to it when we ourselves become light. Therefore faith, even without charity, is always an inception of divine sonship; it imprints on us an image of our Lord. But it is an image that is somewhat alien to us and lifeless, an image that without charity undergoes no development or transformation; it is not really or necessarily connected with supernature and therefore does not manifest or attest our supernatural life. Although supernatural knowledge and supernature are meant to go together and one implies the other, they are not perfectly united until we, sharing in the divine spirituality, actually attain to the culminating clarity of divine knowledge in the beatific vision of God, which necessarily includes charity. Supernature, as a divinely transfigured spiritual state, necessarily tends toward this clear vision of God, and therefore even during the present life cannot exist without a desire to achieve it. Accordingly, even though faith takes the place of vision during our earthly life, supernature cannot crown our faith unless faith is alive with charity. Faith must do more than imprint a dead image; it must be vibrant with charity and strive for glorification in the beatific vision.

We learn from this last consideration that the union of the grace of divine sonship with charity in this life does not compromise the physical essence of grace but confirms and clarifies it. The grace of sonship is connected with charity during this life because it cannot exist without its natural striving and longing for its perfect physical activity and growth, the full vision of God, including the perfect, filial love of God that necessarily springs from it. Thus even during the present period of probation the physical and intellectual essence of supernature remains intact.

Supernature is called holiness in a special sense and is ascribed by appropriation to the Holy Spirit as His personal gift. But these assertions will be discussed in another chapter.

Supernature is primarily a transformation of our nature and a higher way of existing granted to it. It assimilates us to the divine nature as such, especially as the supremely spiritual and immaterial nature. As a result, we also share in the intellectual power belonging to the divine nature. And because we, born of God as His children, now know Him obscurely by the name of Father through faith, and shall one day see Him face to face at our full glorification, we should even now embrace Him in tenderest filial love with a freedom that will become a holy, blessed necessity when at length we see Him as He is.

CHAPTER IX

QUALITIES AND EFFECTS OF SUPERNATURE

OUR discussions have brought us to this point: we are destined to share in the divine nature. Our participation in the divine nature is not limited to an imitation of God's love and moral uprightness; we are to be like Him in intellectual knowledge and pure spirituality. Penetration into this idea will give us a profound understanding of many Scriptural and Patristic expressions that otherwise would have a devitalized and feeble sense and could give the impression of being nothing but empty bombast.

HIGHER LIFE OF THE SOUL

We are now in a position to understand clearly the sense in which we are God's children. We are truly begotten by Him inasmuch as He communicates His nature to us and makes us similar to it.

As He is light and the Father of light, we also are light: light of light. God has summoned us, not to a natural, material, or even spiritual light, but to His own wonderful light, that we may be light in Him and in His way, to walk as children of this heavenly, divine light. You are "now light in the Lord; walk then as children of the light" (Eph. 5:8; cf. 5:1). God "hath called you out of darkness into His marvelous light" (I Pet. 2:9).

As God is holy, they who are born of Him are holy. This thought recurs often in St. John's first epistle. As God is purest spirit, they who are begotten of Him are to be spiritual (John 3:6), not by spiritual or carnal endeavor on their part, but because they have received a higher, spiritual existence. Indeed, as He is God, we too shall be called gods and divine: "You are gods and all of you the sons of the Most High" (Ps. 81:6; cf. John 10:34). The meaning of these words has been explained in a previous chapter.

DIGNITY AND INHERITANCE OF THE CHILDREN OF GOD

As God's children, we receive a most exalted dignity that is based, not on a mere appellation but on our inner state, which is so noble that it has evoked expressions of rapturous wonderment from the Apostles and Fathers. We also receive the greatest of all rights, a title to a divine inheritance, to the personal goods of God, to goods such as belong to God alone. And this claim does not rest on a simple promise; it is founded on the intrinsic dignity of our participation in the divine nature which we have received. Its natural outgrowth is divine knowledge and love, which yet remain pure gifts of God.

KINSHIP AND FRIENDSHIP WITH GOD

We enter into an intimate relationship with God. By nature we were God's menials and had to serve in His house; now we are His children who stand in His presence and rejoice in His love. By nature we were alien to the Godhead and stood afar off from God; by our rebirth we become closely akin to Him and draw near to Him as citizens of His heavenly kingdom, indeed as members of His household (Eph. 2:19), even as His children and trusted friends, to whom the Son makes known all He has heard of the Father (John 15:15). Formerly we were too unlike God to be able to enter into a true, confident friendship with Him, for friendship can exist only among those who in some way are alike. But now we have come close to God; elevated by His grace, we have been made like to Him as far as is possible for our nature, and so are capable of His intimate friendship.

By nature we are creatures, subject to God as slaves to a master whom we could love and honor only as slaves. But by the exaltation of our nature we rise in full confidence to the condition of freedom that befits God's children; nothing keeps us from appearing before our Father. We have become His children and we do His will, not merely because we are subject to Him who is our Lord or because we love Him only as Lord, but because, as His children, we are one with Him, have common interests with Him, and take pleasure in all that pleases Him. We have been liberated from slavish subjection to God's overlordship; more than that, as children we share in His lordship over all things; we possess and enjoy the same goods and joys as He, King of all creation, possesses and enjoys.

RELATIONS WITH THE DIVINE PERSONS

By our participation in the divine nature, we enter into closest fellowship with the Persons who possess the divine nature essentially, that is, with the Blessed Trinity. We become children of God the Father; yet not as though He alone communicates supernature to us, for the entire Blessed Trinity does this, as it is an external work. The Father in the Godhead originally possesses the nature, and communicates it to the Son; that is why the communication of the divine nature to us is ascribed to the Father by appropriation. We further become brothers of the Son by grace, for the special reason that, as we have said, supernature properly develops and presents itself in us as intellectual, because of our knowledge of God; this is an imitation of the way the Son possesses the divinity as its perfect, infinite Word and the eternal wisdom of the Father. Finally, we become temples of the Holy Spirit. As He is the bond of love between the Son and the Father, He is the Person who infuses into us a love of the Father like that of the only-begotten Son, fills us with a similar filial trust, and draws us to the Father in tenderest affection and unity. Ever fostering and supporting this love in us, He dwells in us continually as in His holy temple.

St. Bonaventure, treading in the footsteps of his great teacher, Alexander of Hales, expresses this thought as follows. By grace the soul is made a child of the eternal Father, a bride of the Son, and a temple of the Holy Spirit. The soul becomes a bride of the Son by being made like to Him and by receiving His image, not by being begotten of Him, but because He takes the soul, which is already ennobled as the Father's daughter, closely to Himself in holy love, to share His beauty and wealth with her in pure embrace.[1] This point of view suggests to us an idea of the divine excellence of the soul's mystic union and betrothal with God, specifically with the eternal Word, as described in glowing terms by Sacred Scripture, the Fathers, and the mystics. Nature does not invest the soul with the nobility needed to be a worthy bride of the Word and to enter into this exalted, inconceivable, mystic union with Him; otherwise the union would straightway cease to be truly mystic

[1] Cf. St. Lawrence Justinian, *De casto connubio Verbi et animae* (Basel: 1560), 200–320. The passage from St. Bonaventure occurs in *In II Sent.*, d. 29, a. 1, q. 1 (Quaracchi, II, 696).

and to surpass nature. Natural love (that is, love proceeding from nature and based on nature's dignity) cannot make the soul capable, still less sufficiently worthy, of claiming so intimate a union with God's Son. The soul must first be ennobled and must be a daughter of the same royal Father, whose Son is the eternal Word; before she can advance to meet the Son of God, her Bridegroom, she must be adorned with heavenly beauty and be equipped with a higher, nobler, and freer love. The fruit of this chaste union must be something interior, and must be of such a nature that the soul, illuminated by the light of her Bridegroom, engenders in herself His likeness. With her beauty thus transfigured, the soul not only does not lose her virginal fairness and purity, but for the first time blossoms forth into true beauty and purity.

SUPERNATURAL IMAGE OF GOD AND THE TRINITY

One of the conclusions of this discussion is that supernature makes the soul a perfect image of God and of the Trinity; this is not a product of nature. By nature the soul is an image of the divine essence. It is spiritual, as God is a spirit; therefore it has reason, knowledge, will, and freedom, as God, who is a spirit, has knowledge, will, and freedom. But the spirituality belonging to the soul by nature is its own; although it has something in common with God's spirituality and can even, to some extent, be called a participation of this ideal, all the opposition between created essences and the uncreated essence remains. The soul's natural knowledge and love are likewise in contrast with God's knowledge and love, and retain their proper limitations. The special purity and beauty of the divine splendor are not reflected in the soul.

We can imagine a picture of a man that is painted with

unsuitable, lifeless colors, and contrast it with a picture of the same man reflected in a clear, polished mirror. The mirror gives back the image in the natural brightness and character belonging to the original, in the same colors and light. But the picture painted with colors is considerably different. The paints may be skilfully blended and artistically applied; but the resulting picture will never be able quite to reproduce the life and the natural coloring of the original.

Let us transfer this comparison to our subject. As long as the soul remains in its natural spirituality, it is an image of God; yet an image that can reflect the divine beauty only in created beauty and that is unequal to the divine splendor characteristic of God. But let supernature spiritualize the soul in God's way; then it is a perfect, living image of God, and a person beholding it might almost think he were looking at God. As this image is fashioned by God's own light, the soul will be able by this light to contemplate the original model in its own essence and thus to reflect it faithfully.

The Fathers, particularly the Greeks, often distinguish between these two kinds of godlikeness. Some of them favor the idea that the distinction is indicated in the words of Genesis which inform us that God created man to His image and likeness.[2] Even if we prefer to regard these two terms as synonymous, the doctrine itself suffers no detriment. The Fathers did not derive this truth from the double expression; they merely appealed to it because it seemed very suitable for thoroughly clarifying the deep, pregnant sense suggested by the terms. In company with St. Cyril, the Fathers taught that man, even as man, is similar to God

[2] See the detailed discussion in Scheeben, *Handbuch der katholischen Dogmatik,* II, 116–41.

by nature. Yet there is another resemblance to God by
reason of which man no longer remains a mere man in his
own nature, but is transfigured into an image of the divine
nature and is, as it were, divinized, so that he no longer reflects an image of himself, but lets the image of God shine
through him.

Some of the Fathers place the image of God in the substance of the soul and the likeness of God in the virtues of
the soul. But we should not understand this as though such
virtues were only the development of nature and its faculties, without being at the same time a higher endowment
including a sort of higher nature. The terms themselves
could, perhaps, provide a basis for such a distinction; but
it would not be the distinction the Fathers sought. They
found the image in the nature we receive from the Creator,
and discerned the likeness in the seal of the Holy Spirit, in
the reproduction of perfection and holiness, in that spirituality which the Holy Spirit imparts to us as His gift. We
shall soon have occasion to go into this matter more fully.

Some sort of relationship can be discovered between the
image of God's essence and the image of the Trinity; the
latter, however, is found only in a spirit that has been elevated above its natural condition. According to the explanation of the Blessed Trinity that is derived from the certain
and unquestionable teaching of Sacred Scripture, the Fathers, and almost all approved theologians, the Second
Person in God proceeds from the First Person as the Word,
the expression, the witness, and the image of the infinite
knowledge in which the First Person contemplates Himself. The Third Person proceeds from the other two persons
as the flower and fruit of their infinite, reciprocal love in
which they meet and embrace each other. Consequently
the image of the Trinity in created spirits will have to con-

sist in the fact that that divine process is mirrored and re-produced in the process of knowledge and love occurring in the created spirit.

Some remote analogy with this divine process is found in that activity of the soul in which knowledge and love work together. A far closer analogy is perceived in the reflexive activity in which the soul, from its inner depths, engenders its own image in the knowledge it has of itself, and in the love of itself to which it thereupon awakens. But the existence of a true image of the Trinity in the creature requires that the entire process in the creature, like the Trinitarian process in God, should have the divine essence as its object and center. Knowledge of God, as an image of Him, must be engendered in the creature out of the light in which God is brought near to the creature, and through this image the soul must be united with God in holy love. If the soul produces the image of God in itself out of the natural light with which God shines in it and embraces Him with love through this image, a certain resemblance of the Trinitarian process is discerned. But this resemblance is not fully brought out until the essence of God becomes the immediate object of knowledge and love; only such faculties as are fashioned on the divine model can carry out the process. For in the Trinitarian process itself the divine essence is the immediate center around which the process revolves; it is the immediate object of the activities of knowledge and love that are manifested in the process, and these activities are moments in the process only so far as they are specifically divine and proceed from a specifi-cally divine power. Consequently that process cannot be imitated unless a divine life unfolds in the created spirit.

If the soul, raised to divine spirituality, shares in God's

spirituality, God the Father illuminates it with His own divine light, and so the soul can know the Father's essence immediately in itself. Thereby the soul conceives a word that expresses the divine essence, a word that in its own way perfectly resembles the substantial Word in the Trinity, attaches itself wholeheartedly to that Word, and echoes and reflects it in itself. That is why the Fathers and theologians say that the blessed in heaven see the divinity *in Verbo*, in the divine Word. As divine, filial love for the Father, and also the sweet fruit of this love, the Spirit of love, the Holy Spirit, proceed from the eternal, infinite Word, to unite the Son with the Father in indivisible unity, so a filial love proceeds from the word which the created spirit stammers in imitation, a love that is the faithful image and counterpart of the love existing between Son and Father, with the Holy Spirit as its terminus. This is a love that plunges directly into the essence of the Father and savors His beauty and sweetness; ardently pulsating, it rises up to the heart of the Father at the side of the only-begotten Son, thus merging, so to speak, into one fire with the fire of divine love whose flame is the Holy Spirit.

The process of knowledge and love of God takes place in this supernatural, spiritual, and divinized nature. Since the nature itself comes directly from God, its knowledge and love can be directly referred to God. Thus there arises in the created spirit a most perfect and faithful image of that exalted, wonderful process by which the one divine nature is possessed by the Trinity of divine persons. But, what is even more astounding, the soul also knows the ideal which it imitates and represents. It knows this ideal as it is in itself, not from the image of it that is received. The same light that reveals God's essence to the soul enables it to perceive how this simple, infinite essence enters into that marvelous, harmonious process. Knowledge of the ideal is the only way the soul can come to an understanding of the image it bears in itself.

Accordingly, if a process very similar to the Trinitarian process is brought about by the light of supernature, and if this process is known, an image of the Trinity that leaves nothing to be desired is reproduced in us. Like a polished mirror of pure crystal, supernature engenders an image that faithfully reflects the Blessed Trinity. In all other images, even in that of the natural process which occurs in the created spirit, nothing more than an unconscious, imperfect, and remote analogy is discernible.

In this last sense alone the created spirit is by nature an image of the Trinity. Yet we must not forget that the soul is by nature an image of the Trinity to the extent that in its three basic aspects it naturally has some analogy with the Trinitarian process in God; in its essence, intellect, and will, the soul has a natural obediential potency by which it can receive the highest perfection it is capable of, and thus can become a true image of the Trinity, in the way we have described. This was the sense Augustine had in mind when he said that the soul is by nature an image of the Trinity. He closes his masterly investigation of the manner in which the soul is the image of the Trinity with the assertion that a perfect image is found only in the state of the supernatural, beatific vision and love of God, and holds that all other images are imperfect and deficient.[3]

SUPERNATURAL SPIRITUALITY

Closely connected with this relationship to the divine persons into which we enter through supernature, is the teaching developed by the Greek Fathers on the various ways

[3] *De Trinitate*, XIV, c. 19, no. 25 [*PL*, XLII, 1055].

the divine persons cooperate, by appropriation, to raise our nature to a participation in the divine nature and take up their residence in the created spirit. In this discussion we must also consider the teaching on the missions of the divine persons to our souls, and must advert to the question raised by Petavius on the substantial indwelling that is ascribed to the Holy Spirit personally rather than by mere appropriation. For the Holy Spirit is pre-eminently the divine Person who is mentioned in Sacred Scripture and the Fathers as the author and cause of grace. He is the Person who especially dwells in us and whose name is often identified with the higher vital principle produced in us by Him.

Vast confusion reigns about this point. I hope to contribute toward dispelling it. I shall try, as thoroughly and comprehensively as I can, to give a nominal and real analysis of the main concepts that come into consideration. Special attention must be paid to the two concepts that make up the name of the Holy Spirit: "Spirit" and "Holiness." As these two terms are no less important for further clarifying the idea of the supernatural, as has frequently been indicated, we shall here take the opportunity of discussing them at some length and also of explaining, with all the detail needed, the two main properties of supernature, true spirituality and divine holiness.

According to its first meaning, the German word *Geist* [ghost, spirit] signifies an aeriform substance, or gas. The Latin *spiritus* and the Greek *pneuma* manifestly have this meaning, but strongly stress the idea that this gas or air is in motion and at the same time moves other bodies.[4] This

[4] M. Grabmann, in his edition of Scheeben, *Natur und Gnade* (Freiburg im Breisgau: 1941), 109 note, points out that this etymology is incorrect, and quotes in support H. Paul, *Deutsches Wörterbuch* (3rd ed., Halle: 1921), p. 194.—Tr.

connotation is less prominent in the etymology of the German *Geist;* yet it is there. With regard to this connotation, *spiritus* and *pneuma* further imply the breathing of air that occurs in living beings and is a sign of life, sometimes also an organic phase of life, the so-called *Lebensgeister,* or animal spirits. The Latin and Greek words likewise include that exaggerated, heavy respiration observed in men in consequence of strong emotion (for example, *spiritus irae,* the spirit of wrath). In this way the notion of spirit has been generalized, and the word has been transferred to the movements of feeling, to the affections, and especially to the first of all affections and emotions, that is, love. The term is even used to signify vital movement in purely immaterial beings (as in the angels and God), movement that is not manifested in the stirring of any bodily *spiritus* and remains interior.

If this aspect of movement in the meaning of "spirit" is emphasized, the word cannot, of course, refer primarily to the substance or nature of a thing. If that is the meaning we have in mind, we shall not say that the thing is a spirit or is spiritual, but rather that a spirit is in the thing, that the thing has a spirit, that is, an inclination, a tendency, a relation to an end. Thus we speak of a spirit (that is, of a relation to an end, of a signification, etc.) even of lifeless things or of abstract thoughts. In line with this analogy we say that two men are of one spirit when they move jointly toward a goal and agree in all their efforts and wishes. Sometimes we even say that they are one spirit, when they come together in mutual love, or when one moves and lives in the other by knowledge and love.[5]

We apply the word "spirit" not only to movement itself, but also to the active principle of movement, so far as it is

[5] Cf. St. Thomas, *Summa theol.,* Ia IIae, q.28.

in a state of tendency. Thus we speak of an animating spirit in man. However, we likewise use the word to designate the thing set in motion by spiration, or the thing produced by motion; in some such way as this, "ghost" or "spirit" designates the third divine Person who proceeds as the breath of love in which the Father and the Son move in each other. In a special sense, this Person alone is Spirit in God, because He is spirated, or proceeds by way of spiration. The other two persons, who act together as a single spirating principle, cannot be called "spirit" in accord with this analogy, because they are not spirated. Furthermore, they are not related to the Holy Ghost in the way that the human spirit, as the moving principle in man, is related to the man himself and to the body. For the Holy Spirit is, so to speak, the motion of love in God Himself, or more accurately, the product and breath of love, the terminus of the movement, rather than something set in motion. That is why everything effected and moved by God's love is ascribed to the Holy Spirit.[6] To Him we appropriate, as His part in creation, the movement of things to their end and the impulse toward life found in living beings, and in particular anything that is a special effect of God's love (such as forgiveness of sins, and the like); likewise all those gifts that have some resemblance to His personal character, and most of all the love that cannot spring up in any creature out of its nature, but must be immediately infused by God, the source of supreme, eternal love.

Although an aeriform substance is called *spiritus* because it moves itself and other things, or is moved, the term is also applied simply to the substance itself, by reason of

[6] See the beautiful development of these ideas in St. Thomas, *Contra Gentiles*, IV, 20–22, quoted in Scheeben, *The Mysteries of Christianity*, pp. 190–97.—Tr.

its essence. By analogy we can extend the figure verified in such a substance to other objects, according to a different point of view that is seemingly quite independent of the previous one. For example, in the substance we call spirit, we can consider the subtlety, the rarity which excludes from it all that is gross and ponderous and makes it receptive to light; such a thing is likely to escape our sense perception. In accord with this analogy, we shall use the term "spirit" metaphorically of those substances that lack all material crassness and massiveness and are consequently withdrawn from our senses, and possess a receptivity for the light of intellectual knowledge and a freedom of activity such as can be found only when all cumbersome bonds have been loosed.

This analogy is really present. But we must be particularly careful to note that it may not be separated from the previous analogy. For the subtlety of gases is the reason why they are easily set in motion, why they are elastic and therefore can develop a great power of movement. Thus the vigor and range of true movement and movability in a being are proportionate to the metaphysical subtlety, that is, the simplicity of the being, and especially to its freedom from all material and potential factors, which in the ontological order account for the crassness and heaviness of beings and curtail the freedom of their higher activity and movement.

For reasons such as this, immaterial substances are called spirits. They are free from encumbering matter and are simple and subtle, as well as supersensible; they are capable of receiving the higher, pure light of intellectual knowledge, can exercise an uninhibited activity which is not bound up with matter, and are vigorous in movement and the power of movement. As we have remarked, this sort of spirituality in a being can be more or less perfect, according as the being's simplicity and excellence are more or less purified of all burdensome elements. The purest and most perfect spirituality is found in God alone; in Him alone all that is potential and quasi-material is absent. He alone is supremely simple and invisible, supremely intellectual and active in purest movement. In God, therefore, the spirated Spirit, as most perfect and purest movement, supposes a spirating Spirit as most perfect and purest subtlety, that is, supreme simplicity of existence; and although the Holy Spirit is Spirit as breath that is breathed, He could not be Spirit in this sense unless the spirating Principle were spiritual in the other sense.

We are now in a position to draw the conclusion that the phrase, "to become one spirit with God," has a quite different meaning in the second analogy than it has in the first. According to the second analogy the expression means to receive God's spirituality into oneself, to become divinely spiritual in God's way, without becoming one with God in physical spirituality. Thus iron, when plunged into fire, becomes fiery and is on fire with the fire into which it is placed, although the two substances do not merge their identity. According to the first analogy, two become one spirit when they meet and unite in the movement of love or strive for one and the same end. The two analogies have to be kept distinct and even separate, because normally a mutual relationship exists between them.

Because of this fact, we might be inclined to confuse the two and so allow our physical union with God to degenerate into a moral union. If this were to happen, even the moral union would lose its high, priceless value. For oneness of spirit, in the sense of mutual union in love, is intrinsically and completely possible only if the persons to be united are closely related by their spiritual nature and condition. We must recall what we said earlier about the child's filial relationship with its father. As relationship of filial love has to be based on descent from a father or on adoption, so perfect oneness of spirit with God in love has to be based on a previous oneness brought about by kinship and resemblance.

But this distinction among the various shades of meaning found in the word "spirit," expressing a being's nature or movement and striving, has to be considered in yet another way. In itself, "spirit" can mean every motion occurring in the animal or spiritual part of man, and even those movements that tend toward sensible and material objects and draw the spirit out of its own sphere into the sphere of sense. Thus we speak of a spirit of unchastity, of intemperance, of lewdness, and the like; but we specify the meaning more accurately by including the objective of the movement. Therefore not every "spirit" is spiritual, since it does not always proceed from the spirit or lead to the spirit; there is a spirit of the flesh. Only that motion is properly spiritual which proceeds from the spirit, conforms to the nature of the spirit, and finally leads back to the spirit. As nature provides man with a spirit, his spiritual nature provides him with a spiritual desire that is quite opposed to carnal desire. The spirit, as the nobler substance in man, naturally strives against the flesh (Cf. Rom. chap. 7) and endeavors to dominate the flesh, although it is so weak before the challenge of the body's exuberance that it needs the support of a higher spirit if it is to gain a sure victory. For the human spirit as such is only a created image of the pure, supreme Spirit; if it lives in a way conformable with its nature, it does so by the law and the power it has received from the creating Spirit, who incessantly sustains its nature, makes good its deficiencies, and comes to the aid of its weakness.

In the present order of things, our spirit is meant to live and move not only according to its own spiritual nature, but according to the higher spirituality of the divine nature that is imparted to it or is destined to be imparted to it. Therefore its spiritual movement does not stem from its nature, and is not the movement received from God by nature in the act of creation; it is a spiritual movement in a higher sense, corresponding to the supernature and the participation of the divine nature in man; it is a communication of the movement of the divine life that flourishes in the Holy Spirit. That is the reason why "to be spiritual in love and desire" or "to lead a spiritual life" in the Christian sense implies something quite different from a simple opposition between our spiritual inclinations and those of sensuality. To be spiritual in our striving and living, in the Christian sense, is equivalent to being set in motion by the Holy Spirit, that is, to be filled with a love that is similar to the love from which the Holy Spirit proceeds and which He Himself is. It means to live and move in a divine love; a love springing from our nature that has been spiritualized in a divine way; a love that does not stop with drawing us to spiritual things in general, but reaches out to the infinitely pure Spirit, to God Himself, and transforms us divinely. This is the spirituality which the Apostle, in the Epistle to the Romans, contrasts with the concupiscence of the flesh. He describes it as the spirituality that is right for us as God's children, as that by which the Spirit of Christ, the Son of God, becomes in a way our own Spirit, whose spiritual movements and desires likewise become our spiritual movements and desires. In this way we become one spirit with the Holy Spirit, and the Spirit of God and of Christ also becomes our Spirit.

This spirituality, which elevates the nature of our spirit, provides the assistance and strength needed for winning and maintaining control over the spirit of carnal concupiscence. I do not mean to suggest that the spirit's victory over the flesh could be gained in no other way than by its elevation to a higher spirituality; but in the present order of things the spirit is actually called to a supernatural spirituality rather than to a mere natural spirituality, and therefore should expect from God nothing less than this help and assistance.

The point of view we have taken enables us to understand why Sacred Scripture and the Fathers of the early centuries, who speak even more clearly and emphatically, distinguish between the sensual (or natural) and the spiritual man, the *homo animalis* and the *homo spiritualis*.

From the natural standpoint, the animal man is the man who of course has also a spiritual nature, but instead of living conformably with it, abandons himself along with his spirit to his animal nature. The spiritual man, on the contrary, is the man who lives in accord with his spiritual nature (and also in accord with the will of God, the ideal and lawgiver of all spiritual natures), and desires only what is suitable for it, at the same time completely subjugating his animal nature, so that the spirit, and not the animal nature, is the center of his whole life. The *homo animalis* is the animal and sinful man as opposed to the wise and virtuous man. The term invariably connotes something evil that in itself unconditionally excludes all spiritual good.

From the same point of view we can, after the Apostle's

example, divide the one man, as it were, into two men; for every man has two parts or, in a sense, two natures, that struggle for priority, each of them trying to be the whole and only rightful nature. In that case the animal man is not necessarily sinful, but has an inclination toward sin; and the spiritual man is not the embodiment of virtue and justice, but only has an aptitude and longing for virtue and justice.

In both cases, however, the spiritual man is not what Sacred Scripture and the Fathers describe under this name. For them the spiritual man is he who is filled with the spirit of God, is inflamed and propelled by God, is made alive and elevated by God. He is the man who, in response to this divine movement, lives no longer according to his own spiritual nature, but in a way that is conformable with the divinely spiritual nature imparted to him.

This teaching is brought out most clearly in the beautiful passage (I Cor. 2:12–16) in which the opposition between the spiritual and the sensual man is emphasized and sharply defined. The spiritual man is the man who has received the Spirit of God (the breath of life of the Father and the Son) in so full a measure that he has a spiritual life analogous to that of God. The Holy Spirit animates and moves the spiritual man otherwise than He vitalizes and moves merely natural beings. In the latter He evokes their own proper life; but in His sanctifying work He communicates His own proper life. When a man begins to share in the spirit of God, he is introduced into the most secret mysteries of God by a knowledge which the Apostle had previously asserted is natural to God and His Spirit exclusively, hence to no other spirit. Therefore the *homo spiritualis* is not spiritual because he lives in accord with his own spiritual nature; rather, admitted to participation in the supremely spiritual nature of God, he lives and moves in the way that God, conformably with His own nature, lives and moves in the Holy Spirit; in a word, the man lives by the spirit of God, and not by his own spirit.

The sensual man is in a condition either of contrary or of simple contradictory opposition to this spiritual man. In the first case, sensual man signifies the man who generally lives according to the flesh, not according to the spirit; or, if the expression refers to a part of human nature, it means that part which inclines exclusively to what is sensual and material.

As contradictorily opposed to supernatural spirituality, however, even the higher, spiritual part of human nature and of the man who lives according to it, can be called sensual. In the first place, the spiritual part of natural man can never, by its own power, so completely rule and pervade the sensual and material part that it is fully subjected and conformed to the spiritual part and is itself spiritualized. Therefore, even if man behaves according to the demands of his spiritual principle and does not allow it to be dominated by the inferior, sensible principle, he is nevertheless to some extent implicated in the infirmities and deficiencies of animal life and in the weakness of the flesh, whose effect is concupiscence and the eventual dissolution of nature—death. Only by the transforming and elevating energy of a higher spiritual nature does man's spirit become spiritual enough to permeate the flesh with its own power and to spiritualize it. This notion often occurs in the earliest Fathers, such as Irenaeus, Methodius, and Justin, who say that without the Holy Spirit man is not spiritual but animal.

But something else is associated in their minds with this view. The most ancient Fathers regarded God alone as the truly spiritual nature, on account of His eminent spirituality. When they turned their eyes to created natures, they recognized true, pure spirituality only when they saw a clear reflection of the divine spirituality. Some of these Fathers give us the impression that they were unable to regard any created nature as purely spiritual, that is, as completely immaterial. However, we must remember that they did not have in mind the philosophical and analytical idea of spirit which we derive from our observation of our spirit in its natural state. They were interested in the ideal of spirituality as Christian belief in God presented it to them, and as signifying a goal to be reached by the creature in the future state of transfiguration. By comparison, all creatures, including pure spirits, had the appearance of being material on account of their potentiality; they were isolated and far from God; they seemed to be darkness when confronted with God's light, mortal in comparison with His immortality, sinful in contrast to His holiness which excludes the very possibility of sinning. In such a view even the pure spirit is related to God somewhat as the spirit enclosed in the weakness of the flesh and of sensual life, or the merely animal soul of a beast is related to the pure spirit. The latter is an animal being as compared with the eminent spirituality of the divine nature.

This animal existence of man, in the two senses mentioned, is not properly evil and is not opposed to man's nature, since it is this nature itself. It is only an imperfection, a lack of higher perfection (what Leibnitz called metaphysical evil); yet that which is properly evil and malicious is based on it, for the possibility of evil is included in it. Indeed, when man is regarded in his complete nature, with his rational soul and sensuality in opposition to supernatural spirituality, a certain inclination to evil is discerned in him. Since that is so and, on the other hand, the inclination to good which is likewise found in man does not, in the present order of things, independently reach a full development within its own sphere, the inclination to good did not greatly occupy the attention of the early Fathers. This question, which is more scientific than practical, is extremely important for analytical philosophers; but it had little attraction or importance for those Fathers who, with lively enthusiasm and in a more intuitive way (in the Platonist sense) envisioned Christianity in its practical reality and momentous significance.

That is why they did not devote special consideration to man's spiritual part or its natural, interior development, which they placed somewhat indifferently in the middle between the upward attraction of the divine Spirit and the downward pull of the flesh. Man is equipped by nature to follow the downward tug of the flesh, because he has the power of free choice; but he cannot tend upwards unless he is spiritualized in a higher way and is drawn by God. From the viewpoint that was theirs, the Fathers said that the development of our spirit, as opposed to the Spirit of God, proceeds in the direction of sense and of evil. They gauged the animal, that is, the natural existence of man, not by his essence, where it is only negatively opposed to divine spirituality and can even, in its own way, enjoy a development that is good and spiritual, but by his animal and downward drift, which is contrary to divine spirituality.

This line of thought helps us to understand how the early Fathers could assert that nature, without the Holy Spirit, had a tendency toward nothing beyond sensuality and evil, and yet could contend that the Holy Spirit and the spirituality imparted by Him were given to complete nature which was already spiritual. The very fact that they thought that human nature was essentially complete in its own way without the Holy Spirit, must convince us that nature was not regarded by them as really material if it lacked the spirituality to be received from the Holy Spirit, and that this higher spirituality itself was not natural, that is, due to nature.

In the idea prevailing among the Fathers, the higher spirituality of the spiritual man eminently and in every respect excludes from his spirit all the defects and infirmities which cause animal life to be inferior to the naturally spiritual life. Among such defects are the multiplicity, the cleavage, and the dissolubility of life; the darkness on account of which knowledge is concerned with material things, while it remains quite blind to a higher order of things; the baseness of love and desire which are mainly directed to self and to objects of a sensual kind and suffocate all appreciation of what is higher. The created spirit, however, is not so grievously dissipated and split in its life, and is not dissoluble or mortal; it has light to understand spiritual things, and has desires that surmount the material world and rise to spiritual perfections and goods.

Yet, in comparison with the divine nature, the created spirit is imperfect and, as it were, material. The immortality and simplicity of the soul are mere shadows of the divine immortality and simplicity, as long as they rest on nothing but created nature and are not brought into union with God in a special way, that God may support the flow of the creature's life and draw it out of its natural multiplicity into the divine unity. Although an uninterrupted duration is natural to the created spirit, its life is not raised so high above the current of time that it can achieve full development in a single instant or by a single act, as is the case with

God's eternal, unified life, which embraces all activity in a single act and virtually includes the perfection of an infinite number of acts in the one simple act of divine vision. On the contrary, it is a mortal and scattered life. The brightness of the created intellect is darkness in comparison with the brilliance of God, and the supreme spiritual object is concealed from the created spirit in inaccessible light. "The sensual man perceiveth not these things that are of the Spirit of God" (I Cor. 2:14). He is impelled by nature to love spiritual goodness and beauty, but only in a limited circle closely surrounding him. He tends to make himself the center of all things, but is unable to soar to the heights in free flight; or, emerging from his narrow interests, to plunge into the depths of divine happiness.

All these imperfections, which are the reason why the created spirit is related to God somewhat as animal life is related to natural, spiritual life, will be abolished by the higher spirituality that is imparted to the soul when it is admitted to participation in the divine nature. This higher spirituality will endow the soul with the simplicity and the immortality of eternal life; with light and glory in a higher degree, in the way that God possesses them; with freedom and spiritual desire in the noblest sense of the word. According to the teaching of the ancient Fathers, therefore, the spirit will become truly spiritual, that is, simple and immortal, intelligent and free, when it is raised above its quasi-materiality and is given a share in God's spirituality, which alone is spirituality in the truest and fullest sense of the term.[7]

[7] The eternal life we await is not thus called in the Christian sense simply because it never comes to an end. That would be the case even in natural beatitude. Rather it is called eternal life because it is a participation in the absolutely eternal life of the eternal Godhead in which the soul is immersed. Through the gift of supernature the soul achieves supreme

The doctrine we have here presented in sharp contrast is not, of course, ordinarily brought out so clearly by the Fathers of the first centuries in their various conflicts with the Gnostics. But we can easily perceive that the tenor of their teaching can be translated into scientifically exact language. We could prove this in detail if the effort were compatible with the objectives of the present work.

In Sacred Scripture and the Fathers the production of this higher spirituality in us is ascribed, according to appropriation, to the Holy Spirit. This appropriation can be based on a double foundation. If the spirituality we attain is formally conceived as spiritual understanding and spiritual aspiration, as tendency toward the spiritual and consequently as our growth in spiritual life, it is attributed to the Holy Ghost according to the likeness of the hypostatic character by which He is the substantial terminus of the movement of love between the Father and the Son. In that case we can say that He not only gives such spirituality but that in it He gives Himself (not the Father and the Son) by granting us a participation and imitation of Himself; as the principle and rule of our activity He becomes, in a certain sense, our Spirit. But if we regard the new spirituality as the complete elevated state of our nature, as supernature itself, then the Father in the Trinity properly possesses it and gives it to us by admitting us to a share in His nature. However, He gives it to us in the Holy Spirit, for He gives it through love, and indeed the highest love,

---

unity in its supernatural life; it does not, like nature, merely direct its various activities to its one end; when it is united with God in the state of perfection and sensible happiness, it extends its activity to other objects through its immediate vision and love of God. The blessed in heaven know all things in and through God; even on earth the saints love things in and through God, rather than because of the natural goodness in them.

by which He diffuses externally His own intimate, divine goods. Moreover, the Holy Spirit is the inner movement of the divine spirituality in itself, and so He is the one who must transfuse and communicate it externally, as He is also the one who draws creatures to it by means of their activity. In this second respect, therefore, the Holy Spirit does not give Himself, but gives the light of the Son and the nature of the Father.

This provides us with an occasion of explaining more copiously how we are to understand the doctrine of the Fathers and of Sacred Scripture, that the Holy Spirit is in a certain sense the formal cause of our new spirituality, the soul of our spiritual life, and their assertion that He Himself, as distinct from His created goods and the other two divine persons, is given to us.

We must hold firmly that the soul cannot directly and formally be made spiritual by the divine substance that is applied to it. Spirituality is a quality and property of the soul; the divine substance is its exclusive, immediate, and perfect cause. We have to realize that in the production of our spirituality this cause is far more closely united with the soul than in any kind of natural operation, because it here communicates what is most proper to it, and the creature is raised to immediate possession of God by vision and love.

Because of the fact that God is the absolute cause of supernatural spirituality, and that His activity is not a mere movement but an *essentiare,* a production of being, the union into which He enters with the soul must be extremely intimate. This activity is greater the more the cause pours its riches into the effect, and the closer it draws the creature to itself to communicate itself to it.

All the perfections which God gives to creatures He

fashions according to the ideal of His own perfection. Since this ideal is not a lifeless thing projected in the mind of the artist, but produces the perfections in creatures by its very power, they exist as participations of it, that is, as imitations expressed by it through the power of the image: *imitationes vi imaginis ab ipsa expressae*. Every ideal is reflected in its image, every cause is present, by the way it operates, in its effect. In the case of God, ideal and cause are united; therefore God Himself is in all things, and in such a way that He is they (by their resemblance to Him), as Dionysius says. Hence we can call Him formal cause, not in the sense of an inhering, formed, and intrinsic form, but in the sense of exemplary and extrinsic form, virtually containing the form inhering in the thing. Accordingly the Platonists, who were always concerned about the exemplary form of things and orientated their whole doctrine about causality to it, could say that all things are good, beautiful, and true by the divine goodness, beauty, and truth itself.

With much greater right and in a higher sense we can say that we are spiritual through the Holy Spirit, who is the very spirituality (regarded as movement) of God Himself. We can assert this of our divine spirituality as contrasted with the natural, pure spirituality of creatures. Although created spirituality is likewise an image and effect of the divine ideal, it is not such immediately and does not express the characteristic features of the ideal. But supernatural spirituality does express the most characteristic features of the ideal, for it is specifically divine and is produced immediately by God.[8]

[8] Of great interest in this connection is a passage found in St. Augustine, *De Trinitate*, XV, cc. 17 ff., of which some excerpts, torn from their context, are often misinterpreted, to defend the opinion proposed by Petavius, about a certain substantial union between the Holy Spirit and the souls

To some extent God presents Himself as an ideal to all things, but especially to spiritual beings. And yet, in another sense, He withholds Himself from natural things, which express the ideal in their own way, not in His way, and therefore reflect a copy of the ideal rather than the ideal itself. In particular we cannot say that God gives a divine

---

of the just. The opinion as thus stated is new, and cannot be discovered in the Fathers except by misconstruing their words. In this very passage of St. Augustine, which Petavius regards as classical and decisive, the Saint clearly means something quite different. To prove that the Holy Spirit is love (by appropriation), Augustine says that God sends us the Holy Spirit as His supreme gift. But the supreme gift of God is love. Therefore the Holy Spirit is love. He says, further, that if God gives us love, He gives us Himself, because He is love. Consequently, when he says that the Holy Spirit gives us Himself according to His substance and proper character, nothing else is meant than that He gives Himself as the ideal of our filial love that is to be shared by us.

The Greek Fathers insist that God does not sanctify us by means of a creature; but they say this to prove that the Holy Spirit is not a creature, because a creature could be no more than a mediator of grace, whereas He in His own person produces grace and holiness. This does not mean that the soul is made formally holy by substantial union with Him. And although they say that we are made partakers of the Holy Spirit Himself, they intend to show no more than that He causes holiness in us by His own power. He possesses this power as His own, because He is the substantial ideal of all holiness. This is gathered from the very passage of St. Cyril, occurring in the seventh Dialogue with Hermias, which Petavius makes so much of (*De Trinitate*, VIII. c. 5. no. 2). Cyril is asked if we share in an empty, non-subsisting grace; and he replies: "No, we share in the actually existing and subsisting Spirit of God." The opposition is not between created grace and the Holy Spirit, as though Cyril meant, in the interpretation of Petavius, that we share, not only in a grace inhering in us, but also in the Holy Spirit Himself. Rather the opposition is between an imaginary and hence empty, non-subsisting ideal of sanctity in which we would share by imitation, and the true ideal. For immediately afterwards St. Cyril says: "Otherwise man would have to be called an image of grace, and not an image of God and of the Holy Spirit" [*PG*, LXXV, 1088]. Hence we participate in the Holy Spirit as the ideal of our filial love, and do not enter into a special, substantial union with Him that would not include the other divine persons. In general, the participation which figures so prominently in the writings of the Greek Fathers is nothing else than a sharing in the perfections of an ideal by similarity and kinship with it, according to a Platonic mode of expression.

person in giving natural gifts or even supernatural gifts that are not immediately divine and that do not directly refer to God. Since the divine persons are identical with the divine essence as it is in itself, surmounting all relationship to creatures, we cannot say that they are given to the creature in all the perfection corresponding to their hypostatic character, unless the creature shares in such perfection according to its own proper way of existing. The Son, as the Father's Word, is sent into our hearts when we share in the divine knowledge from which He proceeds as Word; to receive Him thus, we must be given a knowledge that is immediately and exclusively derived from the divine intellect and has the divine essence as its direct object. Similarly, the Holy Spirit is given to us only if we are granted a love of God that is like the love from which He proceeds as fruit and term, and if we also receive the love which the Son of God has for the Father; then we can draw near to God as our Father with filial confidence and tenderness, and can be immediately united with Him in intimate affection.

By bestowing on us the power and activity of the Son and the Holy Spirit and by sending these persons themselves to us in this way, God also gives them to us as the immediate object of our possession and enjoyment. When, in heaven, we are granted knowledge of the Word, we shall behold the Word and all things else in Him, and by the

---

In his later works Scheeben changed his attitude toward Petavius. Under the influence of the Greek Fathers he came to conceive the indwelling of the Holy Spirit in the souls of the just as a hypostatic inhabitation that is proper to the third Person. He also taught that this indwelling of the Holy Spirit completed our divine adoption as already brought about by sanctifying grace, and established it more perfectly as a second, higher principle of it. See Scheeben's *The Mysteries of Christianity* (St. Louis: B. Herder, 1951), pp. 165–72. Cf. also M. J. Donnelly, S.J., "The Indwelling of the Holy Spirit according to M. J. Scheeben," *Theological Studies*, VII (1946), 244–80.

light we receive from Him, we shall find our happiness in Him. Likewise, when we receive the love of the Holy Spirit, we receive the Spirit Himself into our hearts; He who fills us with this love and nourishes and inflames it, guides it back to Himself and gives Himself in it for our delight.

We should further note that the supernatural, spiritual life in us is not related to the Holy Spirit, who communicates it to us, in the same way as our natural life is related to God, who is its cause. The reason is that it is not rooted in nature. Natural life is, indeed, given to us by God and received from Him; but it is permanently rooted in the creature's substance, and hence its duration is assured. The relation of God to our natural life is that of a cause existing on a higher plane, the efficient cause, source and Creator of that life, rather than that of a cause which continuously and directly cherishes and sustains it, in the way that the soul, which is continually present in the body, exerts its influence on bodily life. In a sense, supernatural life becomes natural to the creature, by reason of the creature's supernature. But supernature itself is not a substance. It is only a quality of the created substance, coming from outside; its root does not lie in the substance, which has no power to produce such a perfection; supernature is preserved in existence by the higher Being to whom it is connatural. It is like a light thrown on a body from without; the light lasts only as long as its outer source floods the body with rays.

Thus the Holy Spirit is, so to speak, the soul of supernatural life, for He communicates His own life to the creature; He not only brings supernatural life into existence as its primary efficient cause, but preserves it and gives it the power of movement by a continuing activity and care. This is the only sense in which we can speak of the Holy Spirit as the formal cause of our higher spirituality and of our supernatural, spiritual life. Consequently there is no real, substantial union of our nature with His; we can think of Him as formal cause only to the extent that a formal cause, as in other cases, effects, sustains, and arouses the subject's life. And this comes back more or less to what we said before, that the Holy Spirit is the external formal cause of our higher spirituality, the exemplar communicating itself by its own power.

These three points of view, that the Holy Spirit immediately produces, sustains, and nurtures our supernatural life, that the vital energy which He impresses on us is but an imitation and participation of the spiritual energy which He Himself is, and that He bestows this vital energy on those who belong to Him, to admit them to the delight and repose in the sweetness of love which is He, clarify all that the Fathers have said about our special, mystical union with the Holy Spirit.

But these truths dawn upon our contemplating eye only on the supposition that supernatural life has its foundation in a sort of new nature. In fact, the Fathers base all their statements about such a union on the nature of our supernatural life.[9] The mystical union cannot be conceived as a relation quite apart, unconnected with supernature as such, and the relation itself cannot be explained without reference to a supernature in us. I venture to assert, and I believe I can back up my stand, that Petavius proposed his amazing thesis because he had not penetrated sufficiently

[9] The wealth of patristic learning which Petavius has assembled with amazing erudition in the eighth book of his *De Trinitate*, can be well employed to show how exalted an idea the Fathers had of our union with God, and to prove that this union consists in something incomparably superior to the unity which is generally called moral, resulting from the development of man's natural powers.

into the notion of the supernatural; he has tormented the acumen of theologians by confronting them with a superfluous mystery. He could not discover that mystery in the Fathers otherwise than by an inadequate interpretation of their teaching.

A mystery is there, indeed: an exalted, noble, joyous mystery. We have here no simple or empty moral union of our nature with the Holy Spirit, brought about by aligning and harmonizing the orientation of our natural powers with the Spirit of God, who moves and rules all that lives. The union may be called physical, with St. Cyril, because our nature is so closely linked with the divine nature that it shares to some extent therein; begotten of God by grace, it receives a new life modeled on the pattern of God's life, with the result that it is more thoroughly spiritualized. It may be called an essential union, because in it the essence of God, which is self-enclosed and exclusive of all lower natures, opens itself up, as it were, to impart to the creature its intrinsic, characteristic perfections, which are so transcendent that the creature would be God Himself if it had them in virtue of its nature.

It is a union like that of the seal and its impress; for the divine image which reflects the splendor of God can be imprinted on our soul only by the direct power and action of the divine ideal. It is a union by which the Holy Spirit dwells in us, not merely as the source of special, created gifts, but as the divine love which He really is; as the donor of filial love that unites us children of God intimately with our Father, and as the intermediary of the Father's love for us, by which He brings to us the grace of His children. It is a union, lastly, by which we become one spirit with God, not according to essence or personality, but so far as the spirituality which constitutes the nature of God passes over to us as grace and an infused quality—not as the light itself, but as a brightness streaming forth from the light, to make us truly spiritual in our being, our knowledge, and our love. We become one spirit with the Father, who clasps us to His heart; one spirit with the Son, whose image we reflect; one spirit with the Holy Ghost, who brings the love of God the Father down to us, lifts us up to Him by our love for Him, and thus draws our love and the divine love together in a holy kiss.[10]

In all truth, these are wonders and mysteries in plenty. They are marvels so sublime and inconceivable that we dare not go beyond them to assume yet another kind of union with the divine nature and in particular with the Holy Spirit, unless the most definite and decisive texts of Sacred Scripture and teachings of the Church compel us to make this further step. We should have to be forced by the evidence of a higher revelation to postulate a special, real union with the Holy Spirit that transcends the limits already established. Everything, absolutely everything, is common to the divine persons, with the exception of their hypostatic character; the latter alone accounts for the interior distinction among them, and is also the sole reason enabling them to have some special relation with the outside world.

But neither the Scriptures nor the Fathers impose such a doctrine; all the expressions collected by Petavius have been amply explained by us and full justice has been done to them. Indeed, nearly every statement made about the Holy Spirit is applied also to the Son and, although less frequently, to the Father. Where do we find a passage

---

[10] "God and the penitent soul meet in a holy kiss," *Manuale Sancti Augustini.* This manual is a booklet, dating from the twelfth century, which contains passages from St. Augustine, St. Anselm, St. Bernard, and Hugh of St. Victor. It is found in *PL,* XL, 951–68.

about the Holy Spirit similar to this text about the Son: "We are made partakers of Christ, yet so, if we hold the beginning of His substance firm unto the end" (Heb. 3:14)? All the divine persons come to dwell in us; we are made partakers of the Son also; He too is imprinted on us as a seal, as the Fathers very often affirm. St. Athanasius says: "By the fact that we are sealed with the Holy Spirit, we are made partakers of the divine nature, as Peter teaches [II Pet. 1:4]; and thus all creatures become partakers of the Word in the Spirit, and, in the same way, through the Spirit, we become partakers of God." [11]

Since, therefore, the imprint and action of the Holy Spirit on our souls bring about our participation in the divine nature, in the way specified above, this action cannot be personal to the Holy Spirit. It can be ascribed to Him only by appropriation. The reason is, first, that He is the movement of love in the divine nature, so that the communication of love by transmission to the outside world pertains eminently to Him; secondly, that He causes us to share in the divine nature and spirituality regarded as divine, substantial love, and hence also in Himself.

This last reason gains in force when we consider that the divine nature and spirituality, as communicated to us in this life, appear less as glorification in divine light than as repletion with divine love and holiness.

HOLINESS IN OUR SUPERNATURE

Here we take up the second point that was mentioned above. The communication of grace and, through grace, of the divine nature, is usually ascribed to the Holy Spirit because holiness pertains to His hypostatic character, and in Sacred Scripture and the Fathers supernature is chiefly

[11] *Epist. ad Serapionem,* I, 23 [PG, XXVI, 585].

referred to as holiness or sanctity. In this connection a special remark is in order, as it was in the case of spirituality. We said above that the Holy Spirit is Spirit in the Godhead in a particular sense, and consequently that He communicates a spirituality, that of motion, as something proper to Him. We also pointed out, however, that He is only the movement of another spirituality in God, and that He communicates this also to us, not as something of His own, but by His intervention and transmission. In a similar way the Holy Spirit possesses holiness quite uniquely as His characteristic note; yet He is also the revelation of the holiness that characterizes the Father and the Son. Accordingly He communicates to us a double holiness, one of which includes and underlies the other, again in two ways: first, by giving us Himself, and secondly, by imparting to us the holiness of the Father and the Son.

We generally say that the good is holy, but with a definite connotation, implying a special soundness, purity, and excellence.

Two kinds of good or goodness may be distinguished. There is a goodness and perfection of nature, which is the principle and object of love; and there is a goodness and perfection of love, by which we love what is good in itself. Likewise there is a twofold holiness or soundness, purity, and excellence of good.

First, we have the soundness and excellence of the good itself which is the principle and object of love. This holiness appears mainly as high sacredness, as a dignity and moral power, which imposes the most profound and absolute reverence and demands love as a tribute of veneration. In this respect all peoples designate the divine nature as that which is the highest, most sovereign, most sacred; as that which is absolutely holy, with an excellence so inviolable that opposition to it is an abominable crime and unmitigated evil. This sacredness and excellence of the divine goodness, as manifested exteriorly, are based on the inner solidity and purity of the divine nature; the inference follows that it is not a particular kind of goodness, but is the very essence of goodness, goodness itself, which excludes all defect and imperfection, and hence is unconditionally worthy of love and reverence; it is the good in all its purity and limpidity, tolerating no stain, impairment, or diminution.

Secondly, God is holy because He embraces this most excellent and unsullied goodness of His, this holiness of His nature, with a love that perfectly corresponds to its sacredness, purity, and nobility. And this love itself is so strong and pure that it can never be excessive or deficient in the slightest degree, and is so perfect that it exhausts the entire lovableness of the nature, to which it is equal.

The relation between these two "phases" of holiness resembles that which, as we saw previously, exists between the two phases of spirituality in God. The holiness of love is founded on the holiness of nature, as the spirituality of movement is founded on the spirituality of nature, and as the goodness of love in general is founded on the goodness of nature. Although love in created spirits does not necessarily grow out of nature, the extent, possibility, and order of its goodness are conditioned by nature. In God, holiness of nature corresponds to the hypostatic character of the Father, as begetter, and of the Son, as begotten image. The holiness of love corresponds to the hypostatic character of the Holy Spirit. He is called holy in an eminent sense because He represents the holiness of God in this special phase, as He is also Spirit in an eminent sense because He possesses spirituality in a special way. Thus the entire characteristic of the Holy Spirit, as distinct from the Father and the Son, is brought out by the combination of these two names. Although the Father and the Son are spirit and are holy as spirit, they are not spirit in the same way as the Third Person, that is, as spirated Spirit, and hence are not holy in the same way as the Third Person, who is holy as the terminus in which holy, spiritual love in God issues.

Because holiness consists in this special soundness, purity, and excellence of good, it is something divine in itself, and as such is not, like goodness, common to God and creatures. For goodness loses its soundness, purity, and nobility when it takes on the limitations and instability of a creature. Holiness is indeed found in creatures, but only by reason of some special relation to God. We say that a creature is holy when the creature, united to God, belonging to God, as representing Him or dedicated to His service, gains an excellence beyond other creatures and by special divine favor is endowed with a sacredness that comes to it from God. In this sense all peoples apply the term "holy" to their priests, temples, and sacred vessels, and in general to everything that is consecrated to the service of God and accordingly belongs to Him as His property. We can also call that created spirit holy who acknowledges God's holiness with reverence and love, and by observance of His holy law serves the Holy One in a holy manner. By its relation to God as principle and end of the moral law, the moral goodness of man acquires an aura of holiness which even the pagans did not ignore, and which consecrates the soul as a sort of temple of God.

A certain holiness can be discerned in creatures even when left in their natural condition, according to their natural relations to God. But such holiness is more external than internal; it consists in a humble submissiveness to

God's holiness rather than in an intimate union with it or any kind of elevation to its level. We do not discover in this state the lofty idea of sanctity which Christianity holds up to us as its goal, and shows it realized in so many of its disciples. Compared with Christian holiness, the natural as well as the moral goodness of rational creatures dwindles into insignificance. Christian sanctity is essentially something supernatural, stupendous, mysterious.

We perceive this clearly in those people whom we designate specifically as saints. We give them this name because of their marvelous, heroic, mysterious union with God, which reveals itself in many extraordinary signs, and is so exalted that natural reason has no notion or inkling of it and fails completely to explain it. The essence of this sublime union with God is not confined to the high degree of perfection reached by the saints, in whom it stands forth prominently, but is found in all Christians who through faith and the water of regeneration have entered into union with the Holy Spirit. All Christians are called holy by the apostles in their letters, not precisely because all are at least called to heroic sanctity, but because all who observe the fundamental prescriptions of the Christian law possess the substance of true, genuine sanctity. All who are in this state obtain the grace of justification, and this is generally known in ecclesiastical terminology as sanctifying grace, or simply as sanctity.

By this grace we truly become children of God and so are made to share in the divine nature, hence also in its holiness. This is not a mere external denomination, but is our interior condition. We are holy and ought to be holy, because our Father in heaven is holy. Since holiness as such pertains to God alone, the essence of the creature's true holiness consists in the communication of holiness by God through the elevation of the creature to participation in the divine nature.

Through this elevation and union with God the created spirit receives, in the realm of nature as well as of love,[12] a sublime, pure, and stable goodness such as in itself belongs to God alone.

Even by its nature the spirit, as an image of God in its spiritual substance, possesses a high dignity with personal rights protected by God Himself; it ought to be esteemed by all other beings and, in a certain sense, to be considered holy. However, since the spirit is not like God as He is in His own nature, it does not possess a divine excellence enabling it to stand, as it were, on the level of the Godhead and to become one person with God. This is brought about by supernature, by which the spirit is raised to the Godhead in a way that defies description and is united with God, to have part in His supreme glory and sovereignty. By supernature the spirit, as child of God the Father, and brother of the Son, becomes in some way one person with them, and so receives a consecration that commands our veneration; this is what enables us to behold God and Christ in all men who actually possess grace or are at least called to grace.

The natural goodness of the spirit is, indeed, endowed with a certain purity, soundness, and brightness, but only when contrasted with the darkness and cloudiness surrounding matter. As mere image of the divine nature, the spirit does not reflect these qualities in their full brilliance, since the ray streaming forth from the divine sun breaks up, so to speak, into a thousand tints before reaching cre-

---

[12] The term "nature" is used in opposition to love and morality in the same order, as well as in opposition to the supernatural, which pertains to a higher order.

ated beings, and is thus obscured. But by supernature we receive the divine light in all its splendor, as a mirror does; [13] we ourselves become light in the Lord, as the Apostle says [Eph. 5:8]. Our souls thereby become wonderfully glorified and are filled with a heavenly beauty surpassing that of the angels; St. Catherine of Siena was granted a sight of it, and the vision transported her into ecstasy.[14]

The moral purity corresponding to the purity of raiment which we receive as children of God must be far more perfect than is required by the soul's natural beauty. For this heavenly garment is grossly soiled by the slightest particle of dust, and every stain contradicts its splendor as much as it does the divine light itself, which tolerates no shadow of defilement. This brings us to the divine stability of supernatural goodness. In one respect the goodness of nature, like its powers and tendencies, seems to possess greater constancy than the goodness of supernature. For the former is rooted in the substance of the spirit and therefore cannot be separated from it or destroyed, whereas the latter comes from without and can again be taken away. However, if we examine the matter more closely, we perceive that nature does not arrive at full stability of goodness unless it is crowned by supernature, which possesses it in the most perfect way. Natural goodness always remains finite, and so does not necessarily exclude all change and fluctuation. But supernature is a participation in infinite, eternal goodness, and accordingly, when it develops its life completely, admits us to a share in the eternal, immutable life of God, as we remarked before.

In particular, nature does not necessarily shut out every

[13] Cf. St. Basil, *De Spiritu Sancto*, c. 9 [*PG*, XXXII, 109].
[14] See M. J. Scheeben, *Die Herrlichkeiten der göttlichen Gnade* (16th ed., Freiburg im Breisgau: Herder, 1941), p. 111.

defect opposed to its natural tendency and growth. Since its goodness is deficient and is not goodness itself, it is capable of deflection from the good. Error is possible in the intellect, in spite of its natural bent for truth, and deviation from the good is possible in the will, in spite of its natural hunger for goodness. Consequently natural light is compatible with actual error in the intellect, and a natural tendency toward order is compatible with actual sin in the will. In a word, natural goodness can be the subject of a supervening privation and violation of the subject's necessary perfection, without itself being destroyed.

The contrary is observed in the goodness of supernature; and this is the most important feature of its holiness: it cannot abide a fault or defect directly opposed to it, but decisively and unconditionally excludes any such thing. If it is a participation in the divine goodness, which banishes all defect and all evil, it must to some extent resemble divine goodness. This resemblance is obviously verified most perfectly when supernature fully develops all its resources and transforms us into a perfect likeness of the divine goodness, in the state of everlasting beatitude.

In this state the soul is irresistibly drawn to God and is plunged into the fire of divinity, as the Greek Fathers are fond of saying; the dross of its imperfection and defectiveness is burned away and, under the action of God's infinite goodness, it becomes indefectible, like God's own goodness. The intellect is completely illuminated by the fullness of divine light so that it may know in a divine way and immediately behold the divine essence, source and totality of all truth; it can no more err than God Himself can. Furthermore, the vision of God directly presents to the will the supreme, infinite goodness without which and against which nothing can be conceived as good, exhibiting it in its inexhaustible riches and irresistible attractiveness. Since the will is at the same time permeated and filled by the Holy Spirit with the celestial fire of His divine love, it cannot possibly turn from the true good, which is goodness itself, to the love of anything that is incompatible with such goodness.

During the present life, however, supernature is imperfect, for it is still in a state of becoming and development. Since it does not yet thoroughly penetrate and transfigure nature or turn nature, so to speak, into itself, it cannot shut out the possibility of every defect directly opposed to itself. Its proper essence is disclosed by the fact that it cannot exist together with any defect formally in contradiction with itself. Our reason, regarded as a power and tendency for truth, can remain and always does remain, however much we may err against it and abuse it. But the power and tendency for knowledge which accompany supernature can never abide simultaneously in the soul with a formally opposite, actual error, that is, actual heresy, even during the imperfect stage of such knowledge, when it is no more than the light of faith. As long as nature is not completely transfigured, it can withstand the supernatural as well as the natural inclination for truth and can swerve from truth. When this happens, our supernatural faculty is not merely, like our natural faculty, inhibited from influencing activity, but is entirely smothered and dissolved; it must withdraw from nature.

Something similar takes place in the will. The power possessed by supernature for loving the good (the supernatural virtue of charity) and its tendency toward its last end cannot abide with a formally opposite movement of the will, an aversion and deflection from the ultimate end, and is therefore cut off along with the latter. Such an estrangement dissolves habitual grace, or supernature itself, together with the virtue of charity; it kills the source of supernatural life in the soul, and is therefore called mortal sin.[15]

Thus even in its imperfect stage supernature preserves an implacable opposition to all defects that formally contradict its divine truth and goodness. When it unfolds all its power and completely pervades nature, it excludes even the possibility of such defects. As long as it does not yet thoroughly pervade nature, it cannot, indeed, prevent the revolt against the good which it will be able to prevent in the state of its perfect development; yet it must guard its divine spotlessness, and this it does by retiring from the defiled soul so as not to be contaminated. Therefore, too, supernature is called rectitude and innocence in a higher sense: rectitude, because it is not only, as always, a habitual inclination toward what is right, but because it cannot coexist with what is wrong; innocence, as indicating not only that the soul has committed or contracted no actual sin that still encumbers it, but also that something is present within it that excluded any such guilt.

We have seen that supernature, regarded as a quasi-nature, shares in the divine holiness by imparting to our

---

[15] In this way we arrive at a theological concept of mortal sin and of its essential difference from venial sin. A person commits a mortal sin when he abandons the divine order so as to give up God as his last end and withdraws from subjection to Him. He commits a venial sin when he does not carefully pursue the line of conduct leading to his goal, but at the same time does not abandon the goal itself and consequently his union with God. Venial sin is a violation of the order leading to the end, but not of the end itself. Therefore charity, as love of the end, and with it grace, is not extinguished by venial sin. Venial sin defiles grace in the way that gold is exteriorly tarnished without any interior decomposition. That is why charity and grace are not substantially diminished by venial sin. Only mortal sin can assail their substance, and when it does so, it not merely weakens but destroys.

nature an excellence, purity, and stability in goodness, such as belong to the divine nature alone. Just as the holiness of love which God has for Himself is based on the holiness of nature as the source and object of love, so too the holiness of love in us must be based on and proceed from the holiness which our nature requires because of its transfiguration.

Thus we observe in the Christian saints that wonderful, mystical union with God by love which enables them to live wholly of God, in God, and for God, because Christianity has brought human nature to a close association with God in the elevation and higher consecration of nature by grace. Only in this way does Christian love attain to the divine excellence, purity, and stability basically required of all Christians and fully developed in the saints.

The natural man, too, can love and revere God's holy nature; yet this is a love that is subject to the beloved object and is not raised to its height and therefore cannot embrace it as it is in itself. But supernatural love is so sublime that it can freely soar above all created things up to the highest and most lofty good, embrace it, savor its sweetness, and repose on the heart of the heavenly Father. Nature knows divine beauty and lovableness in broken rays of light and in the faint images of creatures; its love cannot be dissociated from creatures and therefore cannot be wholly pure and heavenly. A purity of love in which the divine goodness in all its fairness and beauty is directly, independently, and exclusively the object and motive, is essentially supernatural, because it raises nature above itself and its natural connections. It corresponds to the purity that, as we said above, belongs to supernature, by which the unsullied splendor of divine light is received into the soul.

The closer man comes to God and the more intimately he is united with Him, the more he recoils in horror at the prospect of separation from Him; for the higher the pinnacle on which a person stands, the farther he can fall. The better we know the sublime purity of the divine goodness and that of its image in our soul, the more abominable the dishonoring of God and the defiling of the soul must appear. Indeed, if we, as God's children, are made partakers of His nature, sin becomes a double murder, an attempt against the life of our Father and a deathblow delivered against our soul, for we snuff out its true and most precious life. Therefore supernatural love engenders a greater abhorrence of sin, and so receives a higher kind of stability that makes sin comparatively impossible, or at least leaves less room for its possibility than natural love does.

All the elements that go into the sanctity of Christian love, its inconceivable sublimity, its chaste and tender purity, its opposition to sin and strong detestation of the same, find their clarification in the holy, supernatural consecration of our nature that results from its participation in the divine nature. Starting with this principle, we can conceive and explain everything; apart from it, we cannot account for anything. If we face the situation from the standpoint of natural, unspoiled reason, we shall, like unbelievers or rationalists, listen to the language of Christian sanctity with speechless amazement, and at best will be interested in it as the expression of exalted, enthusiastic emotion. Because man is regarded merely as man, and no attention is paid to his higher, divine, holy dignity and consecration, esteem and understanding of specifically Christian morality and of its genuine representatives, the saints, have gradually sunk to abysmal depths and have been replaced by complete indifference. Christian holiness had to make way for a so-called human righteousness and up-rightness. If we can restore the idea of Christian sanctity to its full importance in theory and practice, it will be a powerful impetus to a newly-inspired resurgence of religious life.

If we really have in supernature a holiness of nature or a nature of holiness, with which no lapse from goodness is compatible or simultaneously consistent, we attain to a further clarification of various truths, and also of some very strange yet widespread aberrations of the human mind. This subject opens up the meaning of all those passages in which St. John so vigorously insists that they who are born of God do not sin and cannot sin. It also enables us to account for the origin of all those Gnostic, Manichaean, and Beghardian heresies which regarded all or some men as absolutely incapable of sin and error, and consequently as endowed with a holy nature. In this they were not really wrong; indeed, they took as their point of departure the orthodox teaching that there is in us a holy nature which cannot coexist with sin and which, in its eventual state of perfection, renders sin and error completely, essentially impossible. Their mistake was that they regarded this holy nature as man's own proper nature (which is possible only if man is viewed as an emanation from God), or at least considered it in the perfection of its full development, when it entirely pervades nature and consumes the faultiness and deficiency of nature. Therefore "spiritual" men, who are born of God, were thought to be absolutely impeccable; they could not become "animal" men, because they were set apart from such people by their higher nature; and that, too, is why merely animal men could not ever rise up to the level of higher nature by their free activity.

Against such errors the Greek Fathers taught, quite characteristically, that holiness is, indeed, a sort of nature, but that it is not the proper nature and substance of man, although it is in some way engrafted upon man's nature by the Spirit of God. Accordingly "spiritual" men are in themselves also "animal," and "animal" men are capable of receiving a holy nature and are destined for this elevation by God. The reason why some have a "spiritual" nature while others have only an "animal" nature cannot be found in their own nature and substance, and it cannot be accounted for by saying that God wished to give the higher nature to some but not to others; the truth is that some acquire it through the cooperation of their nature, whereas others do not.[16] Although spiritual men have obtained spirituality and holiness by the free cooperation of their nature, their nature still remains in them after they have been made spiritual and holy; further, it is not fully transfigured by supernature here on earth and certainly does not merge with supernature. Their own human activity also remains, and so they are always capable of performing an act that will contradict and banish supernature, with the consequence that "spiritual" men can again become "animal" men. We shall later return to this beautiful doctrine of the Greek Fathers, which manifestly expresses our own view.

Another radical and widely influential heresy, related to the one just mentioned, receives light from the teaching about the holy, sinless quasi-nature in us. This is the heresy of the Reformers, which has so many points of contact with Gnostic and Manichaean tenets. The Reformers, too, take over from Catholic teaching the doctrine that there was found in the first man a holy nature which was called innocence in a higher sense, because it was not only a simple

---

[16] To understand the sense of this statement, consult what we have to say later, about the union of nature and supernature.

negation of guilt, but could not coexist with guilt at all. Like the Manichaeans and Gnostics, they taught that this nature was proper and essential to man. But instead of joining the Manichaeans and the Gnostics in their logical denial that man, who possessed it, could have committed sin, the Reformers borrowed another proposition from the Church, that the first man sinned and by his sin lost holiness, as holiness is incompatible with sin. Since, according to their teaching, this holiness was nothing else than the very nature of the human soul, they had to hold, in consequence, that the nature of the human soul was destroyed by sin.

Viewed from the philosophical angle, this monstrous error is utterly inexplicable; man's natural inclination toward what is good does, indeed, stand in opposition to actual sin, but cannot be destroyed or eradicated by such sin. The theological viewpoint, on the contrary, discloses the truth that there is a tendency toward the good which is torn out by sin down to its very roots. If this tendency arises from the essence of the soul, the soul must necessarily be shattered and killed in its own proper nature. Since that tendency is at the same time the only power of higher life the soul possesses, the soul becomes wholly incapacitated for any good, and inclines exclusively toward evil. Its freedom, too, as the power of choosing good, perishes completely.

It is therefore a matter of the utmost importance to perceive as clearly as we can that supernatural holiness, as also supernatural spirituality, is a sort of second nature or a supernature in man. This perception is needed in order to penetrate into the depths of Catholic truth and, on the other hand, to account for some of the most extravagant aberrations the human mind has ever been exposed to, with a view to refuting them at their source.

Chapter X

POWERS AND ACTS OF SUPERNATURE

I BELIEVE I have brought out the main points of view that have to be considered if the great wealth and range of Catholic teaching on the supernatural are to be clearly grasped. We shall gain an insight into other aspects if we take occasion to link this doctrine more closely with the chief mysteries of our faith. Accordingly we still have the task of examining in some detail the acts of the supernatural life along with the powers corresponding to them.

In general we should note that supernature is the foundation of all those acts which are comprised in the so-called mystic life of the soul, and that a study of these acts is necessary for a clear, thorough, scientific understanding of Christian mysticism. After all, what else is mysticism than a life which transcends the powers and capacities of nature? It is a life that "is hid with Christ in God" [Col. 3:3]; a life by which the created spirit receives a share in the life of God that is by nature concealed and blocked off from it, and is raised from its own sphere to a higher domain where it exercises acts of knowledge, love, and joy that of itself it could never have conjectured. It is a life which, in the stage preceding the full development of its riches and glory, covers even those who possess it with a holy, yet awesome pall of darkness.

"Mysticism," in the beautiful words of Görres, "is an

intuition and knowledge under the influence of a higher light, and an operation and activity under the influence of a higher freedom; just as ordinary (natural) knowledge and activity are brought about by the spiritual light granted to the soul and the personal freedom implanted in it." [1] Rightly, then, we may say that every Christian is truly a mystic (though without scientific knowledge of the fact), at least if he lives the life of faith. For faith, love, and hope are truly mystical acts. In the narrower sense, undoubtedly, only they are called mystics in whom the light of faith, the fire of love, and the strength of hope are manifest in a higher degree, and in whom the supernatural life is already pervading nature, as is borne out by phenomena resembling those which will be in evidence when the lowliness and weakness of nature are transfigured and all that is mortal is swallowed up by life (Cf. II Cor. 5:4). But that only confirms the statement. Mysticism in the narrower sense is but a higher development, that has passed over into the realm of experience and phenomena, of the basic supernature which is common to all true Christians. And even those supernatural works of God in the world and in man which are not immediately and intrinsically connected with supernature, such as prophecies and the miracles wrought by the saints, are closely related to mysticism. For God works such supernatural effects in and through certain men in order to make known the special, supernatural union they have with Him, and to invite others to seek and receive the same favors for themselves.

Accordingly the acts of supernatural life are all mystical. Indeed, in the present state of wayfaring there can be no acts of a higher kind than those that are common to all

[1] J. Görres, *Die christliche Mystik* (Regensburg und Landshut: 1836), I, 1.

Christians. This is particularly true of acts of the theological virtues, because they have God as their immediate object and motive. They can be more intense and perfect, but only within their own order; they can also be accompanied by greater clarity and sensible experience in those souls that have been singled out by God. This mystical character is the reason why the unbeliever can gain no concept of such acts, and why even believers find it hard to form a clear and sharply focused idea of them. And this is why, too, the intuitive language of souls who are at home in this mystical atmosphere is incomprehensible to the uninitiate, and seems to proud rationalists to be folly and nonsense.[2]

Often enough theologians who desire to define more accurately the nature of supernatural acts and to determine their motives, their proper objects, and similar points that have nothing in common with natural acts, are confronted with the objection that such considerations are excessively subtle. The ordinary Christian, says the objector, understands little or nothing of all this, and would not even know how to set about performing a supernatural act; and especially those who have but a vague idea of the supernatural order would not be able to lead a supernatural life. But we can reply in all truth: not our understanding or our reflection, but the unction of the Holy Spirit teaches us all that is necessary in order to lead a supernatural life.[3]

Supernatural life is not produced by our will and our reflection. The power and the impetus for it are supplied to us by the Holy Spirit. The will needs but to follow the inner light and the guidance of the Holy Spirit, and the

---

[2] Cf. I Cor. 2:14: "The natural man does not grasp the secrets of the Spirit of God, for they are folly to him; and he is unable to comprehend them, because they have to be judged of spiritually" (Spencer's translation).

[3] Cf. I John 2:27: "His unction teacheth you of all things."

supernatural life unfolds of itself. In the natural order, too, the natural life of knowledge and of volitional activity can develop normally, although the subject is not conscious of reflecting on the nature of these acts, and even if false views about them are formed in the reflective process. How many people love, and do not know what love is; they love with spiritual love, and are unable to explain how it differs from sense love. All men know in a spiritual and intellectual way; but how few grasp the real distinction between spiritual knowledge and sense knowledge. The reason is that natural and even rational powers have a spontaneous impulse toward their proper activity; and this impulse manifests itself with or without the cooperation of the will, according to circumstances. The will follows the natural, direct, and immediate perception of the objects which arouse the impulse, and may remain unmoved by reflective consciousness of them. What takes place in nature, takes place also in supernature; except that in the latter the influence of reflection stays even more in the background, because the impulse toward movement and activity comes down from above, and by its very nature has a mystical character.

What we have said is verified most of all in the deepest and most secret life of the soul, in which our acts depend on nature for their content and tendency. Nature prevails over reflection in the basic movements of the soul, that is, in knowledge and love. Even natural love is not the product of the free will, except in the sense that it proceeds from nature as a tendency, and is accepted and made a rule of conduct. Since we have arrived at the point where we are going to reduce supernatural acts mainly to supernatural knowledge and love, we should not give way to the fear that a person is unable to lead a supernatural life merely because of a lack of reflection and because he is unacquainted with our theory.

Reflection, to be sure, is predominant in acts which proceed from the will, in the activity that is performed at the direction and by the decision of the will. But the action of the will, especially the activity directed toward its natural ends, has its basis and starting point in a natural connection with those ends, and consequently in the natural knowledge of them and the natural desire and love for them. Therefore acts that may be called external are modified by the nature of internal acts, which better indicate natural activity and are expressed in external acts.

In examining supernatural acts from the viewpoint of their specific difference from purely natural acts, we must focus attention chiefly on those acts which entail the inner, basic operation of supernature, that is, on knowledge and love and hope which is connected with love; after that we can pass on to moral acts, properly so called. The object of supernatural knowledge, hope, and love cannot be attained by nature; but moral acts do not transcend our natural powers; examples of such acts are the worship of God or obedience to Him. But if they proceed from natural powers, they are only a manifestation of natural life. To be acts of supernatural life, they must be sustained by the basic supernatural movements.

Undoubtedly the moral relationships which these moral acts imply are only materially the same in the natural and the supernatural orders; such are, for instance, the relation of subjection to God, the relation of parity and equal rights with our fellow men, the relation of the spirit's dominion over the flesh and its concupiscences; formally they differ in their foundation. Subjection to God can be that of a menial to his master or that of a child to its father. Parity and equal rights in respect to our neighbor can exist between two rational creatures that are natural images of God, or between two images of God that have been supernaturally elevated; between two citizens of God's earthly kingdom, or two citizens of the heavenly kingdom—fellow citizens of the saints and members of God's household, as St. Paul calls them (Eph. 2:19). Briefly, our moral relationships, as we know them by the light of reason and by the light of faith, are distinct, not only materially and subjectively, that is, with regard to our knowledge of them, but also formally and objectively, in their very nature.

But once the supernatural relationships are known, they can, by reflection, be made the object of a natural act proceeding from our natural powers. Such an act, however, will not fully measure up to the supernatural relationships or correspond to them. It will not be the sort of act it ought to be (*sicut oportet,* Rom. 1:26); it is such only if it proceeds from the power and inner movement of supernature, and hence is a manifestation of the interior life of supernature, which is the foundation of these relations. But the acts of supernatural knowledge, love, and hope which, as we said above, underlie supernatural moral acts, and not only imply a supernatural relation but involve a union with a supernatural object, cannot be performed by nature at all, to say nothing of being performed *sicut oportet.* These are really the acts to which and by which nature is elevated; hence they are the acts in which the true character of the supernatural life is chiefly revealed.

These acts, too, have their counterparts in the natural order, and the counterparts bear the same names; but the analogy between them is very weak. Even though the natural acts unite us materially with the same object, God, the union is so different in kind that, in comparison with supernatural union, it is more like a separation than a union. Accordingly the distinction between these two orders of acts is not merely accidental; it is specific and substantial. It is a distinction like that which exists between the acts of two different natures, or of two different levels in one nature (as between sensory and spiritual activity in man), and must therefore have two different natures or quasi-natures as its foundation.

We can now appreciate the importance of the definition of supernature in the strict sense, which we have so insisted upon. On the one hand, it is certain that those theologians who, like Scotus, renounced that definition, also gave up the specific difference between supernatural and natural acts, and substituted an accidental difference for it. They thus exposed themselves to considerable embarrassment; they could neither state exactly what this accidental difference consisted in, nor justify in a scientific and satisfactory way the teaching of the Church about the absolute supernaturalness of those acts. On the other hand, if we employ that definition, we perceive at once how beautifully and logically the supernatural character of those acts can be explained, and how neatly the teaching of the Church can be scientifically formulated.

The acts which chiefly come into consideration here are those of the knowledge and love of God; and we can add peace or confidence in the consciousness of our power to possess and rejoice in Him by our knowledge and love, either by clinging to Him if we possess Him, or by attaining and reaching Him if we do not yet possess Him. This latter is hope.[4] These are the three acts of the soul's innermost life. They are acts by which we possess and enjoy God (and

---

[4] Some aspects that may seem obscure in the general theory of these acts will become clearer when we come to treat of them individually.

in which, consequently, perfect as well as imperfect beatitude consists); they are acts by which we are united with God, and which, therefore, as we said above, are the foundation of the true moral life that is a manifestation of them.

Nature, too, has a power and an inclination for the knowledge and love of God, by which it can securely pursue and adhere to its end, if only the will consents. But this power and inclination are not virtues, because they can be present even though the will does not heed them as the principle and norm of its activity, and hence even though the person possessing them is not simply and absolutely good. Further, natural knowledge and love are indeed referred to God, but within the limits of nature and according to the measure of the union which created nature can of itself have with its Creator. God is recognized merely as the author and cause of created nature; only as such is He known and loved, only as such is He the source of our confidence. God is the object of knowledge and love; but this knowledge and love are neither immediate nor absolute.

The knowledge is not immediate, because the creature knows God only as Creator; it knows Him in and through His creatures. And the knowledge is not absolute, that is, the highest kind of knowledge possible, by which the essence of God is known in itself, even though it is not fully comprehended. For the light of reason, on which it depends, is the creature's own and enlightens only the creature, that is, the soul itself to which the light belongs (when the soul is not shackled and imprisoned by the bonds of matter) or its sensible environment (when it is immersed in material conditions). But that light cannot illuminate God as He is in Himself, for it is not a divine light, and God can be revealed as He is only in His own light.

Similarly, the love of God which is natural is not imme-

diately within us, because nature directs its love first of all
toward itself; it reaches up to God, not because He is of
like nature with us, but because He, abiding in His higher
nature, is the cause of our nature. And the confident hope
of attaining or retaining possession of God by natural
knowledge and love is likewise based primarily on the
power and tendency of nature, and is referred to God only
so far as He is the external prop and support of our natural
strength.

By nature, therefore, we can know God through our natural light, love Him with our natural affection, and trust
in Him as the support and guide of our natural powers. But
we do not know Him immediately, because we are not
transformed by Him and so do not know Him by His own
light; we are not directly united to Him by love, because
we are not closely akin to Him; our confidence is not an-
chored in the full power of His divine might that surpasses
all creation, because we are not able, by nature, to possess
Him as He is in Himself.

Briefly, since we have our own nature and not His, we
live immediately in ourselves and not in Him. We can direct
our lives toward God; but no creature's interior life has
God Himself for its immediate object, because the creature
is not divine. Everything in our lives centers on God, but
He is not the deepest root of life and its proximate object
that characterizes its activity. Every nature concentrates
primarily and immediately on itself, moving within its own
circle, the creature within the created sphere, God within
the divine sphere. Yet the created sphere, which is dependent, must attach itself to the higher sphere; and the
higher, because of its superiority, must dominate the lower;
but the lower does not share in the higher except to the

extent that it is the mirror of the higher, reflects the higher, is subject to it, and is rooted in it.

But if we have truly been made partakers of the divine nature and have become closely akin to it by the fact that our supernature raises us up to it, we have been taken into the ambit of its life; then God immediately and in His own nature, as He is in Himself, becomes the object of our activity. Then, illuminated by His light, we shall know Him by coming into His presence; we shall no longer be limited to seeing Him as He is mirrored in creation. Permeated by God's fire and elevated to kinship with Him, we shall embrace Him directly with our love; for we shall love Him as God who communicates His nature to us, not merely as the Creator of our nature. Our confidence will be directed exclusively to God Himself as He is in His own divine might which transcends all creation, that might by which He leads us toward an end that no created power can attain or hinder, by which He wills to bring us to the possession of Him in His divine glory; and thus we shall repose on the heart of our Father. In a word, if we are made partakers of the divine nature, our lives and our activity must be specifically similar to God's. Therefore our activity must have the same specific, formal object that characterizes the divine activity. The divine essence must be the immediate object and motive determining supernatural activity in our own lives.

As the supernatural power given to us is not dependent on created nature, its activity is not restricted to created nature; the latter does not have to be its proximate and formal object. Rather, since supernatural power comes down to us from God, it leads directly back to God. Because supernatural activity moves wholly toward God, it has a specifically divine quality; it resembles God's own activity, which excels all created activity. And that is why the three supernatural powers by which we share in the divine life are called divine powers or theological virtues. Virtue is really nothing else than a vigorous, perfected power tending securely and steadfastly toward its objective; the Latin *virtus* is a *perfecta vis*. These virtues are not called divine because they refer to God in a general way or are opposed to all other virtues that refer to other objects, such as the cardinal virtues, although this aspect is not excluded. They are thus called, primarily, because they refer to God in a divine manner, that is, they unite us immediately with God as He is in His own exalted nature; the divinity itself, as divinity, is their object.

The specific character of supernatural activity is therefore best defined by the fact that it does not, like natural activity, proceed from nature, and hence does not refer directly to nature, so as through nature to mount up to that Being on whom nature itself is dependent. Rather, supernatural activity proceeds from God immediately, not through a created medium, and therefore leads back to God immediately, not through a created medium; [5] it unites us with God in His very divinity.

To understand this, we must consider the activity of supernature as it is found in its pure and absolute perfection and reflects the divine life perfectly, in the state of heavenly beatitude. Supernature, as the image of God's infinitely spiritual, intellectual nature, realizes its full po-

---

[5] This is clear in the case of knowledge, for by nature we know God through creatures as through a mirror. But in the case of love, misunderstandings can arise. The sense is not that we have no natural power of loving God for His own sake, but only that we are united with God in this love through nature, that is, through the relationship we have with Him by our nature which is specifically distinct from His nature.

tentialities in heaven. The close relationship with God into which we enter appears in all its greatness. The soul, illuminated by God's own light, becomes "light in the Lord" (Eph. 5:8), and God's essence becomes so intimately present that the soul beholds that essence in itself; the divine essence is not merely the object confronting the soul, but shines forth in the soul as the principle determining its knowledge. Through this relationship the soul, pervaded with divine fire as with a sort of magnetic force, is drawn toward God by His own beauty, goodness, and sweetness, and is wholly immersed in the ocean of divine happiness. The soul perceives that God has employed His divine power that so vastly surpasses all power of creatures to communicate Himself to it and to maintain and assure for it the possession of the infinite good itself. And thus the soul reposes in God's heart and enjoys therein the certainty of its eternal life.

In heaven the essence of God that towers infinitely above all other natures, in respect of which it is supernatural, is clearly the source and object, the formal object that proximately and immediately determines the creature's act. It is the source from which power flows, the object to which power returns; the divine essence, which is present without any medium, becomes the motive of knowledge, love, and confidence. Consequently an activity that is quite parallel and similar to the divine activity is exercised by the creature.

All this is best perceived in the act of knowledge, that immediate vision of God without mirror or darkness, by which "I shall know even as I am known" [I Cor. 13:12]. In this vision the intimate presence in which God comes close to us by the communication of His nature is most clearly grasped, and through it our union with God by love receives its characteristic stamp. The beatific vision is the cardinal point of supernatural activity, the proper occupation, the crown and flower of supernature, and the true inheritance of the children begotten of God according to His image, because it brings their divine life to its final consummation. It is the substance of beatitude, the most characteristic feature of divinity, and consequently the highest good attainable by the creature, who receives it by the grace and favor of God, but cannot reach it by the efforts of nature. It is supernatural activity par excellence; and pantheistic heretics show their true colors by the fact that they ascribe the beatific vision to nature.

The perfect activity of supernature in the state of beatitude is therefore the faithful image of the divine activity and has the same motive as the latter, namely, the divine essence that reveals itself clearly and immediately to knowledge, draws love directly to itself, and presents itself unreservedly for possession.

But as long as the soul has not yet advanced to the perfect possession of God and full union with Him, as long as it has not received all the power it needs to reproduce the activity of the divine nature, it must, in striving for this happy consummation, find support and help in God's own activity. Responsive to God's guiding hand, it must grow in perfection and be transformed into the divine image.

During our pilgrimage on earth, the divine essence is not present to us in all its glory, and hence is not the motive determining our knowledge and trust. The chief motive for the activity of supernature is rather God's own activity. As long as our supernatural light does not reach far enough to disclose God's essence clearly, it cannot know God immediately unless it attaches itself to the knowledge God has of Himself and clings to it by faith, through which

God's knowledge proposes and imparts to us the object of future vision, thus introducing and foreshadowing the vision itself. We are not yet fully able to experience the joyful consciousness of securely possessing the divine nature or of being predestined to it, because our nature has not yet completely entered into the possession of the divine nature and is not thoroughly transfigured by it. Therefore we must still count on God's mighty power and activity to lead us to the full possession of Him and establish us in it. Thus we pin our hope on God's powerful action, which consequently becomes the direct motive of our confidence and peace. During the interval, while our own supernatural activity is imperfect and potential, it is supplemented, so to speak, by God's activity, and can develop only in direct correspondence with it.

The essential perfection of love alone is independent of the imperfect state of supernature, because it is independent of the presence or absence of the beloved object. It is based on the intrinsic goodness of the object, and is dependent only on the relationship which the lover has with it. We already have this kind of actual relationship with God by supernature. We are truly His children; we have the dignity and rights of children, and enjoy the Father's full love. Charity during our present life and charity in heaven are substantially the same,[6] and have the same motive. The

[6] This remark, that love in this life is substantially the same as love in heaven, and consequently that love even now implies a full participation in the divine nature, helps to explain the existence of a sort of supernatural vision of God in mysticism, a phenomenon about which the mystics have so much to say. In this love, the most perfect image of God, we behold Him who has revealed to us that His nature is love. "God is charity" [I John 4:16]. St. Augustine says in the eighth book of his *De Trinitate* that if we behold the charity by which we love God and our fellow men, we behold God. [Augustine's actual words: "Vides Trinitatem, si caritatem vides"—*De Trin.*, VIII, c. 8, no. 12]. This is the vision of God which pure souls have; they see as much as is compatible with man's

only difference is that, as our sonship is not yet manifested in all its splendor, our love does not yet appear in all its tenderness and intimacy, and does not produce that perfect, interior, and uninterrupted union with God which will issue from it when we, reposing in the Father's heart and beholding Him face to face, shall joyfully savor His goodness and beauty. Therefore charity during our present life and charity in heaven differ only in their condition. Their motive is the same, but has a different effect; in heaven it brings about a perfect union, on earth it draws us to this union by our yearning for it.

That is why the Apostle says that charity (as charity) remains, and will not be taken away but only perfected, whereas faith and hope will cease [Cf. I Cor. 13:8–13]. For these two virtues are not only accompanied by imperfection; they imply imperfection in their very substance, because they are something imperfect that was designed to substitute temporarily for what is perfect; their motive is not the divine essence itself but a divine activity that influences us. Thus we have an essentially perfect supernatural activity which well imitates God's activity and has the same motive, and an imperfect supernatural activity which depends on God's activity, is sustained by it, and has it as its motive.

We wish next to consider the supernatural faculties and acts individually, especially the imperfect ones. They all have definite features which manifest their supernatural and divine qualities.

---

present state ("Tantum cognoscis quantum es," says Hugh of St. Victor). It is experimental knowledge which savors God as He is in Himself and which gives a foretaste of what God has prepared for them who love Him, of what cannot naturally enter into the heart of any man.

Chapter XI

FAITH

Nothing more sublime or profound can be said about faith than that it is a preparation and anticipation of the beatific vision. The supernatural character of faith is brought out by comparing it with the vision of God: as we are perfectly raised up to God's own knowledge by the beatific vision, we are imperfectly raised up to the same knowledge by faith. Faith enables us to know God in His own light that is inaccessible to nature. If we grasp this truth we can well explain, understand, and defend the sublimity and depth of the firm teaching of Sacred Scripture, the Fathers, and the Church, that faith is like a new creation built on the foundation of the old; it is like a marvelous light shining in the darkness; it is one of the noblest gifts of God, lying completely beyond the reach of nature.

Ordinarily this teaching is not well understood. This is owing in part to rationalist views, in part to the lack of a sharp distinction and analysis of the words and ideas by which the doctrine is conveyed. The Latin *fides* is connected with *fidere*, to trust, count on, rely on something. It can signify, in general, tranquil certainty with regard to knowledge and, in particular, tranquil certainty about knowledge which is the basis of other knowledge that rests on it and is deduced from it; I mean knowledge of truths that are certain by immediate vision rather than by reasoning. But in its proper and usual sense it signifies the untroubled certainty which a mind attains when it relies on the knowledge of another mind, depends on it, entrusts itself to it (*ei se credit*), and so, in a sense, supplements and replaces its own light by another's light. This can occur in two ways. Either the light of the one possessing vision can never pass over to the other, because the latter is not capable of the vision or is not destined for it; or, as is more usual, one person entrusts himself to another (as to a teacher in a school) to be led by him to his own knowledge. In the latter case the learner begins by depending on the teacher's knowledge and receives truth from him for the sole reason that the teacher declares it is so; but the learner's aim is to be gradually prepared and made capable of receiving the teacher's knowledge in order eventually to know as he knows.

Understood in this latter sense, faith, by which we believe God and give ourselves to Him believingly in order to join our knowledge with His, to adhere to it, and thereby to share in it fully at some future time, is a theological and absolutely supernatural virtue.

But we must guard against confusing the act of this virtue with other acts that have an illusory similarity with it. St. James speaks of a faith which even devils have, though it fills them with dread [Cf. Jas. 2:19]. This is certainly not a supernatural faith, for no trace of any supernatural gift remains in the damned.[1] It is not even a faith that would be an ethically good act in the natural order. We may apply the term "faith" to a cognitive act that is based on the

---

[1] I mean here the supernatural as sanctifying, by which we share in the divine life, not the supernatural as essential, such as the sacramental character, which is but a sign of supernatural deputation to the service of God.

knowledge of another person to the extent that it serves as the premise of a reasoning process, even though it does not involve any real adherence or union between the two minds. Thus faith is the name we give to the certitude we acquire when, for example, many men so agree in their witness of a fact that it cannot be false. We regard their evidence as a sure and incontrovertible proof of the fact, although we are not influenced by esteem for the witnesses and although we do not enter into their views or take them as our teachers. We employ the conviction of these men as an a posteriori argument for the fact, in the way we regard the rays of the sun as evidence of its rising.

If devils, and men too, for that matter, in the presence of unmistakable signs of the fact of revelation and also in consequence of their own reasoning, acknowledge God's veracity and so are compelled by their reason to admit the revealed truth as truth, we may say that they have faith in a wide sense. Yet their acquiescence is not faith in the strict sense, because such assent to the truth does not include consent to God who speaks to us. Faith is no mere assent; it is essentially consent, and is assent to the truth only so far as such assent leads to consent with the mind that declares it. Faith is not agreement to a truth because the truth is manifest to our knowledge in its motive, or in itself, or in its consequences and effects (and another mind's conviction may be regarded as such); it is agreement to a truth to which we dispose ourselves in order to conform ourselves to another intellect. As such it is essentially an act evoked in the intellect by the will for this purpose, an act which presupposes a more or less perfect knowledge of the speaker's veracity and the fact of revelation, but differs from such considerations as heaven from earth.

I will go even farther. We cannot deny that after nature, by its own intellectual power, has acknowledged God's truthfulness and the fact of revelation, it can decide, and according to natural law must decide, to conform and adhere to God's judgment, and thus to move reason to assent and subjection. In this sense I maintain that nature is capable of an act of faith to which the philosophical notion of faith corresponds perfectly. Truly, no one can deny this; and if the Semipelagians had asserted no more than this and had given a sufficiently clear account of their teaching, they would certainly not have been condemned by the orthodox Fathers and by the Church. The Church has declared that saving faith, the faith which is the door to the everlasting vision of God, *sicut oportet ad vitam aeternam*, the faith which is divine in the full, proper sense, is supernatural; but faith as we have been describing it is a purely human act that can proceed from human nature, and hence does not pass or exalt itself beyond human limits. It is a subjection, an act of homage which the creature offers to the Creator; but it is not a union or a close, interior adherence of human knowledge to divine knowledge, such as would place the creature in direct contact with divine knowledge or would so introduce the creature into this knowledge as to illuminate it with divine clarity. It is a consent whose intrinsic value is measured by the determining principles of nature and, like nature as left to its own devices, does not share in the infallibility of its motive, the divine truth. God's infallible truth is the motive or rather the goal of this act only to the extent that it is the naturally known cause and object of the creature's homage. Therefore it is only a moral motive, in the sense that it is the object of due reverence which our acknowledgment of God's pre-eminence requires of us. But it is not, I should say, a physical motive that moves us and draws us to itself to unite us with itself.[2]

The divine truth, in this case, does not attract the creature by its own light and power so as to impart its excellence to the creature. In human faith we do not come close to God, we do not mount up to Him; we merely acknowledge the excellence which God's knowledge has as compared with ours. By supernatural, divine faith, on the contrary, we are raised up to God's eminence and share in it. By human faith we hear only the voice of our Master; by divine faith we, as God's friends, are ushered into the light of our Lord. In this faith the light of the Godhead rises before us like the dawn; the glow it sheds on the soul is still no more than a faint, subdued glimmer, but it is of the same kind as the eternal brilliance of the ascending Sun.

Supernatural faith is as much a participation in the divine light as the immediate vision of God, except that as yet it is only a dull, feeble gleam that has to await the future before it bursts into full radiance. Therefore it must be a consent freely offered to the divine knowledge, which is its direct and exclusive motive; it must adhere closely to this motive, receive its full power, and be raised to its high level. This is something that lies forever beyond nature's grasp; nature can never adhere immediately to the divine knowledge as such, unite with it, or take on its divine attributes. We are mysteriously drawn to divine knowledge by the Father, who summons us from darkness to His marvelous light and opens up the ears of our hearts. The witness of God's revelation reaching us from outside is not enough; an interior revelation of the Father and an illumi-

---

[2] A motive is the determining cause of movement; a moral motive, by the esteem it inspires, determines a moral act as a tribute that is due.

nation of the Holy Spirit must be added by that light which we call the infused light of faith. A mystical act must be performed; and this act is performed easily under the guidance of the Holy Spirit, although its nature is hard to describe, because it causes such a dazzling light to rise in our souls.

In faith we are made acquainted, by anticipation, with God's knowledge, which is to become ours in the beatific vision. As the beatific vision is caused, not by our light but by God's light, so the knowledge which we receive at present and which is an introduction and preparation leading to that future knowledge, cannot be the product of our own light but must be effected by divine light. Even the truths we learn now elevate us above our nature, for our Teacher is not content to impart to us a few details of His own knowledge, but wishes to raise us up to the eminence of His own wisdom. Therefore His knowledge must be brought close to us in all its sublimity, and we must rise up to it, or rather be raised up to it. It must be revealed within us and be made known to us in its own splendor, not in mere external signs.[3] At the same time it must draw souls to itself by its own power, to impart its own peace and infallibility to them. And lastly, it must even now fill the soul with some rays of its light, that the mind may be able to grasp so exalted an object with a light that is akin to the object and on the same plane with it. The light of faith is

[3] This interior revelation, this sort of internal listening to God who speaks within the heart that He Himself has opened up, does not do away with the necessity of external revelation or of the rational conviction of its reality. External revelation is not superfluous, because the ordinary light of faith supposes a correct grasp of it. Conviction about the fact of revelation is not superfluous, because man must make the act of faith freely, and is responsible for the way he discharges his duty in making it; hence he must consciously reflect upon its objective conditions. The supernatural light of faith is not sufficient for this, as it is obscure and mystical, and transcends reflection.

therefore a grace by which God directly makes Himself known in the soul as the One who speaks to it; it is a grace by which God draws the soul to Himself to enable it to repose in Him, and makes His own truth understandable and conceivable with a higher intelligibility. All this resembles the light of glory, which makes God's essence present to the soul, elevates the soul to the vision of God, and empowers the soul to penetrate into the depths of divinity.[4]

The interior union by which we establish contact with divine knowledge in faith, so that our act is charged with the power of its motive, is brought most clearly to our notice by the fact that theological and divine faith is essentially infallible. That is, there can be no act of supernatural faith which is not essentially true, whereas that faith which, as we said, can proceed from nature, is not necessarily true and infallible. We can and must make an act of the latter kind of faith when our reason convinces us that God has revealed something. As reason can err in this judgment, it can wrongly decide in favor of that merely human faith and so can err in the act of faith even when it is morally good. Why? Because, although divine truth and infallibility are to some extent the goal toward which such an act tends, and also motivate the act as morally good, divine truth does not draw us by its own light or unite us with itself. Hence it is not by itself the immediate motive of the act regarded as an act of knowledge.

But when the mind, following not only the judgment of

---

[4] These three factors are signalized in Sacred Scripture as external hearing, internal revelation—the drawing power exerted by the Father—and an interior illumination of the heart. The latter gives rise to a certain kind of revelation by which man is made "spiritual" and is enabled to understand supernatural as well as natural things: "The spiritual man judgeth all things" (I Cor. 2:15), including things that are beyond the comprehension of the sensual man.

reason concerning a tribute to be paid to divine truth, but also the light and guidance of divine truth itself, surrenders to it and unites with it, then unquestionably its act is infallible as is divine truth itself, because then it is really and directly based on divine truth as such.[5] Then, too, the certainty we long for becomes incomparably more elevated and sure, not only because we are infallible in this light and hence cannot err, but because our certitude arises no longer from created light but from divine light and shares in its perfection and purity. The certainty of faith far surpasses the certainty resulting from the external proofs of revelation that are open to reason; more than that, it even transcends, in intrinsic perfection, the certainty of the most evident and primary truths which we know by unaided reason.

This assertion about the intrinsic infallibility and certainty of faith should not be misunderstood, as though the person who has faith cannot err in the truths he believes or cannot doubt about the faith. Such lapses can occur because, as we have pointed out, supernature does not so thoroughly pervade the whole of nature during our present life that nature always operates supernaturally. Nature can still operate by its own powers, and therefore can doubt about the faith itself; furthermore, it can err, in good faith, and hence without ruining divine faith, with regard to the

[5] Cf. Pseudo-Dionysius the Areopagite, *De divinis nominibus*, cap. 7, no. 4 [*PG*, III, 872]: "This word [God's knowledge] is the simple and really existing truth, about which, as the pure and infallible knowledge of all things, divine faith is concerned; it is the unique support of believers, establishing them in truth and truth in them in steadfast identity; for they who have been won to the faith possess a [divinely] simple knowledge of truth." See also St. Maximus Martyr, *Capita theologica*, centur. II, cc. 7–13. We may also consult, with reference to the supernatural order, II, 68–74; IV, 12–20; and I, 1–50 [*PG*, XC, 1224 f., 1245 ff., 1308–13, 1084–1101]. The most beautiful passages will be given later.

truths of faith. But when it errs about the truths of faith the light of faith does not cooperate; and when it doubts about faith, the light of faith is even snuffed out and extinguished.

We also stated above that faith is in accord with the beatific vision as regards the principal object of its knowledge. This is true not only in the sense that both, as always, know the same object (*obiectum materiale commune*), but also in the sense that the aspect under which it is known (*ratio formalis sub qua obiectum cognoscitur*) is the same for both. Faith is an anticipation of the vision of God. Faith, like vision, knows God, not only as mirrored in created nature and as knowable by way of ascent from created things, but as He is in Himself, independently of any connection with created nature as such. Consequently, what is known about God by faith is something supernatural, not for God Himself, but with regard to the manifestation of God in created nature. Later we shall see more in detail that this consists mainly in the interior revelation and disclosure of God in the Trinitarian process. Indeed, faith knows everything natural in a supernatural way; in its own obscure manner, like the beatific vision in its clear fashion, it knows all natural things as they come forth from their supernatural cause and are led back to it, and especially how they enter into supernatural union with it.

All these supernatural objects are, in a sense, made akin to us by the light of faith, somewhat as natural, intelligible things are made akin to us by the light of reason. That is why the light of faith enables us easily to grasp them when they are held before us, although we cannot see them or conceive them as they are in themselves until the light of faith is transfigured and passes into the light of glory.

Accordingly faith is supernatural in its origin from divine

light; it is supernatural in its interior motive, divine truth, to which faith clings in its sublimity and infallibility; it is supernatural in its object; and lastly, it is supernatural in the culmination toward which it strives, and that is nothing else than the beatific vision. Faith is supernatural as vision is supernatural, and hence is divine; it is a participation in the knowledge that is proper to God.

CHAPTER XII

CHARITY

THE supernatural character of Christian love is, in some respects, easily defined. On the one hand, it has supernatural faith as its foundation; on the other hand, to know how it is a participation in divine love, we do not have to recur to its perfect state in heaven, since it is substantially perfect even in this life. We could content ourselves here with the simple statement that supernatural love is the love which is infused into our hearts by the Holy Spirit and which is based on the light and knowledge of faith, as natural love is love which proceeds from nature and follows rational knowledge. This distinction is true and fundamental. But we must penetrate into its depth and meaning; otherwise it may be understood as a purely external distinction, that is, with reference to the knowledge which precedes love, or the description of its genesis. Actually the distinction is interior and radical, and refers to the nature of love itself, by which the relation to knowledge and to its cause must be specified. Therefore those theologians who do not admit that supernature in the strict sense is the basis of charity are unable to produce a satisfactory or searching analysis of the distinction between natural and supernatural love. In the following pages I hope to succeed, at least to some extent, in facilitating this important and interesting analysis.

We have repeated several times that love is a unity of affection, that is, a unity of a subject, by affection or sympathy, either with another subject (that is, a possessing good), or with an object (that is, a good to be possessed). A subject can be at one with another subject, if both wish a good for the same person; or with an object, if a subject wishes to take the object to himself and be united with that object. There is a love for a person for whom one wishes good, and there is a love for a thing which one wishes for some person, because of its substance or a quality in it. The first kind of love is usually called love of friendship (*amor amicitiae*). However, this designation is very inaccurate, for friendship arises from love only when both subjects are fairly alike and are intimately associated. Thus the name of the species is substituted for that of the genus. We have no better name for the latter than love of benevolence (*amor benevolentiae*). The second kind of love may be called love of desire (*amor concupiscentiae*), for it refers to an object (quality, form, or thing) which we desire for ourselves or for other. In this connection we should note that a thing can be desired either as a means leading to the object that is really sought, or as this object itself; and again, that the thing we wish and enjoy can be such that it either loses its own nature and beauty by its union with us, like the food we eat, or, as happens more frequently, that the enjoying and uniting subject does not consume the thing by union with it, but takes on its beauty and qualities.[1]

This is the chaste desire, *concupiscentia casta*, so often spoken of by St. Augustine; it is the desire which the soul

---

[1] St. Augustine, *Confessions*, VII, 10, represents the Son of God as saying: "You shall eat Me; yet you will not change Me into yourself as when you eat bodily food, but you will be changed into Me."

has when it rejoices in God as its Food and its Bridegroom. It is chaste because it is free from all corruption, and also because the person who delights in God does not lose his own beauty in his happiness, and does not sacrifice the goodness and beauty of the object to his own enjoyment.

The two kinds of love we have distinguished depend on a certain identity, harmony, kinship with the beloved object. As regards the first kind, love can motivate us to wish good for another as for ourselves only to the extent that we look upon that other as one with us or ourselves as one with him; and well-ordered natural love can regard two persons as one only if they really are one in some way. Thus we naturally love and ought to love all men as our neighbors because they are all one with us in nature. And we love especially those to whom we are closely bound in one state, one nation, one family, and above all those who are associated with us in a like capacity and a like vocation to a single common good. That is, when we possess a common good or have to strive for it, we wish that good for others as well as for ourselves; and our love is specified and involves a different unity of affection according as the objective union in the good or the fellowship varies. But we are one in a different way, for example, with our parents. We are not only one with them in a third thing, our nature, to which we pertain along with them in coordinate fashion; we are one with them as belonging to them and subordinate to them. We love them as our cause; in addition to having a capacity and destiny for good in common with them, we receive from them our very nature, the foundation of such capacity and destiny.

In general, therefore, love for another is dependent on the connection or fellowship by which we are associated with him with regard to the good. We are one with him either in a like capacity and tendency for a definite good, or, what is more important, we are so much at one with him that we receive this disposition from him and so belong to him. In the first case our love is simply a love of mutual fellowship; in the second case it is a love of full surrender to the beloved object, based on the fact that one person belongs to another. The difference in love is dependent on the difference of the connection betwen the persons who love. Thus the love of a servant for a master is radically different from the love of a child for a father, not because a good servant fails to desire good for the master for the latter's sake, but because this desire rests on a different ontological union and hence on a different affective union with the person of the master. The degree of closeness and intimacy of this affective union is proportionate to the degree of closeness and intimacy of the ontological union.

Accordingly we have a twofold love for God on account of our twofold relationship with Him, our twofold union, kinship, and fellowship with Him. We share in divine goodness, first, by nature, as God's rational creatures to whom He has given existence, life, and intelligence. In this respect we love God as our Creator and Lord, rather than as our Father, because we are not one with Him in His nature and consequently in His riches, as the child is one with its father. Our kinship with Him is so remote that it does not invest us with the sublime dignity of His children. We are one with Him only in the more general, not in the special prerogatives of His nature, and hence have no aptitude and claim to be one with Him in the happiness proper to His nature. By the gift of supernature, however, we receive a share in His nature and thus are called to His own beatitude. We are made one with Him in the basis for possession, and therefore in the possession of the good itself, as a child is one with its father, in dignity and heritage; we become one with Him in closest unity, like that existing between the only-begotten Son and His Father. When, consequently, in union with the only-begotten Son, we love God as our Father and not merely as our Creator who is remote from us, our unity of love with God must be incomparably more intimate, excellent, and noble.

This love is called love of friendship, not because it wishes good for God in a general way [2] (this is within the powers of natural, servile love), but because we love God as our Friend who has, in a sense, made us like to Him. He has admitted us to participation in His nature and has called us to His beatitude; He has united us closely with Himself, with a union like that of friends who love each other.

This is the love by which we love God as the Author of our supernatural beatitude, in the language that has become classical in the Church since the days of St. Thomas. The point is not that we love God on account of the supernatural happiness He bestows on us, but that God, by destining us to His life and beatitude, and, with a view to that destiny, by communicating His nature to us in the gift of supernature, becomes our Father and so is most intimately united to us.

This is the love with which we love God by the knowledge of faith. Faith, as a new way of knowing, is more than a simple principle enabling us to love in a different way; divine faith, in the sense explained above, supplies us with a specifically higher knowledge than is available to us by reason, and therefore brings the divine goodness itself

---

[2] That is, with a love of benevolence; benevolence is, indeed, a kindly disposition toward someone, but it is not necessarily a friendly disposition. The latter implies great intimacy and the confidence of mutual relationship.

close to us in a way that surpasses the power of natural knowledge, that is, in its sublime perfection to which we are made akin by our supernature.

This is the love with which we love God as He is in Himself. Nature, too, can love God for His own sake and because of the good He has in Himself, otherwise than Vasquez thought. But the love we are speaking of loves God in His own goodness as it exists apart from all relationship with created natures as such and independently of them.

Briefly, this is a love by which we are joined in affection with the goodness of God, not according to that unity and union we naturally have with the highest cause of nature, but according to that unity and union which we have with God in the supernatural state by our participation in the divine nature. This is a union that makes us nobly-born children and friends of God and joins us to God's essence.

In a similar way the love of desire by which we love God for our own sake with chaste affection, that is, by which we desire to possess God as the object of our beatitude and the ideal of our perfection, into whose image we long to be transfigured, is a twofold love, natural and supernatural. For if we are united in two ways with God as the principle of our twofold existence, we can also be united in two ways with Him as the object of our beatitude, the goal of our activity, and the ideal of our perfection. We can take God to ourselves and possess Him by a twofold knowledge and consequently in a twofold likeness: by the knowledge which proceeds from nature and beholds God as in a mirror, and by that other knowledge which is suitable to supernature and reflects God in the soul according to His own essence. But the power to possess and enjoy an object as our good determines our kinship with it, that is, our relationship and tendency to it and its suitableness for us. Thus the raw materials of vegetation are related to us by our vegetative powers, the objects of the various senses by our animal powers, and intelligible objects by our reason. Along with those powers, therefore, there are found in nature a tendency corresponding to them and a natural love for appropriate objects; such tendency and love vary necessarily according as the powers pertain to a particular level in our nature.

Thus there is in us a double love of desire for God, corresponding to our two kinds of union with God: one which nature has and by which it strives to know and possess God by its own powers, so far as it can; and another, rooted in supernature, by which the supernaturalized being strives to know God as He is in Himself, with a knowledge that, of itself, befits the divine nature alone.

Before developing these remarks I wish to observe that, with regard to God, in the natural as well as in the supernatural order, love of desire and love of benevolence are not as far apart from each other as they are when referring to other objects, the analogy of which can lead us astray. In fact, to a certain extent they coincide because of their purity. One does not exclude the other; on the contrary, one includes the other, or at any rate leads to the other. In the first place, love of desire in the present context does not draw and unite its object to itself in such a way that the object is consumed in the process of enjoyment or is subordinated to the possessor. Rather we long to be united to God that we may receive His likeness into ourselves and be transformed into it. By this love, therefore, we do not draw God down to ourselves but are drawn up to Him. If this love is such as it ought to be, it is a chaste desire, which does no violence to God's pure and eminent goodness, but is based on it.[3] This desire, by which we long for God as our end with which we are to be united, as the good and object which we are to attain, is closely bound up with the love of abandonment which we offer to God as our first cause. For God is the end, ideal, and object with which we are to be united, because He is the principle of a nature or quasi-nature in us that is similar to His own, and therefore, like His own nature, is to have Him Himself as the object of its activity. Our activity is guided back to God as its end because the power to act comes from Him.

The goodness of God's nature presents us with a nature that is capable of good, a nature that is like His, makes us akin to Him, and enables us to love Him because we belong to Him as our principle. God's goodness also becomes the object and ideal of the perfect activity by which the goodness of our own nature is perfected; for God's goodness belongs to us and we love it as the object of our possession and the goal to be reached by our growth in perfection. The two aspects are manifestly so closely connected that in all reality they quite coincide. For God is the principle and cause both of our nature and of our activity; consequently we possess Him by belonging to Him in virtue of a special title. Again, we belong to God by the fact that He communicates to us a nature like His, so that we share in His nature in our way or in His way; but this means that we are also able to possess Him that He may belong to us. Therefore perfect love is a *unitas affectus* with God,

[3] Here we may apply a beautiful illustration suggested by Dionysius, *De divinis nominibus*, cap. 3 [*PG*, III, 679]. If a golden rope were let down to us from the sun and we tried to pull it toward us, we would not draw the sun down to us but would be drawn up to it. In the same way, when a sailor on a ship pulls on a hawser fastened to a dock, he does not move the land to the ship but moves the ship to the land.

a union of affection by which we cling to Him in such a way that at the same time He possesses us and we possess Him. If we truly love God as the one to whom we belong, we must necessarily desire to belong to Him completely, by uniting ourselves with Him as the object and ideal of our activity; and if we truly wish to possess God, we necessarily desire to belong to Him. At bottom, therefore, pure and perfect love is a single basic movement, a tendency toward God's goodness, by which the divine goodness is united to us and we are united to it.

To resume the thread of our discourse: we often say that pure love loves a thing for its own sake and not for the sake of something else. And we conclude from this that there cannot be two loves of God that differ essentially and in their motive, since God's goodness is but one. Truly, pure love loves the good for its own sake, that is, the good regarded as the possessing subject, when it wishes the good (regarded as quality and possession) not for the sake of someone else but for the subject's own sake, because the latter takes pleasure therein. And it loves the good regarded as the object to be possessed when it takes pleasure in the object's intrinsic beauty, and hence does not love the object merely as a means for the attainment of other ends, and does not sacrifice its goodness to the enjoyment found in consuming it. At the same time I should like to remark that benevolence is not properly love itself; it issues from love, it presupposes love as affective union.

The intrinsic goodness of the beloved object is the motive, not absolutely, but because it has some relation with the lover, with whom it is one or with whom it is to become one.

Yet love may be called the pleasure which the thinking spirit takes in the beauty, the order, and the good found in all the domains open to his universal observation. In the narrower sense love, which aims at real union with the beloved object, is the pleasure we take in the goodness of an object with which we are united or are to be united, that is, whose goodness is related to our own, either as the goodness of a subject or nature with which ours is related and connected, or the goodness of an object that is proportionate to the powers of our nature.

Therefore we love God's goodness with spiritual love in two ways, because it is related to our spirit in two ways, by reason of the spirit's own nature and by reason of the participation in the divine nature which is given to it as supernature. Through our own nature, God is related to us as the supreme, intelligent nature that has brought our nature into existence according to His likeness, and as the supreme intelligible object to which all other created and natural objects may be referred. By our supernature, however, God is far more intimately related to us, both as nature, because we, made sharers in His nature, have in a sense one nature with Him, and as object, because the light which we receive by our participation in the divine nature has its proper, proportionate object in the divine essence that we are to behold without any interposing medium.

However, the goodness of the thing itself, not its kinship with us, is really the motive of love. The goodness is what exercises a power of attraction, although it can be effective only with regard to beings that have a kinship with it and to the extent that they have such kinship. The good by which we are related to God, for example, the nature we receive from Him, is much less a motive of pure and perfect love for Him. When we love God on account of the nature received from Him, our nature is not a more powerful motive of love than it is when we love our neighbor because he has the same nature as we. When, therefore, it is said that natural love loves God as the source and end of natural goodness, whereas supernatural love loves Him as the source and end of our supernatural goodness, the good proceeding from Him and referring back to Him is not presupposed as the motive of love of Him. The meaning is merely that the one divine goodness is the motive of love in two ways; it motivates love on the basis of a twofold unity of our soul with it (by nature and by supernature), and in order to bring about a twofold unity with it (by natural and supernatural knowledge).

Here a difficulty appears to arise, like that which confronted us when we were discussing the supernatural character of faith. Our natural, intellectual knowledge and our will can, by reason of their universality, range over all the orders found in the scale of being. Rational knowledge can also reach beyond the domain of sense which is subject to it. Indeed, we have seen that, when it is supplied with external aids, it can rise even to the supernatural and the revealed. Similarly the will, the spiritual appetite, can extend over the domain of sense and can love and wish things that in themselves pertain to sense love and desire. Why should the natural will not be able to reach out for the supernatural, so as to love God as the principle and end of the supernatural order? And if it can, what becomes of the essentially supernatural quality of charity, even if the necessity of a supernatural motive is granted?

This difficulty gnaws at the very root of the matter. We may start out with the first point brought up. The will can love sensible good, which properly pertains to the sense appetite. But does the will love such a good in the same way as sense appetite does? Does the will strive for the sensible good by natural impulse in the way sense appetite does? Is it the will which, somewhat like the polarized end of a needle, is attracted by the related good? Is it the will that unites with such a good, enjoys it, tastes its sweetness, and is satisfied? Is it also the will that experiences the peculiar pain which arises when a suitable good is withdrawn from an appetite seeking it?

Every degree in the scale of nature has its corresponding good, and the universal good (God) is communicated to each according to the capacity of each. Every grade of being tends toward its own particular good, and each in its own way also strives for the universal good. In purely material things this tendency is lifeless, as they themselves are. In plants it is alive, and aims at their development. In animals it is guided by sense knowledge and is connected with sensation; but it is always directed toward the material things akin to them. In spiritual natures it is guided by intellectual knowledge and is directed toward appropriate spiritual things. In God, finally it is supremely spiritual, pure, and perfect, but finds its end and repose in God Himself.

On the various levels of nature, among the individuals of each nature and between the nature itself and its proper good, there is a special kind of attraction, a kind of magnetism, that is based on a special relationship. If the various grades of nature are combined in a being, as they are in man, its highest and most universal tendency (the spiritual), can extend in some measure over all of them. But its love for the good corresponding to the several grades will never equal the tendency corresponding to its own grade, which, drawn by the particular attractive force of the object related to it, unites with that object, relishes it, enjoys it, and comes to rest in it.

The will ranges over the domain of other appetitive

faculties, without descending to them or being moved by the motives proper to their own attractive force. When man is elevated to supernatural kinship with God, his natural will could love God with reference to such kinship [4] without rising to the supernatural tendency corresponding to this kinship and without being moved by the motive proper to its attractive force (God considered as the supernatural good). For supernature as such is a sort of special grade in the scale of being and raises man above his natural spirituality as the latter raises him above sense. Through his sense faculties man contracts a different relationship with certain goods and acquires an inclination toward them that is different from his spiritual inclination; in like manner he receives through the gift of supernature a relationship with the divine goodness which he does not possess as a natural spirit, and consequently is drawn by this goodness in a way not possible for nature. God manifests His special, supernatural power of attraction in elevated nature alone. Only elevated nature savors the charm and sweetness of the divine beauty and goodness; it alone is truly united with them, reposes in them, and attains to happiness in them. Although the natural will can reach out for God's supernatural goodness, the divine goodness as such is not the motive attracting the will. The will embraces the divine goodness under the general category of good that in any way may be open to man by reason of the richly

[4] In consequence of the knowledge we acquire of the supernatural beatitude appointed for us in the vision of God, we can desire that beatitude. But it is not an efficacious desire, leading us to this goal and uniting us with it. As Gratry points out, it does not embrace the object and is not engendered in the soul under the effective guidance of the supernaturally knowable and desirable. The same author continues: "Between the two kinds of desire there is a distinction like that between reality and shadow, fullness and emptiness, the positive and the negative." A. Gratry, *Ueber die Erkenntnis Gottes*, II, 103.

complex gradation of his being; but it does not raise him out of himself to union with God's goodness.

Love is that *affectio* (*ad-fectio*) by which we, powerfully drawn by the beloved object, are bound to it as by cement or irresistible magnetism, taste its sweetness, and rejoice in our kinship with it. Yet the Apostle says: "Eye hath not seen nor ear heard, neither hath it entered into the heart of man, what things God hath prepared for them that love Him" (I Cor. 2:9). The sweetness which God bestows on those who love Him, even in the next life, is nothing else than this very love which is poured into our hearts by the Holy Spirit and is, also in the present life, not an earthly or human, but a heavenly and divine happiness. It is the love by which we so cleave to God that we become one with Him.

Since the love issuing from supernature unites us with God as our supernatural goodness, relishes and enjoys His sweetness, and is drawn by His power of attraction, it is the only love which really has God, source and end of supernature, for its motive, as we brought out previously in a similar discussion about faith.

But again a difficulty arises. If we love God with supernatural love as the principle and end of supernature, why are we so often instructed by Sacred Scripture and the Fathers to love God as our Creator? Surely their exhortations do not refer to natural love, for the love they have in mind is meritorious for heaven and is to prepare us for that highest union of love that will be the crown of all our striving in heaven. Indeed, St. Augustine seems to know of no other love for God than that by which we love God as our Creator; in all the passages in which he speaks of the love of God and particularly of the love for which Christ's grace is absolutely necessary, the love he describes is love of the Creator.

As you see, I am not covering up any difficulties, and I dare not, especially as this very objection is usually brought up by those theologians who, while distinguishing supernatural love from natural love, wish to hear nothing of any distinction in the motive; such is the view of Ripalda, Lugo, Platel, and many others. Yet the objection is not hard to answer, if a biased interpretation of our position is avoided and if the question is not forced out of its natural context by excessive hairsplitting. The distinction we propose brings out the fact that there can be a love of the Creator that is quite separable from the genuine love of God as our Father who admits us to supernatural beatitude. Yet the obverse is not true: the second may not be separated from the first. As supernature, regarded concretely as elevated nature, includes nature itself, so supernatural love of God as the Author and goal of supernature, includes love of God as Author of nature. Elevated nature loves God chiefly as the Author and end of all the good which is found in it, which belongs to it, and without which it could not be what it is. Consequently it also loves God as the One who has given to nature the existence on which supernature is constructed. Thus it also loves God as the Creator of nature, not as natural love does, but because God must be our Creator in order to be our Father, and because God gives us nature, not to leave us stranded on the plane of nature, but to make us, while still retaining our nature, His children by the grace of supernature.

Furthermore, supernatural love loves God as Creator if He is thus called, not exclusively because He brings the substance of nature into existence out of nothing, but because God alone has all goodness of Himself, whereas the creature has nothing of itself, and consequently because God is the sole and absolute source of all the good that is found in creation, whether such good pertains to nature or to supernature.

Again, supernatural love can be called a love of the Creator if the term means, not precisely the love which is rightfully due to the Creator as Author of nature, but the love by which the creature can be intimately united with the Creator and be drawn by Him, as in the present order of things we ought to be drawn to Him. For the supernatural quality of love consists in the fact that the creature is to be drawn up to the Creator and to be united with Him, not in servile love, but in friendly, filial, bridal love. But if love for the Creator is so intimate and exalted, it is no longer based on the mere relationship with Him arising from created nature, but is rooted in a higher relationship communicated by God to His creature by special grace. Accordingly love has less the appearance of a duty laid on the creature as such; it is perceived to be a precious gift of grace, which allows the creature to approach closer to the Creator than is permitted by nature.

Therefore supernatural love is, in truth, a love of the Creator; it is a love which unites us with the Creator. But it is more intimate than our mere created relationship to the Creator grants and requires. It is also a love of God the Creator because, as we said above, God the Creator of nature gives to supernature its necessary substructure. In other words, God is here called Creator in the sense that He is the exclusive and total source of all good outside God. Quite simply we can say, finally, that supernatural love loves God as Creator because He brings forth from nothingness supernature in the concrete, that is, the whole of supernaturally elevated nature.

These various aspects sufficiently clarify the expressions used by the Fathers, particularly St. Augustine, especially since he, as we have pointed out elsewhere, hardly ever regards supernature in the abstract in contradistinction to nature, but considers it to be one with nature as originally established by God; it is the only true nature created by God according to His ideal of man. In his controversy with the Manichaeans, to be sure, God as Creator was for Augustine the Author of the created substance as such, and in this context nature, too, meant nothing else for him than created substance. But in his polemic against the Pelagians the Creator meant to him the Author of all good that was found or could ever be found in man. Consequently love of the Creator signified in his mind not merely love for the Author of our natural goodness, but also and especially love for the Author of our best good, supernature. Very often, too, he thinks of love of the Creator in opposition to inordinate love of creatures, and this opposition is even more marked in supernatural than in natural love of God.

After this discussion, no one will any longer be able to raise the objection that, if supernatural love has for its object and motive the divine goodness regarded precisely as supernatural, that is, in its supernatural relationship with us, the love of most Christians would not be truly supernatural, since they seldom or never attend to this motive in its purity and special quality. I have already given the answer. To arrive at this love, we have only to follow the lead of grace, which is a sort of magnetism by which God polarizes and attracts our souls. Grace proposes to us our object of love, draws us to it, and unites us with it. The unction of the Holy Spirit instructs us about all this. The Holy Spirit, the Spirit of the Son who comes into our hearts, He it is who teaches us to cry out with filial love and confidence: "Abba, Father" (Rom. 8:15). He teaches us to sigh and long to behold the Father's countenance and to be transformed into Him. Moreover, by faith we always have a direct, if not reflex knowledge of God's supernatural goodness; for this is what faith holds before us. Faith reveals to us God as our Father who loves us in His only-begotten Son, has adopted us as His children, and wishes to give Himself to us as the immediate object of our possession in the beatific vision. Under this point of view every believing Christian has a direct and sufficient idea of his supernatural relation with the divine goodness to be able to love it in a fittingly proportionate manner. In general, if we follow the lead of grace and love God's goodness as it is really made known to us by faith, we love it in a supernatural way.

But if we also find tinder for the fire of divine love in natural things, our love does not on that account cease to be supernatural. If we marvel at God's love for us in the natural benefits and goods He has lavished on us, this, to be sure, is in itself an incentive to merely natural love. But to the believing eye even such benefits and goods are messages and assurances of the love of God by which He wishes to make us His children. They thus receive a supernatural dedication and lead our love to God as our Father, and not only as our Creator. In the same way, if we consider the beauty and splendor of creatures in order to learn from them the beauty of the Creator and to enkindle love for it in our souls, our love is natural as long as God's beauty is thus known by our natural light or is restricted to that light.

But if we have begun to know God as He is in Himself by faith, and if we use such reflections of His beauty as aids to illuminate the darkness of faith and to discern from afar and even now to represent in our poor way God's infinite beauty and splendor, as brought out by contrast to all these created beauties rather than by similarity with them, the love nourished and inflamed by our contemplation is not natural but supernatural.

For the most part, I repeat, this process does not go on in us in virtue of our own reflection and initiative, but is accomplished by the grace of the Holy Spirit who moves us and works in us. The Savior tells us not to worry about what we are to say, as the Holy Spirit who is in us will teach us (Luke 12:11 f.). In the same way we do not have to evoke love of God within us by reflecting and thinking about the procedures of His love. Of course we ought to meditate about the matter when we have the opportunity and invitation to do so, and our endeavors to kindle this love within us can be highly profitable for us. But the important thing is that grace enlightens our hearts and thus brings the object and motive of love close to us. Many sincere and unsophisticated souls are clearly enlightened about God's lovableness by grace and are permeated by His fire; they are raised up to Him and are united to Him in so indescribable an intimacy that neither they nor anyone else can form an idea of the perfection of this union.

Indeed, supernatural love, like its object, transcends rational concepts precisely because it is supernatural. It involves an intimacy or rather unity with God, a delight, a perfection, a freedom, a confidence, and a strength that natural reason cannot conjecture.

Although the love that can spring from rational nature refers to God who is above nature, it does not transcend nature and reason. It remains within the limits of nature and reason, within the limits of natural relationship to God, and within the limits of natural knowledge of God. Therefore those exquisite hymns of love into which holy souls break forth in the transports of their charity are not within the power of natural love. In its own way such love is, no doubt, a great and priceless good. But it is not the love of which the devout author of the *Following of Christ* (Book III, chap. 5) writes in holy rapture: "Nothing is sweeter than love, nothing stronger, nothing higher, nothing wider, nothing more pleasant, nothing fuller or better in heaven or on earth. For love is born of God and cannot rest but in God, above all created things. . . . Whosoever loveth knoweth the cry of this voice. A loud cry in the ears of God is that ardent affection of the soul which saith: 'O my God, my Love, Thou art all mine and I am all Thine.' "

Natural love is not the love of which the Apostle speaks when he prays that we, being rooted and grounded in love, may be able to comprehend with all the saints what is the breadth and length and height and depth, that is, to gain an idea of the love of Christ which surpasses all knowledge, to the end that we may be filled with all the fullness of God (Eph. 3:18 ff.).

Surely the love that is in nature's power is not the love which, as St. Bernard says,[5] is unmindful of the creature's due reverence and subjection and boldly ventures to mount up to God as Father, Brother, and Bridegroom; which abandons itself to God and plunges into God as God gives Himself to it and sinks into it; which soars above itself to embrace God ardently and tenderly, becomes one with Him, one spirit with Him, and is so closely united to Him that the soul lives of Him and in Him, is completely per-

[5] Serm. 83 on the Canticle of Canticles [PL, CLXXXIII, 1184 ff.].

meated with His divine life, His light, and His warmth, is transformed into God and, we may almost say, dissolves in the depths of His goodness and sweetness.

Doubtless we could maintain, in a certain sense, that fully developed natural love also loves God for His own sake, adheres to Him above all else, reposes in Him alone, is united with Him, becomes one spirit with Him, and experiences a kind of ecstasy by which the lover lives in God and is made conformable to Him. Especially the latter effects, namely, that love unites the lover with the beloved, becomes one with him, and causes the lover to live in the beloved, are marks of every true love. Love is universally a unifying force, as Dionysius says so beautifully,[6] and to some extent always has these effects. In particular, every true love of God must love Him above all things for His own sake and find repose in Him alone.

However, as we have already stated, the unity which love contains and causes is modified and limited by the measure of unity on which love is based. Therefore natural love unites one with God only in the measure of the creature's proximity to the Creator. The creature loves God as his supreme, generous Lord; he clings to God with all his strength; so far as he can, he conforms himself to God by his natural knowledge and by conducting himself according to the divine will; he subjects his will to the will of the highest goodness; he goes out of himself, so to speak, by subjecting himself to God, and enters into God by living and laboring for Him; he loves and reveres God as the highest good surpassing all other beings and goods, and hence above all. But such unity is more a subjection of the lower nature to the higher, it is more a unity of subordination

[6] *De divinis nominibus,* c. 4, 15 [PG, 714].—See also St. Thomas, *Summa theol.,* Ia IIae, q. 28, a. 1.

than a unity of fusion and inner union, which in a sense abolishes subordination and causes a kind of equality between the lover and the beloved by transforming the one who is of lower station.

The Apostle's words, "He who is joined to the Lord is one spirit" (I Cor. 6:17), have a much higher and nobler meaning than the simple fact that our will wishes and rejects what God wishes and rejects. Although two persons may agree in willing and not willing the same thing, they are not on that account one spirit in the full sense of the term. They are one spirit only if the conformity of their wills arises from the trustful intimacy of their union in affection; the term signifies this intimacy of loving union. But such intimacy is gauged by the closeness of the lovers to each other and the union they aim at with each other. That is why the Apostle, in the context preceding the text we have just quoted, uses the illustration of the union between husband and wife, and he does so of set purpose, to bring out our union with God in love. God and the soul, we may almost say, fuse together; God fills the soul with the plenitude of His goodness, and the soul, permeated with divine goodness, is all but transformed into God. God so gives Himself to the soul that He communicates His own nature to it and makes Himself the object of its beatitude. And God gives Himself to the soul unreservedly so that He belongs to it entirely; and the soul, in turn, gives itself unreservedly to God and loses itself in Him. Drawn out of the circle of its natural life, where it had moved about mostly within itself, the soul now belongs to God so completely that it lives immediately of Him, in Him, and for Him.

Here is found the true unity of love; here, too, is found the true unity of the lovers in their close relationship; and here their union is so perfect that each of them appears to be the other. Here we have a true fusion of love, in which the lover is transformed into the likeness of the Beloved. Here we have the true and supreme ecstasy of love, in which the lover, raised above his own nature, takes on the nature of the Beloved, receives from Him a new life that revolves unobstructedly about Him alone, and is more in the Beloved than in himself, is active by His power more than by his own, works more for Him than for himself, and lives for himself only to belong to the Beloved. For nature, even when loving God, according to estimation, more than itself and as being more deserving of love, yet loves itself for its own sake; this is the love that enables it to love God as its cause. Nature itself is the proximate object of love.

But in supernatural love God is not only the highest and noblest, but also the proximate object; in supernatural love the soul loves itself for God's sake, as something belonging to the human person, God's child. This is the love which truly loves God above all things in the Christian sense, that is, which not only esteems God as superior to all creation, with whom no other good can be compared, in the way that even nature can love Him, but which rises to His level, embraces Him ardently with a divine strength surpassing all created force, and clasps Him so closely that no creature can separate it from Him (Rom., chap. 8). This is the love that is not content unless it rests in God; for He is not only the universal good to which all created good must be referred, but is the good which our love must fully possess and enjoy as it is in itself, in all its divine perfection.

Blessed is he to whom it is given to taste the interior sweetness of this love even during the present life. To such a one is revealed a glimpse of the mystical life that is hidden in all Christians who are in the state of grace and divine charity. Yet even to him that life will never be so clearly made known that it will fully dissipate the darkness of faith in its mystery. Nevertheless pure and saintly souls experience their unity with God so keenly that in the holy intoxication of their love they break forth into a language that is unintelligible to the uninitiate, and to the proud and sensual man of nature appears to be folly and nonsense. For the language of love, especially of that love which issues from grace, is folly to the unloving. That is why the writings of the greatest mystics invariably contain passages that sound pantheistic to outsiders. In fact, pantheists have often taken refuge behind the mysteries of mysticism. This does not invalidate the deep significance and truth of mysticism, but rather confirms it. Where truth is absent, no one can appropriate the fair appearance of truth to cover up error.

The supernatural, transfigured love of God has as its counterpart a supernatural, transfigured love of oneself and one's neighbor. This is but a florescence of the love of God; we love our fellow man and ourselves with the same love with which we love God: in God, through God, and for the sake of God.[7] We can, indeed, love rational creatures for God's sake with natural love. Yet all the while our own nature remains closest to us; at any rate we can, by nature, love ourselves and so also our neighbor because he has the same nature as we have. This love, however, is not well-ordered if it is not subordinated to the love of God to whom we and our neighbor belong, and if it is not directed to God Himself and regulated by His law; still, we naturally love first our own good and created good that has a connection

[7] Most theologians teach that the Christian's love of his fellow men is not a virtue distinct from his love of God. The same motive is operative in both; we love our neighbor for the sake of God, for he is a child of God and His supernatural likeness.

with us. By created good (not as motive, but as cause dis-
posing us to love) we rise to the uncreated Good, and then,
descending again, we can love created good because of its
relation with the Creator. But supernatural love, the love
that properly goes with the grace of supernature, immediately and proximately loves the divine nature itself; and
for its sake, in it and through it, loves all those who share
in it and therefore belong to God as His children. We love
ourselves and our neighbor with supernatural love only if
we regard ourselves and him as God's children in actuality
or at least by vocation, as sharing in the divine nature or
as destined to share in it.

Here we have the explanation of that noble, Christian
love of one's fellow men that is inconceivable to the world
and its philosophers. On this basis we discern its essential,
immense difference from even the purest, most sincere
humanitarian love. This is the love that links us all together
as brothers and sisters; the love by which the Christian
beholds in his neighbor not a man or a creature, but something divine that belongs to God; indeed, the Christian
sees God Himself in his neighbor, and treats him as something sacred to be revered with deep respect and holy esteem. It is the love that associates us on a footing of equality
with the highest choirs of angels in one vast, holy society
or family of God, in which the differences of the various
natures level off and vanish in the beauty of the divine
nature that has raised and transformed us as well as them.
This is the love which makes us all one in perfect unity
(John, chap. 17) with one another, as it makes us all perfectly one with God; which makes us all one spirit in our
united love, as we are one spirit with God and one body
with Christ. Because we are all transformed into God, the
one divine nature pervades and energizes all our lives, and

all contrasts existing among the various natures, even among individuals of the same nature, retire into the background. Thus arises that mystical, heavenly kingdom of deep divine peace and unity, where God is all in all, and all creatures love and live in all. That is the peace and unity of all things with God and with one another, which God in His wisdom and love has revealed in their true colors to the humble and the believing, but has hidden from the haughtiness and arrogance of the worldly wise. The latter claim for themselves a natural unity with God, and thereby cut themselves off from God; the former acknowledge the lowliness of their own nature, and are therefore taken up by God into unity with Him by His grace.

We have said enough of the pure perfection of supernatural love. We have also pointed out the distinction between the consummation of this love and our progress toward it (*caritas patriae* and *caritas viae*), and have shown that this distinction is accidental, not substantial. Further clarification might be added to indicate how love can be essentially perfect or imperfect. However, if we wished to bring out adequately the various views concerning this question, we should be carried too far afield. I shall merely recall attention to a point previously made, that even chaste desire (*concupiscentia casta*) is not imperfect but pure and perfect love, and at bottom is necessarily connected with the love of friendship (*caritas amicitiae*).

Love of friendship necessarily longs for union with God and transformation into Him by vision; and chaste desire, by uniting us with God, by longing for transformation into Him through vision, and by thus rejoicing in God's beauty, abandons itself to Him in order to belong to Him and to love Him as Father. For whoever desires to possess God on account of His goodness, thereby desires to be taken up by that goodness and to be possessed. The substance of love, surrender to the divine goodness, is contained in both acts; only the external appearance varies somewhat. Although many theologians consider only one of the two aspects, they include by implication the whole substance of love; thus, for example, Augustine, Bonaventure, and at times even Thomas, assert that the object of supernatural love is God as the object of supernatural beatitude. This conception predominates when love is represented as a tendency toward our perfect good in which we are to find repose. But to have a full and adequate representation of love, we must say with St. Thomas that we love God as object, as the end or *finis* in which our beatitude is consummated, and at the same time as the principle of beatitude and eternal life; consequently we love Him as the Father to whom we freely give ourselves.

In both respects theological love is known exclusively by the name of charity, because it is exercized on a good that is singularly valuable and precious. Love for our fellow men and for ourselves is charity only when we love ourselves for the noble, precious, and heavenly worth that is ours as God's children, and when we wish for ourselves that good which alone is supremely estimable and which eminently includes all other goods.

This charity is, of course, not merely act but habit. We should note well, however, that it is not a habitual inclination produced and sustained by our acts of love; rather it is supernature's own inclination toward its proportionate good, a tendency that is the root and principle of all the particular acts of love. Nature, too, has an intrinsic tendency toward the good; but this tendency is compatible with perversion of the will and aversion from the true good. Charity, on the contrary, is incompatible with such a cast of will, because it unites us directly with God and, in a certain sense, receives God into our nature. The reason is that by supernature we share in the divine nature which is essentially holy, and so God, the supreme and infinite good, in a way becomes natural and intrinsic to us. Yet charity closely resembles nature's tendency toward its good. Natural tendency permeates all the inclinations and activities of nature and is their foundation, even though we do not have to consider it reflectively as the rule and basis of our conduct. In a similar way, charity, as the basic tendency of supernature, is the source of all supernatural acts and operations, sustaining and influencing them, even though we do not have to direct all our other acts to God by an explicit act of love.

By the habit of charity, the soul belongs to God; therefore everything pleasing to God that is done in this state, is done for God. By the habit of charity the soul strives for union with God; therefore all its supernatural activity is aimed at this goal. Consequently we may say that everything done in the state of charity is done out of charity and by virtue of charity, although it is neither directly nor indirectly referred to God by an act of love. In this sense, too, we may say that nothing is truly good and meritorious except charity and what is done through charity.

This line of reasoning also indicates the true meaning of the assertion that has become classical, that all acts of virtue, to be fully pleasing to God and meritorious for eternal life, must be informed by love. To be such, they must be done for God and be directed to eternal life. This is accomplished best of all, undoubtedly, when our virtuous deeds are called forth by an act of love and thus are formally (mediately or immediately, actually or virtually, because of a previous act) presented to God and directed to the possession of God. But the same result is achieved if the person who acts belongs to God by his state; such a person works for God and strives after God even when he acts out of motives of another supernatural virtue.

Therefore every action of a person who is in the state of grace, if it is in any way performed in the spirit of faith, has a truly divine character; even the moral virtues are invested with a far higher dignity and meaning than they have in the natural order. In their own fashion they become divine virtues, for they are sustained by the theological virtues; the relations they involve also take on a glorified, divine, and holy quality.

The moral virtues are referred either to God, or to other men on our own level, or to ourselves. The purpose of these virtues, as we said previously, is to safeguard, by appropriate action, the dignity of God and of our neighbor against our encroachment, and the dignity of our own souls against the encroachments of sensuality.

God's eminence cannot be enhanced in itself any more than His goodness can. But it is manifested to us more vividly when He communicates the wealth of His nature to us than when He leaves us in our own nature. The more we receive from God, the more we must realize our own nothingness and subject ourselves to Him; we ought to perceive more clearly that God is everything and that we come from nothing. And when God unites us most intimately with Himself, our worship and subjection to His majesty must be most complete. When we worship and glorify God as the author of supernature and the father of supernaturally elevated souls, our adoration is more perfect and different in kind than when we worship and glorify Him as the author of nature. Then our adoration and glorification are so noble and sublime that they faithfully reflect the glorification which God's Son, the eternal and infinite doxology, as it is sometimes expressed in patristic terminology, gives to Him. The Son of God came into this world to establish among us a supernatural, heavenly cult that we might glorify the Father's name as He does (see John, chap. 17 and frequently elsewhere), and that the common priesthood of rational creatures, ceasing to be servile, might be a free and royal priesthood, like that of the Son Himself.

The dignity of spirits that stand on a footing of equality with us and the dignity of our own spirit are truly excellent and glorious. Our neighbor no longer faces us as a citizen of God's earthly empire but as a citizen of the heavenly kingdom, as a familiar friend, even as a brother in the heart of God the Father and a joint heir of the only-begotten Son. He appears before us, no longer in his natural spirituality but in his transfigured spirituality, as a person who has received a holy, divine character by his oneness and union with divinity. As a subject of rights, he has been endowed with a specifically higher title to rights than he previously possessed because he was a human being. Therefore his rights have a quite different quality, and merit a far higher respect and esteem from us than they could formerly claim.

The dignity of our own soul relative to the lower elements of our nature has been no less enhanced. Its dominion over these inferior faculties is more solidly grounded and assured by its transformation into a higher, divine spirituality. The importance and influence of sensual life, sensual love, and sensual pleasure have greatly decreased since the soul, elevated above its native condition, has shifted the central interest of its life directly to God and endeavors to live, love, and find happiness in God alone. God Himself is the soul's Food, changing the soul into itself; God Himself is the soul's Bridegroom in whose loving embrace it reposes and by whose light it is made fruitful, to bring forth in chaste union the image of God within the soul. This truth enables us to appreciate the exalted, divine, heavenly character of Christian continence and chastity, especially of virginal chastity which, far from regarding carnal union as a high good, contemns such union and keeps it afar off, so as not to tarnish and impair spiritual union with God.

Who can fail to perceive, even from the few points here suggested, that the doctrine of supernature, which is an elevation of human nature above its own level, clarifies and specifies the transcendence of Christian morality over all philosophical, rational, and rationalistic morality (if exclusive of a higher morality), no matter how painstakingly these systems have been constructed? The difference between them is intrinsic and specific, not merely extrinsic; it does not arise from the various ways by which they are known, or from the fact that in Christian morality Christ is taken as a model and as the cause of grace for a moral life that in itself is rational. By becoming man, Christ did not reintroduce a human ideal into mankind or leave it with its own meager strength. He has brought to us the ideal of the children of God (John 1:12), and has given us the power to become and live as God's children; He has given to our moral life a new, intrinsic, and superior structure.

Philosophical ethics, in the sense of a system set up in opposition and defiance against theological morality, is unquestionably not a true and genuine morality. For in the present order purely natural relationships do not exist alone and apart, and therefore cannot be made to prevail in isolated self-sufficiency. In themselves, however, these relationships are not false or fictitious. Even a deistic morality that is divorced from Christianity has to treat of love and divine worship as rationally known. But when deists wish to set their ethics against Christian morality and to supplant the latter, their love and worship of God cease to be true and correct, because they refuse to love and worship God in the way He prescribes.

We have added these remarks about supernatural morality to the discussion of charity because charity is its source and formative principle. Our efforts to reach the goal of morality in a perfect and natural way are supported by the love that energizes them.

However, a true, honest acknowledgment and pursuit of a moral goal are possible in the supernatural as well as in the natural order, even though our efforts are not called forth by an actual union of love with the goal. In other words, we can sincerely try to reach such a goal, not only when the object itself attracts us by love, but also when something else gives us the impulse to aim at it. Yet such a striving after a moral goal must always at least intend a loving union with it, even if our endeavor does not proceed from the motive of love. Hence we may say in general that all supernatural striving must proceed from supernatural love of God, either from perfect love, actual or at least habitual, by which we unite ourselves with God actually or habitually, or from imperfect love, that is, from some desire for God that directly or indirectly envisions this union of love as its end and leads to it. To be supernatural, our love must either embrace God Himself in His supernatural goodness (and this is charity), or must be directed to this unification by charity and therefore have God's supernatural goodness as its goal if not as its motive. Every such striving that includes a preparation for love I should call imperfect charity.

As supernature itself is an intimate union and kinship with God's supernatural goodness, so all its activity is a striving after God; and all activity, all endeavor that is directed to supernature must also be directed toward God. That is why Augustine usually designates love of God as the proper effect of grace, the effect for which grace is absolutely necessary; and he proves the necessity of this grace for every truly good striving on the ground that it must be a divine charity. All supernatural effort must aim at God as the supernatural good, and must in some degree be charity; that is, it must be love itself or a tendency toward love.

This tendency can also be instigated by self-love and servile fear (of course I do not here mean that fear which is called *serviliter servilis*). It can be found in any supernatural act in which a person turns to God's goodness, as by faith, hope, and active longing for supernatural beatitude, or in which one submits to God as the author of all our goods and the powerful, just lawgiver of a supernatural world economy. Even servile fear, if it is sincere, if it leads us to acknowledge God as the supernatural lawgiver, and if it subjects us to Him under this aspect, includes a tendency to the love of God which is the crown and fulfillment of the law.

Thus there is also a supernatural self-love, if I may use the expression. This is not only that noble love of self by which we love ourselves for God's sake as His children and wish to be transformed into Him from the motive of pure love, but is also the love by which we desire for ourselves the removal of evil and attainment of the highest possible state of perfection and beatitude. In this kind of love we do not, indeed, as yet embrace God Himself, but we seek our happiness in Him, and so we turn to His love and ear-

nestly long for it. This love, which is not to be confused
with that perfect desire that is charity itself and joins us
to God, is also, in our opinion, an imperfect love of God, if
such a term is allowable and desirable. It is the love which
disposes us for the reception of justification in the sacrament. It includes a desire for the real love which is infused
into us in justification.

Repentance is likewise supernatural. I do not mean only
that repentance which, proceeding from supernatural love,
abominates sin as an evil committed against our beloved
Father and highest good. I include also the repentance
which detests sin as a transgression and violation of the
supernatural order of the world and rebellion against the
Lawgiver, the repentance evoked by the wholesome fear
of losing the end and good of that order, supernatural beatitude, and of receiving a positive punishment corresponding
to the heinousness of the transgression.[8]

[8] What is ordinarily asserted without further qualification about supernatural repentance, that it is supernatural when referred to God, is not
quite accurate. Even natural sorrow is referred to God, if it is sincere.
God is also the object of natural love and the lawgiver of the natural order.
We should properly say that repentance is supernatural when it is referred to God as the object of supernatural love or as the supernatural
lawgiver. Of course this is implied when God is being regarded in the
light and spirit of faith.

Chapter XIII

HOPE

Hope, the third theological virtue, still awaits our attention. The theological virtues or rather virtuous powers are, as we have said, the basic powers of supernature. Ordinarily we distinguish two basic faculties in nature, knowledge and love, in which and by which its perfection is developed. Holding to this view, many theologians draw hope into the orbit of love. They say that hope is nothing else than the longing involved in love to have near at hand and to possess securely the object of love that is still afar off, or the yearning of imperfect love for perfect happiness. However, although hope is connected with desire, since we hope to attain only what we desire, it is not identified with desire; it is rather the confidence of actually and surely gaining possession of the desired good. This confidence is properly the formal element in hope, and specifically distinguishes hope from love. Although, like desire, it is an act of the will, it is not an act of inclination toward the good (*appetitus concupiscibilis*), but an act of the power of endurance (*appetitus irascibilis*), because it defends and clutches a possessed good or steadfastly pursues a desired good.

If we hold that this confidence is the essential and formal element in hope, we may say that natural confidence, by its power of firmly grasping its proper good, has two stages, as love has in desire and fruition, and as knowledge has in faith and vision. For nature, conscious of its power, either strives energetically and surely for the desired good, or triumphantly and steadfastly embraces the good that has been attained.

This seems to be the most natural and appropriate conception, as well as the one best calculated to bring the trilogy of theological virtues into close harmony. Thus confidence is given a definite place relative to the other two acts regarded in their perfection, and is not merely an intermediate stage in the process of their development.

The formal object and motive of confidence are evidently the reason underlying the possibility of attaining what is desired. As the proximate formal object of a pure spirit's knowledge and love is the spirit itself, so its essence is the proximate and formal object of the hope and confidence of obtaining and retaining the good that befits nature. For the good that befits nature is either nature itself or something that lies within and depends on the power emanating from the essence. Nature trusts in God, to be sure, but indirectly, so far as He is the ultimate cause of nature and the energy that guides and reinforces nature's activity. Now supernature is a participation in God's nature. Of itself, it has no power that is its own; and the good it is to attain and possess is God Himself. All its power is derived from God's nature in which it shares; God's nature is the immediate and direct source of its power. Consequently the confidence of supernature, its peculiar divine goodness (that is, its supernatural quality, implying union with the divine nature), and its proper object (namely, adherence to the Godhead that is to be possessed and enjoyed by knowledge and love), rest immediately on the divine nature and its power.

In the state of glory, in which the divine nature is fully

united with our nature and the divine beauty is perfectly possessed by knowledge and love, God Himself is the direct motive of our confidence in the security of possession, as He is the direct object of possession. Then God's activity, by which He draws our nature to His, and also our activity, by which we strive for the possession of Him, reach their culmination. We are most intimately united to the divine nature, and the infinite, invincible power with which God embraces and possesses Himself in divine beatitude gives us the blessed and exultant confidence that nothing can separate us from the possession of God with whom we have become one in supreme degree.

Even during the present life when we have not yet arrived at perfect union with the divine nature and complete possession of God by knowledge and love, our confidence rests on the union with the divine nature that is ours here on earth by the grace of supernature. Relying on the power and activity of the divine nature, which even now has admitted us to close union and has granted us some knowledge and love of God, we expect and we hope that God, on His part, will in time to come, unfailingly and with triumphant might, unite Himself perfectly with us and will welcome us to the full possession of His divine goodness and beauty.

Accordingly supernatural, Christian hope has the distinguishing mark of not only aiming at the loftiest goal, the possession of God, but of relying directly on the infinite, omnipotent, unconquerable might of the divine nature itself to attain its objective. The result is that supernature is true to itself and strains after its difficult, exalted objective with less timorous, or better with far more vigorous sureness and firmness (even with divine assurance and invincibility, so far as lies in its power) than nature provides for its own life in advancing toward goods that are within its reach and are proportionate to its own capacities. This is the basis of that holy pride by which the true Christian rises above all creation and can cry out with the Apostle: "Who then shall separate us from the love of Christ? Shall tribulation or distress or famine or nakedness or danger or persecution or the sword? . . . But in all these things we overcome because of Him that hath loved us [in such a way as to make us His children]. For I am sure that neither death nor life nor angels nor principalities nor powers nor things present nor things to come nor might nor height nor depth nor any other creature shall be able to separate us from the love of God, which is in Christ Jesus our Lord" (Rom. 8:35–39).

This is the true divine hope of possessing and embracing God Himself. It trusts in God's omnipotence which surpasses all created forces. It relies on God's power, which is not only creative and preservative of powers belonging to created natures, but reveals itself in its infinite range. This is the power the Apostle speaks of when he begs God to grant us knowledge of the exceeding greatness of His dominion over us who believe through the exercise of His mighty strength, and to give us the hope that comes with our vocation to share in the wealth of His glorious inheritance (Cf. Eph. 1:17 ff.). This is the power by which God accomplishes far more in us than we can ask or understand, and fills us with the plenitude of His divinity (Eph. 3:19 f.); the power St. Peter mentions when he says that God has given us all the goods of His divine might through the knowledge of Him who has called us by His own glory and virtue, that we may by His promises "be made partakers of the divine nature" (II Pet. 1:3 f.).

For the power of the divine nature is revealed in its true sublimity and divinity, not by imparting life and light to the creature, but by giving itself to the creature, by divinizing and filling the creature with supernatural energy. As the divine power is manifested with incomparably greater clarity in the substantial communication of the divine nature to the Son than in the creation of beings outside God, so it is manifested more clearly by the divinization of the creature through transforming grace than by the bestowal and preservation of the creature's own existence, life, and light. That is why many theologians and Fathers regard the justification effected by the communication of sanctifying grace as a greater miracle of omnipotence than creation and all other wonders occurring in the material and spiritual world. St. Augustine assigns the grace by which sinners are saved to the higher, marvelous world order that has its cause, not in the seminal principles of creatures,[1] but directly in God Himself.

Christian hope, then, is based directly on God's glorious omnipotence. Accompanied by God's infinite love for us, this divine omnipotence unfailingly and necessarily, with all-conquering might, leads us toward the end held out to us. No opposing force, not even our own feebleness (which is banished by God's power, since the fullness of God's might is drawn down to us by our humble acknowledgment of weakness: "For power is made perfect in infirmity" [II Cor. 12:9]) can hinder us from attaining this end. Thus we come to the firm, unshakable, unerring conviction that that end already belongs to us, that the inheritance of the

---

[1] *De Genesi ad litteram*, IX, cap. 17. In Augustine's theory, God created matter and placed in it certain seminal forces (*rationes seminales*) from which the empirical world with all the beings found in it were to be formed according to definite laws of growth and structure.

children of God is already ours, that we are and will always remain God's children, if only we ourselves do not draw away from the influence of the divine power.[2]

This confidence and assurance by which the soul is grounded on God as on solid rock, imparts to Christian holiness a firm and unshakable foundation, a certain immobility. In all the storms of life, not only in those which assail him from outside, but even in those which rage in the deepest recesses of his soul with devastating, shattering fury, the Christian stands unflinching in his faith and love. With the inflexibility of a diamond, he withstands all blows, and exhibits to the world that noble spectacle which Stoic apathy dreamt of and sought in a false ideal.[3]

This confidence crowns holiness during the present life by investing it with strength and durability. It crowns beatitude and glory in the next life by giving us conscious assurance of their eternity and unchangeableness. It coincides with our awareness of being children of God the Father, who repose securely on His breast and are safe under His all-powerful protection; there we have no enemy to fear, but can draw from that source all the strength we need to reach our exalted goal. With the Apostle we can even now "glory in the hope of the glory of the sons of God" (Rom. 5:2), and we shall one day glory that, as sons, we share with God the Father and the Son their eternal, unassailable sovereignty.

Knowledge and love of God and the confidence of successfully attaining and retaining the possession of God,

[2] Grace equips and elevates our will with this victorious, infallible, irresistible power, but does not smother or suppress the will itself.

[3] Cf. the homilies of Macarius the Elder [St. Macarius the Great], PG, XXXIV, 449–822. J. Stiglmayr, S.J., *Sachliches und Sprachliches bei Makarius von Aegypten* (Feldkirch: 1912), regards these homilies as spurious; B. Altaner, *Patrologie* (Freiburg i. Br.: 1950–51), admits only the letter, *Ad filios Dei* (PG, XXXIV, 406–10) as genuine.

make up that precious trilogy of truly divine powers and activities which pertain to supernature regarded as a participation in the divine nature. These three virtues are the spirit and the substance that fashion and shape our lives and make them genuinely Christian, patterned on the model of Christ the Son of God. We are already God's children during this life, and we have all three virtues: "Now there remain faith, hope, and charity, these three; but the greatest of these is charity" (I Cor. 13:13). Above all we have charity, by which we even now embrace God; our knowledge of God and the development and transformation of supernature into its stage of divine durability and immortality are but imperfectly anticipated. Thus charity remains, and has nothing yet to attain but full fruition. But knowledge and confidence do not remain in their imperfect state. Faith dissolves into vision, and hope is changed into triumphant, everlasting, undisturbed possession.

This trilogy puts us in harmonious relationship with the divine Trinity. The Father imparts to us the hope and pride of being His children; the Word sheds on us His light, and in it His wisdom and knowledge; the Holy Spirit communicates to us His own special love. In this way, as we remarked before, a faithful, well-rounded image of the Blessed Trinity is fashioned in supernature; likewise the glorious doctrine of the mission of the divine persons to our souls receives a satisfactory explanation of its high meaning. The Son and the Holy Spirit are sent to us to bring us to the Father, whom we shall eternally possess and enjoy through the light of the Son and the love of the Holy Spirit.[4]

----

[4] See the development of these points in St. Thomas, *Summa theol.*, Ia, q. 43.

In concluding our exposition of the supernatural order of grace, or supernature and its activity, we wish to draw attention to a beautiful passage of St. Maximus, Martyr. In majestic, striking language, he describes nature elevated by grace, or supernature, in its highest perfection and realization. We have said that the supernatural order is made known by faith and is laid open before us in faith. Proceeding in a similar way St. Maximus, commenting on the text, "The final issue of your faith, the salvation of souls" (I Pet. 1:9), points out what the salvation of souls is, and discusses their supreme good, their perfect beatitude.

Faith is brought to its consummation in the state of beatitude; it passes over into vision and comprehension, immediately though not adequately embracing the object of faith, God. Love is united with the highest Good; it returns to its principle, which is now its end, and so arrives at the summit of all its longing. Straining hope comes to rest in this union, and wins eternal, inseparable possession and fruition.

Such is the general activity of supernature exercised in the state of beatitude; its supernatural character is more clearly brought out in what follows. Happiness and the possession of God rest on a participation in divine goodness that surpasses the resources of nature. This participation is an assimilation to the Godhead; as the most perfect possible likeness it implies a certain identity in nature with God, and is consequently a divinization of the one who is favored with it by God's bountiful grace. This divinization is, of course, a supernatural elevation of the person to whom it is granted, an elevation that raises him above all creatures and created relationships. It raises him above the world of time and temporal things to a share in the eternal life of God. It raises him above creaturely servility, by which the creature was kept apart from the Creator as his Lord, his highest principle and end, to union with Him. It raises man above the limitations characteristic of creatures to which God, creative principle and end, has doled out a restricted measure of perfection, to the pure and boundless perfection of God.

Such an elevation of the person made worthy of it by God's grace is clearly not a flowering of our own natural power, even if we think of it as supported by God. It is the result of an immediate, infinite activity on the part of God, an activity that is manifested by its tendency to issue in an infinite effect of God's transcendent power.

As this elevation is brought about by a striking revelation of God's omnipotence, which here, so to speak, calls upon and expends all its resources, it can conduct the creature to an exalted and inconceivable union with God and, placing him in the current of God's happiness, enable him to enjoy an inexpressible and more than inexpressible happiness and rapture for which we can find in nature no conception and no expression, no idea and no word. It is the happiness of which the Apostle speaks when he says: "Eye hath not seen, nor ear heard, neither hath it entered into the heart of man" (I Cor. 2:9). All these elements of the supernatural state of beatitude, the salvation of souls, and the supernatural end which is the final issue of faith, are joined by St. Maximus in a running chain; he links one with the other and points out the identity between them.[5]

[5] The passage, briefly sketched in *Capita de caritate*, cent. IV, cap. 12 [*PG*, XC, 1049], is found fully developed in *Eroteses in Scripturam*, quaest. 59 [*PG*, XC, 608 f.].—The Scholia with which the work is enriched are not from the hand of Maximus [Tr.].

PART FOUR

UNION OF NATURE AND GRACE

Chapter XIV

UNION OF NATURE AND GRACE IN SUPERNATURAL ACTS

WE HAVE studied nature and grace or supernature separately, and have investigated the kind of life that is led in these two orders. We must next examine the problem of their interconnection. We do not intend to go more deeply into the question of the extent to which, in the present economy of providence, the natural order of life is capable of an independent development within its own sphere. That is linked too closely with the mysterious question of the way in which God, in His inscrutable decrees, distributes graces for the attainment of the supernatural end. Let us rather inquire into nature's ability to contribute to the supernatural activity of grace or to the acquisition of grace. This will lead us to the mystery of the harmony between grace and freedom, the two main elements of the higher order of the world as it exists at present.

Let us first consider how the acts of our supernatural life arise in us and which are the factors that modify them, especially at the moment when they are associated with the initial entrance of grace into nature.

Generally speaking, every relationship in this domain implies that the acts characteristic of supernature cannot possibly proceed from nature as such. They require, with absolute necessity, a supernatural power.

To grasp this truth more clearly, we should recall that two elements are necessary for the soul's acts: first, a physical power, the real principle of a vital act, such as the faculties of mind and will in the natural order, and secondly, a stimulus and movement of the power for actual activity. Of course, there is found in every natural faculty a tendency to its own activity; but it needs an impulse for actual operation, aroused in the intellectual faculty by the presentation of its object or the movement of the will, and in the will by the attraction of the thing that is to be desired. The power itself, along with its tendency and stimulation, are sustained and guided by the supreme cause, God. In the natural order, too, God is the highest cause of all naturally good actions, because He is the cause of nature itself and has placed in nature an inclination toward the good, to which the will has only to attach itself. Moreover, by His providence He furnishes objects and impulses for good actions. Finally, God upholds the creature in the exercise of its activity, and accompanies it with His so-called universal, simultaneous concurrence. Having mentioned this last point, we need not advert to it explicitly in our subsequent considerations.

All this has to be borne in mind if we wish to understand aright the teaching of the Pelagians and of the doctors of the Church who opposed them. The assertion has often been made that the Pelagians taught a state of pure nature, and the only fault found with them was that they regarded nature, as it was created by God, sufficient in itself to accomplish good, even in a Christian, meritorious way. However, if we scrutinize their doctrine attentively, we discover that they destroyed true nature no less than they destroyed grace. Their basic principle was that there is no such thing as true nature, that is, an inclination and tendency toward good placed in the soul by God, in virtue of which the will would be stimulated freely to strive after the good, and without which no activity in the will would be conceivable. They maintained that the will must of necessity be as indifferent to good as it is to evil in itself, as it was in the first man and in the angels; there must be no tendency toward good, no inclination that precedes free choice and is independent of free choice. They insisted that the good in us proceeds altogether from us, just as evil does. To their mind, therefore, natural freedom was not a potency given by God through any natural power, tendency, or impulse toward good, urging us to embrace, hold, and foster the good; and consequently grace was not a God-given inclination toward good preceding every movement of voluntary decision.

To oppose such an error, the Fathers had the task of showing that the will does not give itself the initial impulse to any good, but can do no more than fall in with an impulse received from God. Especially when the question concerned the good that is profitable for the eternal life won for us by Christ, they had to show that the will must be incited and strengthened by supernatural grace that is likewise received from Christ. How this tendency to good is communicated to us and is aroused in us, was not the object of the controversy; the Fathers insisted that it does not come from us and cannot be merited by us. That is why there was less occasion to inquire whether the tendency is natural or supernatural, habitual or actual.

But in later centuries, when the Scholastics investigated the necessity of grace from the entirely different point of view of philosophy, the problem took another form. They regarded grace in opposition to true nature, and therefore discerned in nature, as in grace, a God-given power and inclination to good. From this viewpoint the necessity of grace in the narrower sense, as distinct from nature, had to appear mainly as the necessity of a supernatural vital power for the performance of certain acts for which no power is found in nature. Thus emerges the interesting phenomenon that in the older Scholastics grace in the strict sense signifies habitual grace, or supernature along with its powers.

In truth, the real reason for the necessity of Christian, supernatural grace is not, as many think, that every good action and motion must proceed from God, because in some way it leads to God (for this is the case even in the natural order), nor that nature, impaired by passions or sensuality, needs a special stimulus coming from God, but that nature possesses no physical power for such acts and therefore must be fortified and raised by supernatural powers. Accordingly the necessity of supernatural grace is eminently a necessity of a new habit that elevates natural power.

This supernatural power, no less than a natural power, has an inner tendency to activity. Apparently, however, it needs a proportionately greater impulse from God than the natural powers do, and this impulse must come immediately from God. Because it is not rooted in our own being but stems directly from God, it is far more dependent on God for its actuation and must be continually under His direct influence. As the branch of the vine, says our Savior, cannot bring forth fruit and exercise its vital activity unless it is connected with the root, since it has no independent life of its own but only a life received from the root, so our divine life cannot unfold except under the continuous influence of the divine nature in which we share. During the present life, moreover, the powers of supernature never openly encounter their formal object and motive, which therefore cannot stimulate and evoke the activity of these powers. Lastly, supernature with its faculties is capable of a continual growth and increase, which it is to achieve by activity and the use of the degree of power that is available whenever the occasion arises. Since this power cannot reach beyond itself, God must draw us and raise us to an ever greater share in His nature by a special action.

For these reasons it pertains to God to stimulate such powers and to set them in motion, and hence the man who is endowed with habitual grace must always stand under the constant, direct influence of Christ and the Holy Spirit. Thus, too, the necessity of actual grace even for the justified man is not compromised but is frankly acknowledged; and the learned Thomassinus displayed a flash of genius when, with a prodigious expenditure of industry and show of erudition, he set out to demonstrate from the teaching of the older Scholastics the paradox that they overlooked the necessity of actual grace because they were so engrossed in the question of habitual grace.[1]

If the supernatural power, as habit, cannot put forth an act without a special, corresponding stimulus and motion on the part of God, must not such stimulus and motion evoke a supernatural act before the supernatural power is infused as a habit?

It is a commonplace that supernature is not conferred on nature as independently of the subject's activity as nature itself is given to him. "He who created you without your help, will not justify you without your cooperation."[2] As we mentioned before, the mistake of the Gnostics and Manichaeans was their contention that supernature was

---

[1] L. Thomassinus, *Dogmata theologica* (6th ed., Paris: 1870), VI, 61–475.

[2] St. Augustine, Serm. 169, c. 11, no. 13 [*PL*, XXXVIII, 923].

necessarily connected with nature or even constituted nature; whereas the older Greek Fathers explicitly taught against them that supernature, or grace in the strict sense in which the Scholastics used the term, is not infused independently of nature's own activity. This common teaching of the Church furnished the Scholastics with the incentive for the celebrated controversy, whether man at his first appearance and prior to all sin was created immediately in the state of supernature, as he was in the state of nature (*non tantum in naturalibus sed etiam in gratuitis*). Both parties to the debate agreed on the main point. St. Thomas, too, along with his school, taught that the first man received grace at the first instant of his natural existence, since in that same instant, responding to God's lead, he prepared himself for its reception. Therefore a relation founded on nature itself rather than on the sinful condition of nature is the reason why the union of nature with supernature is brought about, not by an absolute divine decree, but by a kind of marriage; nature makes itself ready for the grace proffered by God and then receives it.

The explanation of this situation is found in our previous description of supernature as holiness. Supernature itself, as sanctifying grace, as participation in the divine nature and holiness, necessarily excludes mortal sin, with which it is incompatible. If, therefore, grace were infused into nature and would remain in it without reference to the activity of nature and its will, nature would be incapable of grave sin and would lose its liberty of contrariety. We should then be back at the Gnostic and Manichaean system of spiritual men and animal men (*homines spirituales et psychici*). Accordingly, if the liberty of contrariety (power of free choice between good and evil) is not to be extinguished, as it is not meant to be during this life in the present economy of the world, the existence of supernature in nature must be made dependent on a free decision, both as regards its entrance into nature and its continuance. It can enter only if nature, invited by the actual, excitating grace of God, consents to it and is willing to submit to its law. And it must retire as soon as nature withdraws from its influence and rebels against its law by mortal sin.

Only they who are ignorant of the true supernatural eminence of grace and who see in it nothing more than a general tendency and movement toward good placed by God in nature, can join the Jansenists in taking umbrage at the teaching of the Greek Fathers and the Scholastics (that the conferring of grace is dependent on the free activity of nature), or in judging that these Catholic writers ascribe to nature an excessive independence of God and deprive grace of that transcendent excellence which is the reason why it cannot be merited by nature. The independence of nature and its ability to merit grace are not in question. Nothing is ascribed to nature prior to its supernatural elevation except a simple, free consent to the state of grace. And even this consent is not given by nature through its own power, or through a natural movement aroused by God; it is given in response to God's supernatural excitation and attraction. And nature follows God's initiative, not to merit grace, but only to receive it, as it is offered by God's free goodness. God expects nothing else of nature than a willingness to take the gift held out to it.

As long as nature is not yet elevated by supernature, it acts as nature in distinction to grace, not in the sense that grace is a supernatural or natural stimulus and movement consisting in an enlightenment of the intellect and an attraction exerted on the will by God, but in the sense that grace is supernature itself which is still to be acquired. By itself, nature cannot consent to supernature. God Himself, who transports nature to a higher, more excellent, divine state, must draw it up and elevate it by a supernatural attraction and a stimulus of a superior order. Nature has but to follow God's lead in full surrender, not with a proud, Pelagian self-determination which insists on generating good out of its own loins, but in humble submissiveness, interposing no obstacle in the path of grace that purposes to raise nature to so high a dignity, and allowing itself to be borne aloft. This supernatural invitation to supernature is given to all men, for the supernatural state is meant for all. Therefore every man has only himself to blame if he does not reach the supernatural state; but no man can take the credit to himself if he does possess it, because he has not merited it but has received it, and could have failed utterly to attain it if God had not drawn him to it.

What is true of supernature in general—that it is not connected with nature by an immediate, unconditional bestowal, that it is not strictly won or merited by nature but can only be freely received, and that after it has been received it remains united with nature only so long as nature does not sever the bond by a free act opposed to it— holds also for the various powers pertaining to supernature. Faith, regarded as a light and as the physical power of eliciting a supernatural act of faith in the fullest sense, is infused only into those who follow the grace leading them to faith, assent to its requirements, and submit their will. The soul is energized with the supernatural strength to cleave firmly to God by the act of faith at the very instant it begins to cooperate with the grace that beckons and invites it. The same is true of the habits of hope and charity, which are infused the instant nature is at the point of following the lead of grace and of eliciting the respective act of hope or of love. Thus, too, the infusion of supernature itself accompanies the infusion of charity in justification, if nature, under the inducement of prevenient grace, turns itself to an act of love.

However, let us come back to our question. Before the habit of faith, for example, is infused, is the act of faith as a disposition for it already completed? Or is the act performed by means of the infused habit of faith? Against the first alternative the axiom is alleged that a supernatural vital act cannot be executed without a supernatural, physical, and interior vital principle, and consequently that the habit of faith must have been infused in order that the act may really ensue. The second alternative is seemingly blocked by the circumstance that the first supernatural act of faith, hope, or charity is generally regarded as a disposition and as an act of congruous merit for the communication of the habit.

At first sight this controversy may seem to be of slight importance. In the later scholastic period, however, it was vigorously agitated, and in fact it touches one of the main problems in our investigation. The older Scholasticism, in its noble yet profound simplicity, seems to have cast its vote heavily in favor of the second alternative. In fact, it is hard to conceive how nature can elicit a supernatural act unless it is equipped with the corresponding supernatural faculty. Consequently the first supernatural act, that of faith, for instance, is really elicited in virtue of the habit of faith, and therefore supposes that habit for its actual execution. So far, then, as the act of faith presupposes the habit, it cannot really be a disposition for the habit, because it follows and does not precede the habit.

Yet there is one element in the act that can precede the infusion of the habit, namely the decision of the will to elicit the act, and this decision can be made under the intervention of prevenient, excitating actual grace. For when the will decides in favor of the supernatural act to which prevenient grace draws and invites it, it disposes itself to receive the supernatural vital power needed for the execution of the act. Thus the decision of the will to elicit the act and the infusion of the power by which the act is executed meet in closest union. Accordingly the act, so far as it is contained in the decision of the will, can be a disposition for the reception of the habit, and nevertheless can proceed from the habit in its execution. In this way grace, as habit and supernatural power, is an aid for the performance of the act, and yet is dependent on the free decision of the will for its existence and exercise.

Here is the chance for the well-known but rarely understood teaching of the Greek Fathers, mentioned above, against the Gnostics. When they ask why one man turns to faith or love while another man does not, they do not always answer that this happens because one cooperates with the grace given and uses it, while the other does not; rather they say that one has grace and the other has not, that is, one accepts the proffered grace while the other refuses it. To clarify their point, they usually introduce an apt comparison. They say that an eye cannot see unless it has light. Similarly a man cannot act spiritually (in the higher sense of the term, which the Gnostics themselves had in mind) unless he has spiritual light within him. (In the same vein Augustine says: "No one acts justly unless he is justified"). But the eye can either shut itself off from light and thus keep it at a distance, or can open up, take light into itself, and see. Likewise nature can either close itself off from the light of grace by turning away from it, or else, influenced and attracted by this light, can receive it, and by its aid can see and act. And as the first kind of sight is brought about by opening the eye and admitting light, so the first supernatural activity results from the favorable decision of nature and the simultaneously ensuing entrance of grace.

The next step involves the interesting observation which is made too seldom, that at the first turning of the soul to God by grace (the *conversio mentis in Deum*), in which mainly the so-called *gratia efficax* comes into consideration, efficacious grace (that is, grace by which we are actually converted), is physically distinct from sufficient grace (by which we are invited to conversion). For the full grace needed for conversion, the most important grace, is given only to the really converted, and nevertheless the freedom of those who are converted and the possibility the others have of still being converted are not eliminated. On the contrary, freedom appears in its greatest splendor where grace emerges in its fullest light as the true principle of supernatural life. For this reason human freedom in conjunction with the acquisition of grace is so strongly stressed by the Greek Fathers and by the older Scholastics who base their views on the Greeks rather than on St. Augustine, and yet grace shines forth in its most radiant beauty. But in St. Augustine, by whom grace is less regarded as a supernatural power in opposition to natural power than as an impulse and propensity of the will to good in opposition to the stark, Pelagian indifference of the will, grace does not stand out so distinctly in all its divine superiority over the lowliness of nature. Therefore, too, the freedom of indifference which the human will enjoys, as set off against grace, cannot be so clearly brought out.

According to the description of the older Scholastics and the Greek Fathers, grace has the appearance of a physical form that of itself determines the will to good. This teaching was in part the source from which later Thomists drew their doctrine about physical predetermination in efficacious grace; they are fond of citing those passages of St. Thomas in which such a predetermination is most clearly indicated. Their contention is true to the extent that the predeterminist theory could not be thoroughly refuted by the teaching about an aid (*auxilium*) which is physically the same in the case of the converted and the unconverted. And one of their first and most successful opponents among the Jesuits had recourse, not to *scientia media* or to a moral efficacy of grace, but to the doctrine that has been presented above; with its help, and in his own elegant and skillful way, he answered all the objections that have been raised.[3]

For the form (determining us in the direction of good) which is necessary for the acts of faith, hope, and love, and which at the same time introduces faith, hope, and love, is offered to all men by God, but is actually given only to those who are willing to accept it. Therefore even those who do not receive it remain free to believe, to hope, and to

[3] Cf. Gregory of Valencia, S.J., *Commentariorum theologicorum tomus secundus, complectens omnia Primae Secundae D. Thomae theoremata* (Venetiis: 1608), disp. VIII, q.3, punct. 4; q.5, punct. 4. Gregory of Valencia, who won great distinction in the Congregation *De auxiliis*, is not as well known as he deserves to be. Perhaps no other theologian merits so much attention in Germany. He was a second Bellarmine in combating the heresies of the sixteenth century, and devoted almost all the energies of his long life to labors in Germany. He combined in his person all the eminent qualities a theologian could wish for, and had none of those failings which deter many people from the older theologians. He was an excellent Scholastic, a faithful, intelligent disciple of St. Thomas, and had little love for the endless subtleties so common in other commentators. He possessed a calm, correct sense of judgment, and for his time had a remarkable acquaintance with Scripture and tradition. In addition to all this, his style is a model of clarity, preciseness, and virile elegance. Clement VIII, although his sympathies lay with the Dominicans, called him "the doctor of doctors."

love, although they do not possess all that is needed for these acts. And they who actually receive the form are free not to believe, hope, and love, because they are free not to accept and keep it, even though it is accompanied by faith, hope, and love. This, then, is the grace that is chiefly intended in the familiar axiom: "To him who does what is in his power, God does not refuse grace."

The preceding line of investigation brings us to a certain union of nature and supernature, of freedom and grace in the generation of the supernatural life. Let us hold fast to this idea and exploit its full meaning, its great riches. We shall see that the luminous mystery of the development of the Christian, supernatural economy of salvation and of the entire world order consists in this union.

CHAPTER XV

THE MYSTERY OF THE UNION IN THE CHRISTIAN ECONOMY

ORDINARILY we regard the union of nature and grace as a mystery that defies explanation. We feel that it can hardly throw light on other truths; it envelops them in its own obscurity. The reason for this is that, when we hear the word "mystery," our thoughts are likely to turn to the impenetrable veil enshrouding all reality, including natural things, rather than to what is really supernatural. We cannot completely fathom and comprehend even natural things, particularly their relations to God and their hidden substratum. We know them by reason and can form a clear, distinct idea of them, but not one that adequately represents their inner structure. Since such is our idea, we locate the mystery of the union of grace and freedom, not in the supernatural, mysterious character of grace, but in the harmony existing between God's causal influence on His creatures and the indifference pertaining to the exercise of freedom. Consequently the mystery is found also in the natural order, for nature, too, requires God's causal influence for the free exercise of its good, natural activity. This mystery can and must be known by reason, and nature can form a clear, distinct concept of it; yet nature can no more penetrate fully into the mystery than it can fully penetrate into itself.

If the union of nature and grace is to be a specifically

Christian mystery, one of the united extremes must be specifically Christian, established and revealed by the supernatural economy of Christianity; such a mystery is grace, the supernatural elevation of nature. The specifically Christian mysteries are of course much less fathomable than natural mysteries. In comparison with the latter they are called mysteries because they surpass nature and reason, and so are not naturally knowable. Knowledge of them is acquired by the wonderful, supernatural light that is given in divine faith. They become luminous to believers, but remain completely shrouded in obscurity as far as reason is concerned.

Such a mystery is certainly the supernatural order of salvation in the world, because it leads to an absolutely supernatural and mysterious end, the elevation and perfect transformation of created nature by the divine nature. The mystery unfolds as nature is raised up to supernature or grace. This transfiguration is brought about by the union of grace with nature. Consequently the union of nature with grace is the luminous mystery of the Christian economy of salvation and hence of the entire order of the universe.

Let us go more deeply into the meaning and nature of this mystery. Nature and its freedom, as distinct from supernatural grace, can be conceived in three different ways, but can enter into a real union with grace only in one of them. Nevertheless we must also consider the other two ways in some detail. This will enable us to bring our own view into harmony with that of St. Augustine, which seems to exclude a union of grace and freedom, and will also help to clarify all the other aspects of the question.

In an effort to appreciate clearly the standpoint and the relative importance of each of these three ways, let us again have recourse to analysis. Such an analysis will be fairly easy, as the preceding discussion has furnished most of the necessary elements.

1. We have observed that nature is man's being and condition such as he has of himself. If we give the term its full meaning and consider man absolutely, apart from all divine influence and without the reception of anything from God, he is by nature absolutely nothing. His very existence is a communication of God's goodness, a product of grace and not of nature.

If we now take real man and consider in an abstractive manner what he has by himself, or rather what he keeps by himself, we may say that by nature he has everything that still sticks to him from his condition of nothingness: his potentiality, his indetermination to good, and his possibility of falling into evil. But all his being, all his power and tendency and impulse toward good come from God, lead to God, and are effects of His kindness; hence all this is a grace. In these two respects we can and must say, from the standpoint of philosophy as well as of theology, that of ourselves we are nothing good and have nothing good. We can say, with Quesnel, that nature of itself has light only to go astray and energy only to plunge into the abyss. Of ourselves, completely apart from God, we can do nothing but sin. The Council of Orange teaches: "No one has anything of himself [i.e., exclusively of himself, without God] except falsehood and sin." [1] From nature, exclusive of any communication from God, we have nothing but imperfection, the power to fail and to fall. The power of advancing to good and of ascending to the Good of all good, has to come to us from this same Good. To move freely in the

---

[1] Canon 22 [Denz., 195].

direction of good, we have to receive an attraction to it from the supreme Good (as from the final cause drawing us to itself) and an impulse (as from the efficient cause inclining us toward good).

As sin itself consists chiefly in self-seeking, we may say further that by nature we have only self-seeking rather than true love for God. Sin enters when we make ourselves the highest goal of our deeds, the central point of our activity, whereas God alone, the source of all good, ought to be the end and center (I do not say the motive) of all our actions. The malice of self-seeking is not that we desire God and His goods for ourselves. The supreme goodness wills to communicate itself to all things; therefore it wills to be desired by them: "The good is that at which all things aim." [2] But this is to be done in such a way that all things which receive existence and goods from the divine goodness move toward it, repose in it, submit to it, glorify it, and do not draw it down to their level or separate themselves from it. The great mystery of sin is precisely this, that the creature concentrates on himself, forsakes the fountain of life and digs instead empty cisterns,[3] that is, suffices for himself, manages his own life, lives for himself apart from God. Self-seeking is a striving after self-deification, a desire to set up another god against God, to replace the true God by a futile idol or by absolute nothingness. The man who is without God and is independent of God is nothing, whereas God is He who Is; whatever existence and goodness man possesses he has received from God.

[2] Aristotle, *Nicomachean Ethics*, I, 1 (1094 a 3).
[3] Cf. Jer. 2:13: "My people have . . . forsaken Me, the fountain of living water, and have digged to themselves cisterns, broken cisterns that can hold no water." [Tr.].

Such self-seeking is possible only because man is nothing of himself. Thus if we conceive nature in the sense mentioned above, we can say that man is by nature capable of nothing except this malicious, empty self-seeking.

Lastly, a special, intrinsic imperfection is found in man because of the composition of his nature. Not only is matter brought into existence from nothing, but such reality as it has is, in comparison with all other beings, a sort of nothingness, something imperfect, indeterminate, mean, chaotic. In human nature these characteristic traits of matter are modified by the natural power of the higher, spiritual principle, but are not entirely eliminated. This accounts for that weakness in human nature, that affinity for the sensible, those base appetites which burden the spirit and draw it down with almost irresistible force from God and from the spiritual world and its lights in general, to bury it in the void and darkness of matter.

In this sense we can say that man is unable by nature, that is, according to his inherent imperfection (which is all he has of himself alone) to do anything good; on the contrary, he has a frightful, insuperable bent toward evil. By nature he has no charity; he not only lacks supernatural love of God, but has no love of God whatever. More exactly (according to the mind of St. Augustine) he has no inclination toward God; all he has is unchaste concupiscence, a self-seeking and an overpowering hankering for goods of sense.

Obviously grace cannot be said to enter into union with such a nature or, more correctly, with nature thus regarded. Nature in this sense is the very opposite of grace, an antagonist that cannot be united with grace but has to struggle against grace and be cast out by grace. If nature is only a power, or rather a powerlessness for evil, and in no way a power for good, grace, as a higher power for good, can find in nature no footing, no point of contact.

This is the way ascetics regard nature when, in their zeal to lead us to perfect humility, they tell us that by nature, as the opposite of grace, we are nothing and are capable of nothing but sin, and when they stigmatize every impetus of nature as egoistic, sensuous, or proud. That is undoubtedly true, even though we can do some good by our God-given nature without any supernatural grace; likewise this contention does not exclude the truth that nature, as it comes to us from God, by itself aspires after God. Such seems to have been St. Augustine's point of view in his conflict with the Pelagians. When, in his polemic against them, he rules out any union of grace with natural freedom, which he describes as nothing more than a freedom to do evil, he is regarding nature, not in its concrete existence, but in the abstract sense, to the exclusion even of God's natural influence. The position of his adversaries forced him to this attitude. A clearer understanding of this point will be worth the effort needed to gain it. If the situation really is such as I am representing it, nearly all the difficulties that cause so much trouble vanish.

The real core of the Pelagian heresy has seldom been correctly grasped, and therefore St. Augustine, who always heads straight for his objective by the shortest road, without side trips or sightseeing tours, and who is oblivious of all else in his eagerness to reach the goal, is often misunderstood.

I submit that when Augustine insists against the Pelagians that man has by nature nothing but the ability to fall; nothing but lie and sin; that he has no charity but only self-seeking lust; that he owns nothing beyond the freedom to do evil, the Saint does not intend to assert that man does not possess in his real nature any power and freedom for good and for the love of God. What he teaches is that man does not possess such power and freedom entirely of himself, independently of God's influence and natural cooperation, or in the sense that nature is regarded as autonomous and severed from connection with God.

For this is the way the Pelagians regarded nature. Their fundamental contention was that the possibility and power of good along with the tendency toward good, are as fully within man's competence as the possibility of evil and propensity toward evil. Although they often admitted that man has received his freedom from God, the situation is not changed in the slightest; they made this admission more to appease the Catholics than of their own accord; besides, it had no bearing on their main tenet. They placed freedom equally and indivisibly in the power of willing evil as well as good, and good as well as evil. Consequently man cannot receive freedom to do good otherwise than freedom to do evil, or freedom to do evil otherwise than freedom to do good. If, according to Catholic teaching, man receives from God freedom to do good, he likewise receives from God freedom to do evil; but if he has freedom to do evil from himself, he also has freedom to do good from himself. Both alternatives are false. But the Pelagians asserted both: the first, to shelter themselves from the Catholics, the second, to construct their own system.

Accordingly they held that man, of himself, by his own nature, quite independently of God and all divine influence, is able to aim at good as he does at evil. But Augustine rightly says that this is most outrageous nonsense, so outrageous that only the most deluded pride could suggest it. The idea is so monstrous that many theologians at the time of the controversies about grace and free will did not suspect that it could be found lurking in the background of the Pelagian system. Nowadays, after we have seen how the human mind, arrived at the peak of its self-deification and denial of the true God, has declared the identity of being and non-being, act and potency, good and evil, we can also perceive how the practical pride of Pelagianism was able to jumble freedom and power for good with freedom and power for evil.[4]

By this procedure they likewise erased the distinction between good and evil. They denied that there is any other good than that which, like evil, is the product of the autonomous will. But such a product cannot be good in the true sense of the word; it is necessarily evil. Such a good, like evil, must have its highest end not in God, but in man; it is a glorification of oneself rather than of God. As it does not in any way come from God, and as man does not accomplish it in response to a God-given attraction and impulse to good, it does not return to God, is not referred to God, and is not a glorification of God. Pelagian good can consist only in works that are conformable to external law or order, works that are subject to the will's supreme dominion; it cannot consist in interior submission or in the union of our will with the divine will. Therefore Pelagian morality is not a devoted love of God or charity, but is egoistic self-love, cupidity, love of self reaching even to the contempt of God; it is not service of God but service of idols. It is the morality of pride.

The keen mind of St. Augustine penetrated to the bottom

[4] By identifying the essence of freedom with indifference to good and evil, the Pelagians destroyed the concept of absolute goodness and of pure being; for, as Augustine subsumed, the essence of freedom must belong to God. Therefore good and evil, affirmation and negation would have to coincide in God. Consequently the Pelagian God must be the Hegelian God, who is simultaneously true being and true nothingness.

of this affair. Hence he was justified in saying that nature, in the Pelagian version, has nothing of itself but falsehood and sin. Natural freedom, as the Pelagians regarded it, can accomplish absolutely nothing that is really good, because it does not have God as the goal of its striving. The Pelagians themselves admitted that the heathen could not know God without faith, and so they recognized no orientation toward God in pagan conduct. Thereupon Augustine could subjoin that in their hypothesis or from their point of view all the actions of infidels are evil. And when he thus considered natural freedom apart from all connection with God in its absolute powerlessness for good and as challenged, moreover, by the might of sensuality, he could add that it was not only incapable of nothing but evil, but was swept along toward evil with irresistible violence.

In the severe, inflexible terms employed by St. Augustine in this controversy, we can but marvel at the keen acumen of the great doctor. His occasional lack of clarity is explained by the fact that, with respect to the concrete condition of nature as infected with original sin and torn from its primordial union with God, he sometimes raises the hypothesis to a thesis, as though nature really had no other qualities than those allotted by the Pelagian system. The Pelagians intended directly to exclude the grace of Christ, although their system really eliminates all divine influence. Therefore in Augustine, too, the grace of Christ, which alone can and should actually lead man to true and perfect good, generally stands for every influence of the Creator affecting the creature's progress toward good. On the other hand human nature, which was withdrawn from God's original influence by the first sin, represents for him, more or less, nature and freedom as considered by the Pelagians in complete independence of God. Hence he can prescind from the power and tendency to good still found in nature, owing especially to the image of God that continues to remain in the soul, in order to meet the enemy on his own terrain and thus secure a more decisive and triumphant victory.

But when the terms employed by Augustine are transferred to concrete nature as it actually exists subsequent to original sin, they receive in his reiterated and explicit teaching a moral and restricted value rather than an absolute sense. He does not mean to say that man can do no good whatever without the supernatural grace of Christ; all he says is that without grace man cannot do good in the Pelagian sense. What good man is capable of in such a condition is fragmentary and insignificant; the true, supernatural, Christian good is entirely beyond his grasp.

2. We remarked above that nature and free will can be regarded formally as being absolutely our own and as proceeding from us. In that case, as we have seen, natural freedom is nothing but powerlessness, darkness, possibility of evil, or even inclination to evil. But we can also formally regard nature together with its freedom as a definite power communicated to us by God, and then it is the foundation of all good. This is the view Augustine adopts when he says that nature is what God instituted and wished to exist; it is what it ought to be, to have, and to be capable of in accordance with the will and institution of the Creator, conformably with the idea He has of it. By nature man has a disposition to existence, and hence a power and tendency to truth and goodness. Every existence, every power and tendency which man receives from the Creator is natural in this sense; moreover, to Augustine's mind, nature is not only the existing substance of man with its powers and tendencies, but embraces his supernatural existence with

its powers and tendencies. That is why the Saint could say that the first man possessed in his nature, as he received it from God, the power and tendency to all good, including supernatural good.

Likewise free will in this view is not something to be contrasted with the divine influence, but is essentially the power and tendency to good that comes from God (the power of guarding rectitude, in Anselm's phrase).[5] The possibility of deviating from good is also present, but is accidental and incidental, rooted as it is in the imperfection of the person possessing free will. The freedom that we have entirely of ourselves is a mere lack of determination to true activity, to the good, and is a determinability or even a certain determination toward evil, conferring on us the disastrous power to aim at evil and to realize it. We have no freedom to strive after and realize what is good, except in virtue of a God-given determination which urges and draws us toward good.

If we cling fast to this standpoint, we cannot say that grace is added to free will. Grace gives us true freedom, for it gives us the ability and inclination to love what is good, and liberates us from inability to pursue the good and from the calamitous strength of our propensity toward evil. Thus grace does not destroy but establishes freedom. And St. Augustine says that the first man, by virtue of the natural and supernatural perfection of his nature, was free from all evil and free for all good. True natural freedom and supernatural freedom have this in common, that they are not an indeterminate indifference with respect to good and evil, but rest upon a God-given determination to good, which confers on freedom the power and inclination to love what is good.

[5] St. Anselm, *De libero arbitrio*, c. 12 [*PL*, CLVIII, 504].

This was denied by the Pelagians, as though indifference to good and evil or even indifference respecting individual good actions were thereby excluded. Pelagian indifference, which represents the will as being quite as indifferent to good as to evil, so that the will gives to itself the first impulse to good in the same way as it can give to itself the first impulse to evil, and in the performance of a good action does not heed an impulse and attraction to good placed in it by God, is indeed excluded. Absolute indifference to good and evil can at most, as we said above, suffice by way of negation for doing evil, but is not enough to enable us to do good; it is not a perfection but an imperfection. This absolute indifference toward good is never found in the will, because the will inclines in the direction of good by the force of its very nature.

During our present life, however, this orientation toward good is never so decisive that it removes a simple possibility of deflection toward evil. This possibility is not ruled out as long as the orientation itself does not involve perfect union with God, the supreme goodness, in the beatific vision, or as long as the will is not confirmed in good with full, unreserved surrender to God's goodness, as occurs in the decision made by pure spirits even in their natural state. Nor does it do away with the liberty of specification with respect to choice among various good alternatives; otherwise God could not have this kind of freedom. On the contrary, the more closely the spirit is united with goodness itself by love, the greater is its power to choose all the particular goods that are suitable for it. The orientation given us by God, regarded as a power and inclination to good, establishes freedom in us as the power (*dominium*) to love and to realize what is good.

As in the previous sense nature and freedom stood for

our weakness and the principle of evil in us, so they depict, according to this second conception, our true power and the principle of good in us. In both cases we do not have a real union of natural freedom with grace. In the first case freedom implies either absolute nothingness or a negation that clings to existence. Evidently grace cannot enter into union with the former, because it cannot join itself to nothing; nor can it enter into union with the latter, because this negation, this imperfection, this indetermination to good which is also a determinability or even a determination to evil, is more or less expelled by the advent of grace. In the second case, complete natural freedom is something produced and established by grace; freedom as a power and tendency toward true goodness and the true final end, and consequently as the ability to take and use particular goods and means leading to the end according to one's choice, is the effect of grace. Hence we can here speak of an identity, but not of a union of grace with freedom as of two distinct factors. In both cases we can speak only of a compatibility and reconciliation of grace and free will as of two real or apparent opposites, which seem mutually to exclude each other. In the first case there is a real opposition; grace endeavors to banish the freedom to do evil; but so long as it does not completely pervade and transform nature, it cannot succeed. In the second case the opposition is merely apparent; in reality freedom and grace (as power and ability to will and do good) are one, and the exclusion of the opposite, and the most profound and perfect conciliation between grace and freedom, are found in this oneness.

Since Augustine, arguing against the Pelagians, discourses of grace and freedom (as nature) according to these two opposite aspects, he has no occasion to speak of a union between them as two distinct factors in the execution of an act. When, therefore, the Pelagians reproach him with the charge that his teaching on grace jeopardizes man's freedom, he has no thought of clearing away the difficulty by pointing to a real union between natural freedom and grace. He contents himself with replying that true freedom, the freedom to do good, is conferred by grace. But freedom from good and freedom for evil (or enslavement to evil) ought to be suppressed by grace; and grace, by swaying us toward good, bestows on us an invincible and inherently infallible power to avoid evil. But during this life grace always allows full play to freedom; man can always sin, because grace leaves him in some degree to himself, with the result that he can withdraw from its influence.

Because he was dealing with Pelagians, St. Augustine did not dare to speak of a real union between natural freedom and grace, a union in which free will, as a self-moving power, would advance toward grace. If he had done so, he would have aggravated the conflict and would have supplied his adversaries with a screen under which they could easily have concealed their abominable error. According to their notion of the relation between grace and freedom, nature by itself could decide in favor of the good, and so could make itself worthy of grace as a necessary aid for attaining its self-designated end, thus using grace for its own purposes. If, therefore, Augustine had represented natural freedom as being in any way independent and capable of good, even in a sense different from theirs, and had allowed it to take a step toward grace for the purpose of entering into union with it, his language would have smacked of Pelagian terminology. To avoid this, he always described freedom, in opposition to grace, as freedom to do evil, and did not grant that it was freedom to do good unless it operated under and with grace.[6]

[6] We do not wish to pass up the opportunity of giving briefly and clearly, so far as we can, an analysis of the term "freedom" which is so much used and so often misused. The word itself is so vague that it can be applied to all sorts of things. Its meaning is essentially relative; we speak of "freedom from something" or of "freedom for something"; whenever we desire to make the sense definite, we must advert to the other term of the relationship. A thing can be free from evil, from imperfection, from want, from restriction, from outside influences, from constraint, from regulation, from necessity, from impediments, and so on. The word can even denote contradictory things; we speak of freedom from sin and freedom from justice (Cf. Rom. 6:20), of freedom from disorder and freedom from the constrictions of order, of freedom from good and freedom from evil, etc. Whenever that from which a thing is free is something evil or imperfect, the freedom itself is something good or perfect; and vice versa. Thus freedom from indeterminism to good, and likewise determinism to the love of good, are supreme perfections in God and the blessed; on the contrary, the indeterminism to good found in created nature, freedom from an interior determination to love of the true good, is an imperfection.

Generally, however, the word "freedom" is used in such a way that not only the relation to that from which one is free, but also to that for which one is free, comes to light. This occurs when we speak of the freedom a power has with respect to its activity or progress toward a goal. In such usage, too, the word admits of many applications. We speak of a freedom from restrictive factors; thus the soul's intellectual activity is freer and more universal than an animal's activity, and God's knowledge is freer than that of the soul. Freedom from obstacles which hold a power back from reaching the end toward which it naturally tends, is something good. And the same is true of many other kinds of freedom: freedom from violence, that is, from direction and movement imposed from without upon a thing contrary to its nature or inclination; freedom from servitude and subjection, although a thing may be dependent on another thing in its activity, either for needed strength (aid), or a norm (law), or its end (if its activity is performed in the interests of another) —this is a freedom pertaining to God alone; freedom from all external determinism to activity (this too pertains to God alone); freedom from a preceding, necessary determination to activity (liberty of indifference).

In the last sense we ordinarily speak, in the domain of morality, of man's freedom *in abstracto,* as of a property of the will by virtue of which determination to activity rests with the man himself; this is called self-determination, because it is a determination, proceeding from the man himself, with regard to a choice that up to this point was undecided. This property of the will, indifference, varies according as the objects among which a decision is to be made are of various kinds. Thus we have liberty or indifference of contradiction between contradictories (to act

3. If we leave to one side the polemic viewpoint of St. Augustine and interest ourselves in the purely scientific aspect of the question, we may and ought to permit ourselves a conception of nature and free will in which natural

---

or not to act), liberty of specification among objects that differ specifically (such as good actions of the various virtues), and liberty of contrariety between contraries (such as good and evil). The first two kinds of indifference essentially designate a perfection; for, as St. Thomas says, nothing is more perfect than the ability, while heeding the order of the right end, to choose the various particular goods or means leading to the end. Such an ability reveals a certain dominion of the soul over its own activity and the objects of activity. But indifference concerning the end itself, by reason of which it is possible to abandon the order of the right end, is not formally a perfection; it is a perfection only because it supposes the will's dominion in the other two kinds of indifference.

If, however, freedom is regarded as a factor in moral conduct, it is no longer considered in the abstract, as a property of the volitional faculty, but in the concrete, as free choice. Freedom, received from the hand of the Creator as something good, is the power and tendency to love good by which we have the ability to preserve rectitude (as Anselm says) or the order leading to the right end, and in which the ability to deflect from rectitude comes into consideration as an accidental imperfection. Natural freedom is the power and tendency to love and accomplish natural good; supernatural freedom is the power and tendency to love and accomplish supernatural good. The former is the natural faculty of free choice, the latter is the same faculty of free choice as elevated and transformed by grace. Some obscurity seems to be introduced if supernatural freedom, in contrast to natural freedom, is described, not as a power of a higher order, but as a mere condition of liberation from sin, guilt, and the like. In that case supernatural freedom appears to be more a product of the activity of natural freedom than a principle of a new, higher activity. The extent to which the attainment of supernatural freedom and of the transition of natural freedom to it depend on natural activity, will soon occupy our attention.

The relation between grace and free will is encompassed by many deep mysteries, natural as well as supernatural. On the other hand, many of the spirited controversies that have developed about this point seem to us to involve the mistake of endeavoring to locate the mystery where it is not to be found. The delicate, circumspect analysis of ideas and words, which sets St. Thomas so high above other authors, is grievously lacking. Even Suarez, whose great merit has been convincingly brought out by Professor Werner (*Suarez und die Scholastik der letzten Jahrhunderte*, Regensburg: 1861), is very rigorous in applying such analysis; he is extremely cautious and sharp, but perhaps too sharp and not deli-

freedom, in contradistinction to grace, emerges as something independent and good, and as a genuine factor alongside grace. Such is the doctrine which the Greek Fathers,
and even Augustine himself, propounded against the Manichaeans.

This is the conception which is taken as the basis for our
entire treatise: it occupies the middle position between
the two that have been previously discussed. According
to this view, nature is neither our own inherent indetermination and powerlessness with regard to all good, nor the
complete determination to all good, including the highest,
which we receive from God through grace. It is neither
sheer imperfection nor pure perfection. It contains a certain power and determination to good, namely that which
was given to us by God along with our own essence and
substance. At the same time it contains a certain powerlessness and indetermination toward good, and this comes
from ourselves. For our essential goodness is limited, first,
because natural power and tendency to good are weakened
and hampered in the soul by their connection with sensuality; secondly and especially, because the soul of itself does
not possess any power and determination with regard to
the higher good that is proper to the divine nature, and
therefore must receive a new, higher determination to this
good from supernature. Thus nature is something good,
a true, independent factor that is able to achieve some

cate enough. He not only distinguishes related ideas and the various
meanings of words in their mutual interplay, but separates them and
thus severs their natural, inner connection. It is inconceivable to us how
the outstanding contributions made in this matter by the above-mentioned
Gregory of Valencia, a loyal disciple of St. Thomas though not a Thomist
after the fashion of later representatives of the School, could have remained so long unnoticed.—On Suarez, see also P. Dumont, S.J., *Liberté
humaine et concours divin d'après Suarez* (Paris: 1936).

good for itself and can also combine with another factor for the production of a higher good.[7]

At this point a true, perfect union between nature and grace occurs; its fruit in us is the heavenly life belonging to the children of God. Here we have a subject that is susceptible of grace, a subject that is to reach its highest perfection in and through grace, that in the present order of the universe is to expect the satisfaction of all its wants from grace alone, and therefore advances toward grace with ardent yearning, to be enriched, enlightened, and animated by it, and to be introduced by it to the possession of the supreme good. On the other hand, grace itself is not comprised within this subject; it comes from outside as the reflection of divine light which is to illuminate, transfigure, and inflame all rational creatures, in order to transform them into the perfect image of the divine sun. It is offered to all; its vibrations gently brush every spiritual eye, and it requires nothing more than that the eye should open; then it will penetrate into the eye and fill it to repletion with its glory.

The two factors require each other. "Neither divine grace produces the illuminations of knowledge unless there is someone who has the physical power of receiving enlightenment, nor does a person thus equipped produce this effect without the higher operation of grace," says St. Maximus,

[7] The grace with which nature can and ought to enter into union, is grace in the restricted sense of supernature. As we shall show presently, actual grace, which anticipates and precedes supernature, is the intermediary of the union. There can be no enduring union with actual grace itself, because reception of actual grace does not depend on nature, to which it is given by God without nature's cooperation and only too often against its will; also because actual grace, as was shown above, is not able by itself, apart from supernature or its several powers, to produce supernatural fruit, acts of the supernatural life. It is a stimulus and capacity given to natural freedom, enabling the latter to enter into union with supernature and thus to become a freedom of a higher kind.

Martyr.[8] Both factors are necessary for the generation of supernatural life in man. Both cooperate for the single purpose of uniting man with God and of glorifying God in man as in His image.

Grace alone, coming as it does to man from outside, cannot give him the first capacity for the spiritual life or for union with God. It necessarily presupposes that such a capacity is already found in man's nature. It is a higher, more perfect form that is not acquired by an internal development but comes to the natural power and disposition from outside.[9] The subject must be essentially spiritual, intellectual, and capable of love, before it can receive a higher spirituality, intelligence, and love.

However, to find his completion in this higher form, man's own spirituality, intellectuality, and love must be relatively imperfect. We are united to God and are similar to Him by nature; by nature, too, we know God and yearn for the love of God. But this similarity and union, this knowledge and love do not bridge the infinite chasm separating us from God. Finite nature lacks the resources to fill up the void. In the bounty of His infinite love, God descends to the creature and by His infinite might raises the creature up to Himself. Accordingly a capacity to receive divine light and love exists in nature. God must inundate nature with His light, as the sun illuminates a clear crystal globe so that the globe seems to become another sun, or as fire combines with a precious metal to pervade it wholly and set it aglow. God must fructify nature with the seed of His divine life. As we graft a branch of a higher species on to a root and thus impart to it a new, higher power to put forth new

---

[8] *Diversa capita ad theologiam et oeconomiam spectantia,* IV, cap. 12 [*PG*, XC, 1308].

[9] This has been demonstrated above, Part I, chap. 2, and Part III, chap. 8.

blossoms and fruit, so God unites Himself with nature to impart to it the seed for the flowering of heavenly blossoms and fruits.

The basic conditions for a true union with grace are realized: distinction between the two factors, mutual limitation, and on both sides the relation between subject and form, potency and act that is needed for close union. Can we also find a reciprocal desire for this union?

As far as grace is concerned, the light of faith that reveals to us the source of grace, divine love, leaves no room for doubt. Nothing is more common among the Fathers, particularly the Greeks, than the comparison between God and the sun which sends out its beneficent, illuminating, warming rays in richest fullness toward all quarters, to enlighten everything that can receive or wishes to receive its light. God is the "light which enlighteneth every man that cometh into this world" (John 1:9). That is obviously true of the natural light by which God speaks and gives light to every rational creature. However, since this light is found in our nature, we have no option about receiving or not receiving it; at most we can prevent it from displaying its rays in a free and unobstructed manner. If, therefore, we follow the Fathers in interpreting such passages as referring to a light whose reception depends on us, that is, supernatural light, we perceive that God in some secret way sends the rays of His supernatural light into the hearts of all men (supernatural actual graces) to prepare them for the reception of the light itself and to conduct them to it. The inner union of God's Son, who is divine Light itself, with a member of the human race in personal unity, by which He communicated the fullness of divinity with its inexhaustible wealth to the assumed human nature, is a guaranty to us that He wishes to unite the whole human race, the whole of human nature in all its representatives, with His divine light.

But does nature, for its part, desire to enter into this union with God and His grace? Of itself, nature cannot have an efficacious desire that will bring it into the arms of the divine Bridegroom. Nature itself cannot take a single step to cross the boundless gulf separating it from grace; grace must reach out a hand to draw nature to itself. Grace itself arouses in nature a desire for grace.[10] By disclosing to nature the first rays of its light, by touching nature softly and lovingly with the first sparks of its warmth, grace enkindles in nature a longing to approach ever closer to this heavenly light, to be thoroughly permeated by it, and to receive it wholly; the light has no other wish but to impart itself. Grace itself (by the illuminations and inspirations that precede habitual grace) awakens in nature a perception of its inherent lowliness, indigence, and barrenness, and thus incites it to seek help, support, and happiness from grace.

But nature, by its own light, must recognize its limitations and imperfections; it must acknowledge that it cannot attain the complete, supreme perfection and happiness

---

[10] We here understand grace in the proper sense of supernature, the higher state of transfiguration into which nature is to be introduced. When we say that grace draws nature to itself, we mean that the divine nature, of which grace is a participation and which in grace unites itself with nature, attracts nature to itself by communicating to it an actual motion (actual grace as actual illumination of the intellect and inspiration of the will), so as to dispose it for the reception of grace. Consequently actual grace, which precedes the possession of habitual grace, is here called grace so far as it is an impulse, a motion toward the acquisition of grace in the proper sense. Thus we can say that grace in its principle and ideal, the divine nature, disposes our nature for the reception of grace and draws nature to itself. In similar fashion we say that the heat which a cold body is to receive from another body disposes it for the reception of heat by previously drying, illuminating, and warming it until it receives the heat itself.

that may be and actually are destined for it in the vision of God, except by grace. Nature must keenly experience the need for grace; in the present order of things no other means of salvation is at hand against the sluggishness of its natural faculties and its weakness that is like an illness, than that heavenly ointment, that marvelous warmth, that divine energy of life which heals the wounds of the soul in order subsequently to regenerate it to a higher life. All the wants of nature are fully met through grace; and to that extent nature has a natural desire for union with grace. But this desire merely makes nature capable of receiving grace; that it may lead nature to grace, it must, as we said above, be enkindled by the first rays of grace itself.

If nature is the receptive subject and grace is the celestial dew fructifying nature, and if both strive for union with each other, the real union must actually take place as soon as nature humbly and obediently accepts the invitation issued by grace and throws itself into the arms of grace. Nature cannot demand or merit this alliance because, as we have seen, the union is too far above nature's reach. Nature is invited to the union by the light and attraction of grace itself. Invited, I repeat; for nature is not necessitated, much less violently forced, to enter into this alliance. The union is not merely natural, like the union of body and soul; it is a true marriage, and consequently must be free on the side of grace as well as of nature. God gives grace with utmost freedom; grace is not a factor in the natural life of His creature for which he would have to provide. Nature, too, must receive grace freely; God does not force this most precious gift of His on nature against its will, and chooses to give it only when nature is ready to receive it fittingly. Therefore nature must freely yield to the preliminary attraction of grace, and must declare its readiness to observe the laws arising from its union with grace and to remove all obstacles standing in their way.

This is still a freedom of nature, not of grace; for the person who is endowed with freedom and freely advances toward grace is not yet in the state of grace or informed by grace, although he is drawn by grace. Freedom must be found on the side of nature, because otherwise grace, which is meant for all, would actually be given to all, and because grace itself cannot supply the freedom to possess or to lack grace. It is found in nature, but only so far as nature, drawn by a supernatural attraction, ought to pass over to the state of grace. Yet it is not a purely natural freedom; for the acts of such freedom do not in any way depend on grace, and so cannot lead to grace, much less merit it. Even when incited by actual grace, natural freedom cannot merit habitual grace, which is infinitely beyond its reach, because it does not yet pertain to a nature that has entered into the state of supernature. Such freedom can do no more than lead to grace, and hence its act is simply one of humble obedience, submission, acquiescence to the invitation of grace; it receives the gift thankfully, without presuming to demand or in any degree to merit grace.

The act of freedom open to nature is an act of humility; nature acknowledges its lowliness, incompetency, unworthiness, and its infinite remoteness from grace, and so yields to the higher will of grace. This freedom of humility has nothing in common with Pelagian freedom, the freedom of pride. First, it does not elicit its act independently of all divine impulse, for a natural impulse is not enough; a supernatural one is needed. Secondly, it does not put forth a claim for grace as something due to it or earned by it. On the contrary, nature avows that God is not its Debtor but its Lord to whom it belongs entirely; and the consciousness of its own baseness and lack of all claim decides it to submit to the call of His gracious love and to let itself be borne aloft to the heights to which God wishes to raise it.

Thus this wonderful union of the divine nature with human nature in the communication of grace or supernature is brought about by God's merciful, infinite love. It is a chaste marriage. For grace, on its side, unites with nature and fructifies it without violating it; nature, as an image of God, is the undefiled,[11] receptive soil to which grace brings the dew of heavenly energy down from heaven to revive and fructify it, and sheds on it heavenly light to adorn and warm it. Nature is the eye which, without being violated by the action of the light, generates within itself the image of the object from which the light flows into it. Conversely, nature does not defile grace. Grace does not enter into nature until nature is cleansed of all sin that is directly opposed to grace (mortal sin); grace does not come while nature is under the sway of some other principle by which it allows itself to be dominated, or so long as it does not crave union with grace by a chaste desire, that is, a pure, unselfish yearning. Nature must in some sense be virginal; that is, it must not have already conceived the fruit of its sensuality or egoism, that by grace and in grace it may receive heavenly fertility and thus generate the image of divine light and the fruit of divine life, to bear within itself, as it were, the Son of God anew.

Is there not a remarkable similarity between the marriage of nature with grace and the nuptials of Mary, the

---

[11] This can be said of nature even after original sin and, though less aptly, after actual sin. For culpability does not destroy the intrinsic goodness of nature, which is an effect and hence an image of the Creator; as such it is inherently a subject capable of receiving grace. Guilt raises a sort of barrier between nature and God as the source of supernatural light, a barrier that obstructs this light from reaching nature. This conception is well known to the Fathers, and especially to St. Thomas.

Virgin Mother, with the Holy Spirit? No resemblance is more deeply grounded than this, and nothing is more significant for grasping the grandeur of Christianity. The Virgin Mother, as the Church says, poured forth the eternal Light into the world; she bore the Son of God in His human nature and conceived Him in her womb. Through grace the Son of God is to be born again in human nature, not in physical unity of person, but in a moral, personal union, by a real image of His divine light and a real sharing of His divine life. The hypostatic union is the ideal, as well as the principle and end of the union by grace. It is the principle, because by it the Godhead is brought close to all mankind in inseparable union; the fullness of divinity was united with one individual of human nature, to be communicated to all others by participation. It is the end, because the true God-man must be the Head and King of all men who have been made to share in the divine nature through Him, and they must all be associated with Him for the greater glorification of His majesty.

The manner in which the divine nature in the person of the Word was wedded with human nature in the womb of the Virgin Mother corresponds in all details with the manner in which God wishes to be united in grace with nature as it exists in every man.[12] Human nature could have been imparted to the Son of God by creation. In that case no mother would have been needed. But because He wished to be born in human nature, the Holy Spirit had to be joined in a nuptial union with a human mother. She had to cooperate with the Holy Spirit in this work; God could not form a man who was to be born into the human race without her, and she could not give birth to the God-

[12] St. Augustine has also drawn out this parallel, but does not mention the reasons given above for the gratuitousness of grace.

man without God. She was the immaculate soil that the Holy Spirit was to overshadow like a cloud and to make fruitful with the dew of His power.

From eternity He had chosen her to be His bride, and awaited with ardent love the time when He could give Himself to her. And she, on her side, illuminated and incited by His grace, yearned as no other creature could for the infinitely exalted union of God with mankind. But this yearning was joined with deepest humility, for she was well aware of the infinite distance between God and herself; she knew that she could not merit that stupendous favor, and she did not consider herself worthy to see the sublime mystery fulfilled in her.

Then the Holy Spirit sent word to her through an angel and invited her to be His spouse. Although her consent did not decide God to decree the mystery, God was pleased to await her consent, that the nuptials might be celebrated with free love on her part, too. "Behold the handmaid of the Lord," she said, "be it done to me according to thy word" (Luke 1:38). As an obedient, humble maid, she assented to the word that conveyed her Lord's request to her to become His mother. With the same sense of lowliness, the same consciousness of her nothingness with which she regarded herself as unqualified and unworthy of so august a union with supreme Goodness, she humbly subjected herself to God's gracious love, and yielded herself to be raised to the highest pinnacle of dignity, to cooperate with God's greatest work.

Thus is accomplished the chaste marriage of the purest and most responsive creature with the all-pure and all-holy God. The dew and the power of the Holy Spirit flow down upon this receptive soil, to impart to it a divine fruitfulness and to cause the heavenly blossom to spring forth from the root of Jesse. The divine light in undiminished fullness falls on her as on an untarnished mirror, to be born by her and to be poured out by her into all the world.

Mary was a virgin before the marriage, because she had received no other seed, had taken to herself no alien light. She is a virgin in the union, because she suffers no hurt in her own life by receiving the divine seed, but on the contrary flowers forth into a higher life; she is not stained by the heavenly light, but is purified and transfigured with celestial beauty. She remains a virgin after the nuptial union, because she, having borne the most perfect fruit and having been flooded with the very source of light, nevermore can or may receive another seed, another light.[13]

Can there be a greater similarity, can a more perfect parallel be drawn out, than between the marriage of the Virgin with the Holy Spirit and that of nature with grace? The resemblance is so striking and clear in all details that we do not have to pursue the comparison in its individual traits. On both sides the analogy is evident: height and depth, the infinite and the finite, heaven and earth are joined in a most astonishing and intimate union. Both mysteries alike are sublime and wonderful: "Which is more tremendous, which is more amazing: that God gives Himself to earth, or that He gives you to heaven; that He Himself enters into association with flesh, or that He grants

---

[13] The analogy of virginity before and after marriage cannot be applied to the union of nature and grace except with certain restrictions. It is not absolutely necessary that nature should never have been impregnated with sin prior to its union with grace, or that it should never be thus impregnated thereafter. Strictly, all that is required is that nature must have renounced connection with sin at the time it is to be united with grace. And although grace does not exclude the possibility of sin in the future, it demands that sin should never again be granted an entrance; if nevertheless sin does enter, the union with grace is dissolved.

you fellowship with divinity?" [14] The two mysteries are closely related; because of this relationship, both are the starting point, the center, and the goal of the entire supernatural economy of Christianity.

The admission of free nature into the resplendent light of grace and its eventual perfect transfiguration by grace is the great work of the Trinity, the great work of the reconciliation between divine and human nature in the person of the God-man, the great mystery of Christianity. Nature and grace in their mutual interplay, their reciprocal friendly advances, are the factors in the great universal drama. Grace bends down to nature, to make nature share in its divine glory and to enable it to reign with God in the eternal happiness of heaven. And nature mounts up to grace to be transformed and fructified by it, thus to generate the heavenly life of the children of God.

But is not the relation existing between the two more a conflict than a union? A struggle of nature against grace and of grace against nature, destined to end with the eventual victory of grace and the destruction of nature? Does not Christianity stand forth with a sword, to declare war on nature, reason, and its life? Is not its watchword the crucifixion of the world, of nature, and of reason? Does it not require us to give up all natural feelings and inclinations, even our natural processes of thinking? And in the other camp, do we not see, hear, and sense that nature recognizes its foe in Christianity which sets out to combat and annihilate it? Do we not experience how nature wrestles against the influence of grace? Does not nature harbor within itself a law that is diametrically opposed to the law of the Holy Spirit? Do not the ascetics teach us that the

[14] St. Peter Chrysologus, serm. 67 [*PL*, LII, 391].

motions and tendencies of nature and grace repel each other and pursue opposite courses? [15] But where there is war, there is enmity; and where enmity prevails, union is impossible.

This difficulty leads us to the other great mystery of the supernatural order of the universe, the mystery of the Cross, of sacrifice, of the mortification of nature by grace. The mystery of the union of grace with nature cannot contradict this mystery; we must find a close connection between the two; even in the person of the God-man the elevation and sacrifice of His human nature do not cancel out each other. In a certain sense, indeed, we can say that downright enmity prevails between grace and nature—if we think of nature, in the way outlined above, as something pertaining exclusively to man in complete independence of God, as defectibility or tendency to evil, to self-seeking, to pride, to sensuality. Grace cannot but combat nature thus understood, and strives to annihilate it thoroughly.

If we consider man's nature as it actually exists in the concrete, the enmity appears to persist. To account for this phenomenon, some theologians suggest that the battle is waged, not with true nature, but with nature as corrupted and perverted by sin and inclined toward evil. In our view, however, if we prescind from the formal aspect of original sin which is conceivable only on the basis of a higher, supernatural order, and also from the corresponding economy of salvation, nature is now in a condition in which God could have created it. It is still the Creator's handiwork, and as such is good in itself and involves no direct opposition to grace; in fact it is capable of receiving grace. St. Paul himself says that the inward man, the "ego," the higher

[15] Cf. *Imitation of Christ*, III, chap. 54, "On the Different Motions of Nature and Grace."

and more important part of nature, the spiritual part by reason of which nature is even now a natural likeness of God, wrestles and struggles with the flesh, and that the Spirit of God joins forces with this man by supernatural grace to see the battle through to a triumphant victory (Cf. Rom. 7:15–22). The battle is fought within the domain of nature, within nature itself, and rages between its higher and its lower part, ever since the original (and of course supernatural) perfectly peaceable union between them was dissolved by sin. Union with grace is brought about in man mainly according to the spirit; it is not sundered, but rather should support the spirit in the war against the flesh. Grace wars against the spirit only when the spirit, against its own interests, becomes entangled in the law of the flesh, or in proud egoism rebels against grace itself.

I should even go so far as to assert that this conflict actually reveals to us the mystery of the union between nature and grace in all its grandeur. The mystery is now greater and more sublime than it was in the first man.

God had originally so devised the union of nature and grace that all the infirmities of nature were expelled, so long as nature did not haughtily rise in revolt against grace and thus sever the union. In that strong and healthy nature, grace displayed its magnificent power; the union was peaceable, without conflict of any sort. God permitted the insurrection of nature, but only for the purpose of subsequently making the union more intimate and glorious than ever. Cut off from grace, nature was punished with the loss of its interior peace, its inner union and harmony, and so tended to sink back into its native void. God could then have left it to languish on its own level, and giving it nothing but His natural assistance, could have allowed it to plod laboriously toward its natural end. Or after a sincere conversion brought about through the mediation of the God-man, who really inaugurated the union between nature and grace, God could have restored nature to its previous condition.

This would seemingly have been the culmination of God's loving kindness. But His glorification and that of nature itself demanded a quite different order. Nature was to remain in its helplessness and misery, to be a permanent, vivid example showing, not only how poor it is without God (for this is evident even in the state of pure nature), but chiefly to make clear what its fate necessarily is if it renounces the supernatural union with God destined for it. This condition is a tribute exacted by divine justice and a punishment for nature as long as it does not recover the lost union with God. The universal Mediator of grace, the God-man, also took this punishment on Himself, so far as it does not involve any disorder in nature, to offer satisfaction to the Father and to obtain from Him the restoration of grace to us. But as that condition was not a punishment for Him personally, neither is it a punishment any longer for all those who again enter into grace through Him. "There is now no condemnation to them that are in Christ Jesus" (Rom. 8:1). Yet that state continues on, for the greater glorification of God and His grace, and for the greater glorification of nature itself. God is never more glorified than when His creature avows his nothingness before God and offers himself to God as a holocaust by annihilating himself in his own estimation and willingly bearing the consequences of his futility.

This is likewise the greatest glory of the creature, if the creature is so united with God and subject to God that he can offer himself to God as a holocaust; just as it is the

deepest debasement of the creature if the creature rises
in revolt against God, the source of the creature's existence,
power, and life, and so concentrates tragically on his own
nothingness. The fire in which this holocaust is to be offered
to God is grace, along with the burning love of God that
grace enkindles in the creature. The aim of grace and charity is to vanquish the inclination toward sensuality and
sin that is harbored in nature, and completely to eradicate
that autonomy, that self-will, that independence which is
peculiar to nature and which, though not inherently evil,
can be and easily is an occasion for evil; the ultimate purpose is that God alone may live and be glorified in nature.

Grace requires of nature the renunciation of many natural things and relationships, otherwise good, that nature
may belong to God alone. Grace prevails on nature to love
and seek that from which it instinctively shrinks, and not
only to bear its natural wretchedness with joy or even to
glory in it—"I glory in my infirmities" (II Cor. 12:9)—but
to desire ever greater sufferings and humiliations, to love
and prize abasement, contempt, and pain for its own good,
because in the creature's mortifications, voluntarily endured out of love, the honor of the Creator wins its greatest
triumph. In a word, grace aims at crucifying nature for the
glorification of God, as the Son of God Himself wished to
suffer and be crucified in His humanity for the glory of His
heavenly Father. But as He regarded the hour of His passion as the hour of His glorification, so grace, while doing
violence to nature, intends nothing but nature's glorification.

Therefore the yoke of infirmity, sinfulness, and misery
under which human nature groans because of its weakness,
the yoke which it has to bear even on the natural level and
which is no mystery in itself, has mysterious implications

in the present economy of the world because of its relations with the mystery of grace. This mysterious element is not a disorganization of nature resulting from sin; nature as such and its natural development, as well as the havoc wrought in it by its own activity, are not mysteries in the Christian meaning of the word. The infirmity and wretchedness of nature are mysterious only in connection with the higher order of grace; they made their appearance with Adam's violation of the order of grace, and at the restoration of that order are meant to contribute to the greater glorification of grace and of nature itself.

The natural infirmities, sufferings, and eventual dissolution of nature are not, in the present order, a simple consequence of nature's essential imperfection, a result that nature has to bear with in patience. Through grace they become a sacrifice offered by nature in satisfaction for nature's rebellion against grace, to the greater glorification of God and its own supernatural purification and glorification. Nature itself struggles against its own futility, which it would prefer not to recognize; and the idea that sufferings, death, and concupiscence could not plague man except for sin is at bottom naturalistic. But grace, by linking nature wonderfully with God, teaches nature to love, for God's sake, not only its natural goodness, but also its natural imperfection and flimsiness, and to glory in its infirmities with joy. Through grace, God gives Himself to nature with all His greatness and magnificence. In like manner, nature ought to surrender itself to God with all its feebleness; then with full candor it can say: "Thou art all, I am nothing."

Accordingly the mystery of the Cross, the crucifixion of nature by grace, clearly does not provoke any hostility between nature and grace that would preclude union between them; on the contrary, it brings out the full grandeur of the mystery of the union. In the present state of conflict the union is much closer and more marvelous than it was in the first man while he was still enjoying a state of peace. It is more marvelous, because it does not assume that nature is at the height of its power, free from crippling obstructions, but, as St. Augustine says, it comes to the aid of the human will in its weakness, to give it an invincible, irresistible strength by which it can victoriously overcome all difficulties, all infirmities, all evils.[16] The union is closer, because grace is united with nature not only in its goodness but also in its weakness and misery, as in the Incarnation the Godhead is substantially united with the human nature in its passibility and mortality.

Through this infirmity of the flesh and death, nature advances toward the goal of its perfect transfiguration and glorification in its perfect union with grace. That is also the way Christ had to suffer and so to enter into His glory.

Freely, though not without struggle, nature is united with grace even now. But when grace is transformed into the light of glory, the union will become an indissoluble spiritual marriage, a *matrimonium spirituale ratum et consummatum*. The freedom of nature at the side of grace will cease, because it will be thoroughly pervaded by grace and taken up into grace. But its inherent weakness and misery will also cease, because it will be completely transfigured and glorified by the light of grace. Then, in comparison with grace, it will be, as it were, annihilated, but only in its imperfection; indeed, in grace and through grace it will reach its highest perfection. After Christ's resurrection, the power and fire of the divine nature and spirituality consumed the weakness and passibility of His

[16] *De correptione et gratia,* cap. 12, no. 38 [*PL,* XLIV, 939].

human nature and transformed them so divinely that the Apostle could say: "If we have known Christ according to the flesh, we now know Him so no longer" (II Cor. 5:16). Likewise, as the same Apostle indicates, the dishonor, weakness, and animality of our nature are even now besieged and overcome by the power of the divine law that dwells in us when we are in grace, and will one day be fully swallowed up, that God may be all in all (Cf. I Cor. 15:43 f. and Rom., chap. 8).

This glorification and transfiguration of nature by grace are the consummation and end of the supernatural order of the universe, which is designed to lead to the transformation of created nature by the divine nature. The mystery of its unrolling lies in the adjustment and conciliation of nature and grace, in the marriage of the two. It is a mystery or rather an insoluble enigma for the self-sufficient natural reason which refuses to surrender in obedience to faith. The economy of Christian salvation is folly to the animal man. But faith reveals it to us, and in its light equips us to judge all things according to their true meaning. "The spiritual man judgeth all things" (I Cor. 2:15). To the believer, God's will to save becomes a light that illuminates all the other mysteries of Christianity and makes them known in their true splendor.

EPILOGUE

THE spiritual man, enlightened by the Spirit of God, judges all things without exception, especially all divine, spiritual, supernatural things. The more clearly and faithfully he keeps in view the standard according to which he is to contemplate and weigh everything, the sounder his judgment will be.

All the supernatural mysteries of Christianity are related to the position man occupies in the realm of Christianity. In the Introduction we drew attention to the truth that the supernatural character of these mysteries and their importance for the Christian economy of salvation can be known only with reference to man's supernatural position in the universe or to the existence of a supernature in him. In the course of our exposition we found repeated opportunities to emphasize such points of contact between the teaching about supernature and other mysteries.

The divine Trinity, consisting in the substantial communication of the divine nature to several persons, is the beginning, the middle, and the end of the supernatural economy of salvation. For this economy is based on the communication of the divine nature to man through the gift of grace. It consists in a union of man with God as his Father; and this is analogous with the union which the only-begotten Son of God has with the Father in the Holy Spirit. And it leads us back to the Trinity; for, as St. John tells us, it introduces us into a fellowship, a companionship with the Father and with the Son in the Holy Spirit (Cf. I John 1:3), in which we love and glorify the divine Persons and share in their happiness.

The Incarnation of the Son is the mystery of the reconciliation of our nature with the divine nature. The Son of God takes our nature to Himself to make us His brothers by our participation in His divine nature. As the Firstborn, He was to be the head of all the brethren; as such He had to be made conformable in nature to all the members: "It behoved Him in all things to be made like unto His brethren" (Heb. 2:17). In this way divinizing power could flow out from Him into all the members. His real presence in the Eucharist, in which He gives Himself to us as our food, was to become the vehicle transmitting to us the fullness of grace and divine life.

With regard to man, the mystery of the situation and position in which he finds himself is properly discerned, not in his present state as such, but rather in its relation to the original, mysterious, and supernatural state of the first man which was lost to us through original sin, and to that other state into which we are again to be introduced by Christ. In no other hypothesis can the necessity of redemption by a God-man, as well as its significance and method, be satisfactorily understood.

We mention these mysteries only by way of example, because they are the most important and are the ones chiefly brought out by what we have had to say in this treatise. A fuller, more adequate, systematic application of the doctrine about the supernatural character of the Christian economy of salvation will have to await a later work, if the Author of grace blesses our present endeavor and chooses

to favor our future efforts for His glorification.[1] If theology would take over this groundwork and would con-
sistently and solidly erect its entire structure thereon, the
profit for Christian learning and Christian living would be
enormous. If the science of faith were treated formally
and materially as something supernatural, as knowledge
of a supernatural order of things acquired with the aid of
supernatural light, all its autonomy, excellence, and marvelous intrinsic organization would clearly stand forth. As
a participation in God's own knowledge, it would be the
true transcendental science for which natural reason, in
its pride that is typical of our century, so vehemently
yearns.

The seraphic mind of St. Bonaventure devised a masterly
plan for this science in the sixth and seventh chapters of
his splendid book, *Itinerarium mentis in Deum.* With the
resources of our natural reason we have only an ascending
knowledge which has natural things for its immediate
object, and by arguing from them rises to their necessary
cause, God as the Supreme Being, Yahweh in the oneness
of the divine nature. That is the method of philosophy,
which is knowledge of a basic reality derived from its effect
and phenomena; and that is its object, natural things in
their natural relations to one another and to God. But by
grace we become sharers in the divine knowledge, and thus
come to know all reality in and from its cause. In the beatific vision God grants us knowledge of Himself as the luminous ideal of all things, the exemplar from which we can
clearly know and perfectly grasp all reality. But when God
directly communicates Himself to us by faith, He enables

[1] This promise was fulfilled. See Scheeben's magnificent book, *The
Mysteries of Christianity* (St. Louis: B. Herder, 1951).—Tr.

us to know Him as the supreme, infinite goodness. In faith, therefore, we know all things in the light of God, their highest cause, as He produces them out of His infinite goodness. Goodness communicates itself, is self-diffusive. Even natural things flow forth from the divine goodness that communicates itself to them, but our reason knows them immediately in their own reality. Above them exist other communications of the divine goodness, but these cannot be known by reason either in the light of natural things or directly in themselves. The first and highest is the substantial communication and diffusion of the divine nature from the Father to the other two divine Persons. The second is the hypostatic union of the Second Person with humanity. The third is the union of the God-man with all other men in the Eucharist and in grace, with the purpose of conveying to them, from the very source of the divine goodness, all the riches of God. And so the development continues.

That is the method of the science of the faith: directed by God's hand and guided by His own Word, to trace the interior and exterior unfolding and communication of His goodness, and to know all reality as it is connected with its cause, the divine goodness, and the plan of its communication which God Himself has revealed to us. That, too, is the object of this science: primarily and especially the supernatural unfolding and communication of the divine goodness, and secondly its communication on the level of nature, so far as the latter communication is connected with the former and is subordinated to it.

Quite similar are the method and character of Christian knowledge drawn up for us by St. Thomas. God grant us this blessing, that a host of scholars may direct their labors along the lines indicated by these two stars, St. Bonaventure and St. Thomas, shining in the firmament of Christian learning! [2]

Even more than science, Christian life ought to spring up afresh in consequence of the emphasis laid on its supernatural foundation, its supernatural end, and its supernatural activities. How poverty-stricken and mean Christian morality appears when it is regarded merely as the morality of man (that is, the ethics based on man's natural moral dignity as found in his reason and free will) rather than as the morality of the sons of God! How faintly the heavenly, spiritual, holy, even divine character of Christian virtue glows in this view! It is not sufficient to stress the exceedingly great and fatherly love of God for us, or to say in general that we are adopted by the Father through Christ and are made co-heirs with Him. To appreciate the magnitude of that love, we must perceive the magnitude of its effect in us. To grasp the truth that we are really Christ's brothers, we must go into the question of our conformity with Him in His divine no less than in His human nature. And grace may not be regarded merely as a corroborating factor in moral life; it must be apprehended and presented as the new foundation of that life, pertaining to a higher order. Then we shall develop a true moral theology, as distinct from a moral philosophy. Then we shall be able to preach from the pulpit a morality that shares in the excellence of dogmatic theology, a morality rooted in faith, grace, and the mysteries of Christianity.

Such a conception of Christian life is characteristic of St. Peter Chrysologus and lends to his sermons that inspiring ardor, that wonderful unction which so charms and edifies

[2] See Scheeben's own achievement in *The Mysteries of Christianity*, Part Ten: "The Science of the Mysteries of Christianity, or Theology."—Tr.

us. He invariably bases the Christian life on the truth that we are not mere servants of God (although that would in itself be a great honor); we are children of God who have been made a heavenly race by sharing in His nature and therefore do not stand afar off from Him in servile awe but draw near to Him in trusting, filial love and repose in His heart.

I believe I cannot better bring this work to a close than by laying before the reader a few passages from his homilies. These can serve as an example illustrating in what a strikingly intelligible and edifying way this beautiful teaching can be developed. Thus we can make amends to the reader for the dryness and heaviness of our own exposition, which have perhaps detracted too much from the splendor of the doctrine.

Let us see how, in his homilies on the Our Father, St. Peter Chrysologus brings out the supernatural character of our relationship to God, which he admires scarcely less than the Incarnation itself. We can then follow him as he discourses on the various supernatural blessings longed for in the Lord's Prayer, the hallowing of the divine name, the coming of God's kingdom, fulfillment of the divine will, and the gift of bread for our souls. Proceeding in this way, he opens up before our eyes the sublime, heavenly meaning of the noble prayer.

What you are now going to hear arouses the astonishment of the angels and the wonderment of heaven; earth crouches in terror before it, the flesh cannot endure it, our ears do not take it in, our minds do not grasp it, the whole of creation cannot bear it. I hardly dare to speak, yet I cannot remain silent. May God bless your ears that you may hear, and my lips that I may speak.

Which is more tremendous, that God gave Himself to earth or that He gives you to heaven? That He Himself enters into association with flesh, or that He grants you fellowship with divinity? . . . That He is born into your condition of servitude, or begets you to Himself as His children? That He accepts your poverty or that He makes you His heirs, joint heirs with His only Son? It is indeed more awe-inspiring that earth is transferred to heaven, that man is changed divinely, that the lot of servitude acquires the right of ownership.

Although this is all so stupendous, yet, since our present concern is more to obey a command than to listen to instruction, let us, like little children, run to where charity calls us, love draws us, affection invites us. Let our hearts be full of God our Father, our voices resound, our tongues speak, our souls cry out, and let all that is in us answer to grace, not to fear. . . .

"Our Father, who art in heaven." When you say this . . . understand that yours is a heavenly race, whose Father dwells in heaven; and see to it that by living in a holy way you may be conformable to your holy Father. They show themselves to be sons of God who are not besmirched by human vices and who shine with divine virtues.

"Hallowed be Thy name." We are held to belong even by name to Him whose race we are. Therefore we pray that His name, which is holy in itself and by itself, may also be sanctified in us.

"Thy kingdom come." We ask that He, who has always reigned in His kingdom, may now reign in us, that we too may reign in Him . . . as free men throughout eternal life.

"Thy will be done." This is the reign of God, when God's will is the only one in heaven and on earth, when my God dwells, when God lives, when God acts, when God rules, when God is everything in all men, so that, in the Apostle's phrase, "God may be all in all" (I Cor. 15:28).

"Give us this day our daily bread." The heavenly Father urges His heavenly sons to ask for heavenly bread. Christ said: "I am the living bread which came down from heaven" (John 6:51). He Himself is the bread that was sown in the Virgin, leavened in the flesh, kneaded in the Passion, baked in the oven of the tomb, that is stored in the churches, is placed upon the altars, and daily furnishes heavenly food for the faithful.[3]

[3] Hom. 67 [*PL*, LII, 391 f.].

In the seventy-first homily, St. Peter Chrysologus clarifies
the connection between the mystery of the divine Trinity
and the supernatural life of grace in nature, and thus brings
out its great importance for practical Christian living.

The power of faith, the might of belief, the value of profes-
sion, are today made clear in you. Behold, the threefold profes-
sion of faith in the Trinity has raised you up from earthly slavery and has made you a heavenly progeny. Behold, faith expressed in God the Father [belief in the person of the Father
in God as distinct from the Son] has today gained God for you
as your Father. Behold, the word which confessed that the Son
is God, has won for you the adoption of the sons of God. Behold, the belief which proclaimed that the Spirit is God, has
changed you from the substance of mortal flesh into the ever-
living substance of the Spirit [by similarity]. Who will be found
worthy to announce so bountiful a kindness? God the Father
receives men as His heirs, God the Son does not disdain to
accept slaves as His fellow-heirs, God the Spirit admits flesh
into fellowship with divinity. Heaven becomes the possession
of earthlings, and they who were lawfully assigned to the
nether world are welcomed in the highest courts, as the Apostle
indicates when he says: "Know you not that we shall judge
angels?" (I Cor. 6:3).

Therefore call God your Father; and if you are not yet born,
be persuaded that you are destined to be His sons. Consider
well to what extent your life is heavenly, your morals are divine,
and the form of God is manifest in your own entire form. For
the heavenly Father enriches with divine gifts His sons who
live conformably with their race, whereas those who are false
to their race He recalls to penal servitude.[4]

Briefly, St. Peter Chrysologus infers the excellence of
the objects and motives of our faith, our hope, and our love
from our supernatural union with God. On this union he
bases the sublimity of our duties toward God, our fellow
men, and ourselves. In terms of it he accounts for the depth

[4] Hom. 71 [PL, LII, 401].

of our fall into sin, even that sin which is not personal. Through it he brings the whole economy of salvation into harmony with the capital mystery of the Blessed Trinity. Through it he explains how the Incarnation is the supernatural foundation on which the system of Christianity is erected above nature and reason. By it he helps us to grasp the necessity as well as the absolute transcendence of grace. By it he makes clear to us the mysterious, heavenly, maternal dignity of the Church, the marvelous power and meaning of the sacraments, and so on. I need say no more to show that the way indicated in this book, intended to promote genuine Christian learning and Christian living, whether in school or in the pulpit, is the very road which this enlightened Father of the Church, in the company of so many others, especially the Greek Fathers of the first and most flourishing ages of Christianity, has traveled. Ask your Fathers and they will tell you.

INDEX

Action: informed by charity, 273; perfection merited by, 75

Activity
essence prior to, 155
faculties as potency for, 155
of human soul, 60, 71 note
natural inclination toward good, 53
natural and supernatural, 4, 8
supernatural, 27, 42
of thinking, 160

Acts: informed by supernatural love, 272; of mysticism, 221 ff.; of supernature, 220-34

Adoption: divine, 126; human, 126

Amor amicitiae, 246, 270

Amor benevolentiae, 246

Amor concupiscentiae, 246

Analysis of supernature, 33-45

Aquinas; *see* Thomas Aquinas, St.

Appetitus concupiscibilis, 279

Appetitus irascibilis, 279

Aristotle on potentiality, 42

Athanasius on participating divine nature, 205

Augustine, St.
on the beatific vision, 57
on charity, 233 note
on chaste desire, 246
on grace of Christ, 312
on human freedom, 310-14, 316
on love for the Creator, 258, 260
on man's divine sonship, 121
on man's natural endowment, 309, 313
on natural good, 95
nature defined by, 22
nature's rights defended by, 96

Augustine, St. (*continued*)
on necessity of grace, 94, 277
Pelagianism combated by, 2, 309
on power of grace, 283
on soul as image of Trinity, 181
on union with the Holy Spirit, 198 note

Baianism repulsed by Church, 5

Baius, condemnation of, 83, 93

Basil, St.: on godlikeness, 113 and note; on infused holiness, 110 note

Beatific vision
conferred by special grace, 93
contrasted with natural end, 57, 77
elevation of intellect in, 58, 77
eternal life in, 164
faith as anticipation of, 149, 233, 235
God fully revealed in, 148, 341
in history of dogma, 57
as inheritance of God's sons, 146
Jansenist error about, 80
knowledge and love in, 170
life of God's children in, 164
supernatural activity in, 230 ff.
supernatural character of, 58, 79

Beatitude: culmination of supernature in, 164, 170, 232; supernatural, 27, 77; supernatural activity in, 230 ff.

Bellarmine on supernatural order, 156

Blessed Trinity, the
capital mystery of, 347